2005

" the 3ᴿᴰ Day of Christmas "

ITALIAN FAMILY DINING

ITALIAN FAMILY DINING

Recipes, Menus, and Memories of Meals

with a Great American Food Family

EDWARD GIOBBI &

EUGENIA GIOBBI BONE

RODALE

Printed in the United States of America
Rodale Inc. makes every effort to use acid-free ∞, recycled paper ♲.

Illustrations by Edward Giobbi

Library of Congress Cataloging-in-Publication Data

Giobbi, Edward.
    Italian family dining : recipes, menus, and memories of meals with a great American food family / Edward Giobbi and Eugenia Giobbi Bone.
        p.   cm.
    Includes index.
    ISBN-13 978–1–59486–126–0 hardcover
    ISBN-10 1–59486–126–9 hardcover
    1. Cookery, Italian.   2. Menus.   I. Bone, Eugenia.   II. Title.
TX723.G482   2005
641.5945—dc22   2005019366

Distributed to the trade by Holtzbrinck Publishers

2   4   6   8   10   9   7   5   3   1   hardcover

We inspire and enable people to improve their lives and the world around them
For more of our products visit **rodalestore.com** or call 800-848-4735

CONTENTS

ACKNOWLEDGMENTS

*This book is dedicated to the Giobbis: Elinor, Lisa, and Cham; to our spouses,
our aunts and uncles and cousins, our nephews and nieces, our children and
grandchildren; to the ghosts of the past and the babies yet to be born.
We all sit at the family table together.*

I cherish the time I have been allowed to spend with my father in making this book, and I am grateful for the lesson he has taught me by example: that aging need not be a decline, as I had feared. On the contrary, life can become ever more inspired as long as we nourish our creativity and use it to feed the people we love.

Authors get the credit when a book is published, but many people go into the making. It is a team effort, and we are humbled by the team we had this time around. We would like to thank Elise and Arnold Goodman, our agents, who have flawless moral compasses, and have never steered us wrong, and Margot Schupf, our editor at Rodale. In a climate where Italian books are saturating the market, Margot saw how this book was different and necessary, and never lost confidence in it. She remained our champion and became our friend. We owe a tremendous debt to Roy Finamore, a great editor, an elegant chef, the drollest wit in the room—and an Italian! He edited this book with grace and humor. We are grateful to Jennifer DeFilippi, our in-house editor, and Meghan Phillips, our publicist, who combine skill, youth, and charm, and Lois Hazel and Amy Kovalski, who perform the least glamorous and most necessary tasks: production and copyediting. We are also grateful to Andy Carpenter, who designed the cover, and Tara Long, who designed the pages, for working with us to fulfill our vision of the book. All in all, it was a smooth sail.

Our thanks go out to Sal Del Deo, Flavia Destefanis, Jacques Pépin, Marisa Getz, Cham Giobbi, Sal Biancardi, and Giancarlo and Rosa Paciullo, for graciously allowing us to either print or adapt their recipes for this book.

And finally, we would like to thank our spouses, children, and friends, for blaming it on the project whenever we behaved badly. We love you for that.

INTRODUCTION

Since 1971, when my father, Edward, published *Italian Family Cooking,* more and more people have come to prepare and enjoy Italian dishes. Unfortunately, there hasn't been a reciprocal increase in people eating Italian-style meals. That's a shame, because an Italian meal—with its focus on vegetables, its variety of courses, and its aversion to elaborate, sugary desserts—is a delicious, interesting, and healthy way to eat. It is also a meaningful way to eat: Because the Italian meal takes time to consume, friends and families end up talking to each other around the table. Italians use dining to facilitate the creation of familial bonds. Indeed, the Giobbis became a family at the table, and we stay a family by way of the table.

There are a few particulars that define Italian dining. First, it is rare that an Italian will have just one course, even if he is eating light. The courses, however, will be small. I think that when diners anticipate a second or third course, they tend not to eat as much. In the countryside of Le Marche, the Adriatic region where my father's family comes from, each place setting is piled with plates, indicating how many courses will be served at that meal. My dad taught us kids to always count the plates before we reached for the bread; otherwise, we'd never be able to pace ourselves. According to nutritionists, it takes up to 30 minutes for your brain to recognize that you have had one mouthful of food. Multiple small courses take longer to eat, as there is some waiting involved in the transition between courses, giving your brain a chance to tell your stomach when it is full before you have overeaten.

Italians sit down for meals. More Americans should: Research suggests that children who sit down to evening meals with their parents consume more fruits, vegetables, and dairy products; drink fewer soft drinks; and are less likely to skip breakfast. Similarly, a Finnish study found that children with no regular family dinner ate sweets and fast foods more often than those with a regular family dinner. Childhood obesity is a serious health and social problem in this country. Italian-style dining may be part of the solution.

In the Giobbi house, busy weeknights consist of dishes like bean soup, followed by a salad, with a glass of wine. Or polenta on the board followed by a salad. (Italians don't start a meal with a salad; they end it, believing salad cleanses the palate.) Four courses are served whenever there is company, and at Sunday lunch. These meals are composed of a small pasta course; meat, fish, or poultry with vegetables; a salad; and a dessert. On occasion, Italians serve a seasonal antipasto, like mixed cold cuts, family-style at the beginning of the meal.

Eating a large, hard-to-digest meal at night is a recipe for heartburn. So we try to keep our dinners light, or early. Let's say we plan to serve pasta as a first course for dinner. First, you will see that we serve half the amount of pasta that you usually get in a restaurant. If meat, fish, or poultry (versus vegetables or a salad) is the second course, then the pasta sauce we choose will be a light one, made from vegetables or fish. Entrées are served with vegetables, not starch (you've had that in your first course).

It is important to note that until recently, most central and southern Italians rarely ate dairy products from cows. The primary dairy source for these Italians was sheep, which could survive on the tough, weedy ground cover in uncultivated areas, and, to a lesser degree, oxen. As a result, few recipes from our family include butter or cream. With the advent of the common market, butter and cream have become more prevalent in central and southern Italian kitchens. When Edward was a young man studying art in Florence in the late 1950s, one of the most expensive dishes on restaurant menus was pasta with butter.) Likewise, central Italians do not eat beef like they do in the north. You will find few beef recipes in this book.

Maybe one of the biggest misconceptions about Italian cookery is that it is a starch-based diet. Actually, seasonal vegetables predominate in Italian cookery. (In fact, most of the second-course dishes in this book call for a meat or fish cooked with a predominant seasonal vegetable—eliminating the necessity for a side dish.) The benefits of this are obvious. Because seasonal vegetables travel less distance, they have more time to ripen on the plant. As a result, they are fresher, tastier, healthier, and cheaper. We find great pleasure in anticipating the advent of a favorite fruit or vegetable—it's the same enjoyment that comes at the cusp of a new season. As I am writing this, on a snowy January afternoon, I can't wait for the artichoke season to begin, and the warm weather that comes with it. The two are synonymous.

A seasonal approach to cooking benefits menu planning as well. If the primary ingredients of all the courses involved in a meal are seasonal, then the overall menu will tend to be more cohesive and the different courses will almost always work together. A meal should tell us where we are in the year. For example, in the spring, the asparagus, artichokes, peas, strawberries, and rhubarb are in. So, too, shad, lamb, peas, and morels. We can, from these ingredients, put together numerous menus. Risotto with peas and asparagus followed by lamb shanks with artichokes. Or pea soup with fish followed by scrambled eggs with scallops and morels. We can fry soft-shell crabs as a first course, then serve sole with new spinach. Building a menu within a season will almost always prove to be satisfying.

Italians don't eat sweets the way Americans do. They enjoy them at holidays and special occasions, and sometimes as snacks—especially ice cream—but sweets are not offered after every meal. Instead, a meal usually ends with a piece of fruit or cheese, or some nuts. Likewise, it is unlikely an Italian will drink sugary sodas with a meal. Italians drink water, wine (or watered-down wine), or beer with their meals.

Italian meals are structured in a way that keeps family and friends at the table: Multiple courses take time to eat, and wine keeps conversation flowing (although Dad says arguing was never acceptable at the table when he was young, as it was said to ruin the digestion). The meal is the entertainment: It has a beginning, middle, and an end. That is not to say a great Italian meal has to be complicated, or for guests only. We eat simple meals like a fall dinner of spaghetti with botarga and wild mushrooms, a salad, and maybe a poached ginger pear, served after the kids are in bed and the parents need to talk. Or on a wintry Sunday, baccala alla Marchigiana, served with a steaming platter of cabbage and beans, and maybe a walnut orange cake afterward, when the upcoming week is discussed. Even a picnic, simple as it is, can feel like a culinary event. We take prosciutto and fig sandwiches; quartered, salted cucumbers; and chunks of fresh Parmesan cheese up into the mountains to snack and lounge and share theories on the age of mossy rocks.

Creating a shapely meal is an act of love, Italian-style. My dad is from a generation of men who didn't indulge in overt displays of affection, but he has his ways. He got up early to pack lunches for us when we were in elementary school (home-canned tuna, roasted red peppers, a thick piece of Mom's homemade bread). He smuggled food into our hospital rooms (fish soup with rice, veal breast stuffed with prosciutto and ricotta), and cooked for dozens of wiggly birthday parties (pasta with pesto, chicken with honey and lemons). These were meals that spoke volumes, as most Italian meals do.

Meals are the time when a family communicates. To this day, when my brother and sister and I need to powwow, we do it over food. From small, intimate, "what-to-do-about" dinners, to Sunday lunches where we converge at the family house in Katonah, New York, to eat and update each other, to our large Christmas Eve feast of Cena della Vigilia, the Giobbi family has always defined itself at mealtimes.

Throughout this book I tell stories of meals with the family: The oldest are Edward and Elinor Giobbi. Next come their children and the spouses: myself, and my husband, Kevin Bone, a tall, good-natured architect; Lisa, elegant and fiercely loyal, is an aerialist, and her husband, Paul Guilfoyle, the actor; and Cham, a painter and voice-over artist, the humorist of the family, and his wife, Laine Valentino, a film producer. Of the grandchildren, there are five: My Carson, 14, and Mo, 10; Lisa's Snow, 5; and Cham's Val, 3, and Gigi, 1. They are all wild, lovely, pains-in-the-asses in an age-appropriate way. I guess that's true of us all.

We also enjoy, and nurture, our extended family. We travel frequently to Italy, and Dad travels at least twice a year to visit his relatives in Le Marche, a region little known to Americans, on Italy's Adriatic coast. There are marvelous fish restaurants along the seaside promenade, but we usually eat most of our meals at Zia Ada's house in nearby Centobucci. The families from both sides of the Atlantic reconnect over Marchigiana specialties like stuffed, fried olives and home-cured artichokes, linguine with the Adriatic's tiny clams, and a fish stew called Brodetto alla San Benedetto del Tronto. Between sips of Piceno Rosso, the local red wine, we try to communicate. Though many facts get lost in the translation (Dad being the only one who speaks both languages well, and he's often busy eating), the most important stuff gets done: We spend time together. It is during these meals, us stumbling through Italian and they stumbling through English, that all the Giobbis remember who they are.

When it was time to empty my late grandmother's house in Memphis, Tennessee, my mother arranged for a couple of southern cooks to come around and prepare meals for us. It was a wise thing to do, because even the most together families can lose their cool when it comes to divvying up the loot. But at the table, over baby butter beans and corn pones, or white-meat chicken salad served in a cup of iceberg lettuce with buttery crackers, we sorted out all our differences and were reminded of what really matters: being and staying together.

During the course (and courses) of a meal, some of the most interesting things in life happen: the confessions and admissions, the family stories and histories, the hopes and aspirations that bring us closer, that make us feel greater empathy for each other, that make us better people. This book is about two things: how to eat like an Italian, and how eating like an Italian made the Giobbis a family.

How to Use This Book

Italian Family Dining is divided into four parts: spring, summer, fall, and winter. Within each of these parts, you will find first courses, second courses, vegetables and salads, and desserts. The book is split into seasons because we want you to think about menu planning in terms of the seasons. The recipes within each part are interchangeable. In creating a menu during the spring, for example, you can combine any of the recipes in that section and be assured the dishes will go together. Some menu ideas have been included, to get you started.

There are a few things to keep in mind when you start to make up menus. Although radical combinations can be a lot of fun, Italians generally keep first courses and second courses in the same category: a fish first course should be followed by a fish second course, and a meat first course should be followed by a meat second course. Poultry is flexible, and always suitable for a second course. Vegetables, and pasta with vegetable sauces, can be served before any main course, and vegetables alone make a delightful second course in themselves.

Typical holiday menus are included in the text, and the recipes can be located in their appropriate seasonal chapters. Recipes are designated to a specific season based upon their primary ingredients. In the case of a primary ingredient that is always abundant, like onions, we refer to the ingredient's historic harvest time in the Northeast. And of course, seasonality depends on location. The best way to learn what comes in when is to visit your local farmer's market on a regular basis. To track down a farmer's market in your area, try logging on to www.SlowfoodUSA.org.

Hard-and-fast rules of dining are no fun, and Italians like to enjoy their food. This book is a guide for Italian-style dining, not doctrine. Because no one likes to be told what to do.

Especially Giobbis.

A Few Menu Ideas

A Family Spring Lunch
Penne with Asparagus and Shrimp
Stuffed Chicken Legs

A Quiet Spring Dinner
Fresh Pea Soup with Fish
Turnip Greens
Zabaglione with Cream

A Big Sunday Lunch in Spring
Risotto with Peas and Asparagus
Veal Tails with Artichokes and Asparagus
Lemon-Glazed Ricotta Balls

A Simple Spring Dinner for Company
Spaghettini Salad
Monkfish with Asparagus
Strawberry Panna Cotta

A Sexy Spring Dinner
Soft-Shell Crabs with Asparagus
Artichokes Stuffed with Spinach
Sautéed White Asparagus
Fresh strawberries

An Elegant Spring Lunch
Capellini with Steamed Mussels and Clams
Shad Roe with Tarragon
Roasted Asparagus
Jacques' Rhubarb Galette

A Quick Spring Lunch
Penne with Pork, Asparagus, and Morels
Green salad
Slices of fresh Pecorino

A Family Summer Lunch
Summer Minestrone alla Genovese
Chicken Sausages with Pole Beans
Apricot Fool with Peaches

A Quiet Summer Dinner
Cuttlefish Salad
Cucumber spears
Peaches in wine

A Big Sunday Lunch in Summer
Zia Ada's Gnocchi with Chicken Giblet Sauce
Chicken with Ascoli Olives
Polpette di Melanzane
Peaches Stuffed with Ricotta

A Simple Summer Dinner for Company
Zucchini Flower Frittata
Fillet of Sole with Cantaloupe
Cherry Almond Sorbet

A Sexy Summer Dinner
Tomatoes Stuffed with Ricotta and Tuna
Fish Stew with Almond Pesto
Beet Granita with Lucy's Cookies

An Elegant Summer Lunch
Farfalle with Zucchini Flowers and Shrimp
Cabbage Stuffed with Fish
Green salad
Broiled Apricots with Lavender Syrup

A Quick Summer Lunch
Grilled Eel
Baked Zucchini with Balsamic Vinegar
Baked Corn
Cherry Crisp

A Family Fall Lunch
Tagiolini with Saffron
Chicken with Fennel and Mint
Sweet and Sour Cipollini
Torta Adelaide

A Quiet Fall Dinner
Spaghettini in Duck Broth
Butternut Squash alla Parmesan
Chestnut Puree with Whipped Cream

A Big Sunday Lunch in Fall
Timbalo Gigi
Guinea Hen with Chestnuts
Puree of Parsnips and Potatoes
Kale and Cabbage
Almond Torte with Poppy Seeds

A Simple Fall Dinner for Company
Skirt Steak with Lobster Mushrooms
Fall Vegetable Medley
Concord Grape Granita

A Sexy Fall Dinner
*Spaghettini with Botarga and Wild
Mushrooms*
Green salad with Gorgonzola cheese
Ginger Pears

An Elegant Fall Lunch
Stracciatelle Soup with Cardoons
Eggplant Rolls
Radicchio salad
Fig and Pear Tart

A Quick Fall Lunch
Farfalle with Green Tomatoes
Swiss Chard with Squid
Apple Compote Crumble

A Family Winter Lunch
Cranberry Bean and Faro Soup
Sliced cured meats
Endive salad
Homemade Chunkies

A Quiet Winter Dinner
Fish Soup with Anisette
Fennel Salad
Tangerines

A Big Sunday Lunch in Winter
Meat Lasagne
Parchment-Wrapped Sausage with Fennel and Onions
Cabbage with Beans
Butternut Squash with Potatoes
Walnut Orange Cake

A Simple Winter Dinner for Company
Cranberry Beans with Caviar
Codfish with Brocoletti di Rape
Roasted potatoes
Puntarelle Salad
Quince paste with nuts and pears

A Sexy Winter Dinner
Spaghettini with Maine Shrimp
Broiled Sardines with Breadcrumbs
Lemon Sorbet with Spumante

An Elegant Winter Lunch
Risotto with Crabmeat
Monkfish with Leeks
Orange Salad with Olives
Meyer Lemon Tart

A Quick Winter Lunch
Penne with Cauliflower and Ground Pork
Green salad

SPRING

THE WEDDING

Kevin and I had a yearlong engagement. During that time we lived it up, and, very gratefully, handed all plans regarding our wedding to my parents. We had no particular ideas about it, except the date, May 1 — May Day, the pagan European celebration of the first spring planting. I probably took a little too much glee from pointing out the phallic origins of the May Pole to my mother's conservative southern kin, but then, I was young.

That year I worked for a statistical encyclopedia called the *Worldmark Encyclopedia of the Nations,* where I wrote entries on the number of cars in Nauru and the number of chickens in the Vatican. My mother often came to my office to take me to lunch and offer me choices between invitation card stocks and flower arrangements for the tables. I took her advice in all ways, as she has very elegant taste, and I am one of those people who mistake rayon for silk. My mother also registered me for wedding gifts and helped me decide which glasses and forks to select, thank god, as my tendency was toward the baroque and natty—bamboo-handled silver, red goblets, and individual ashtrays—but she diplomatically steered me toward more moderate choices, which I use to this day.

There was some confusion regarding who would marry us, as Kevin and I were both baptized Episcopalian, but we weren't affiliated with a congregation. Plus, I leaned toward Quakerism since my teenage years, when I found some solace in counting the ceiling slats of the meeting house (for the record, there are 139). We finally settled on a benign Episcopalian minister with a lazy eye.

The day before the wedding, I showed up at the house in Katonah, New York, where I grew up. The house, built in the 1900s by a textile manufacturer, sits on fifteen acres of land abutting the Croton Reservoir. There is a lily pad–clogged pond surrounded by weeping willows, and in spring, the low spots on the long lawns are spongy with the fresh water that burbles up from below, mysterious and sweet, home of watercress and small frogs. The house itself is a grand old rickety place, with deeply carved woodwork, textiles on the walls that blossom with fat brown flowers, and an ample, colorful kitchen stocked with copper pots, antique hand-painted Italian ceramic bowls filled with garlic, and branches of dried hot peppers hanging from thick wooden beams. My mother had planted hundreds of tulip bulbs the previous fall, and the flowers were up and bobbing in the cool sun, their petals soft and fresh as a baby's cheek. A huge white tent was set up near the house, filled with round tables and chairs and bowls of petite roses and tiny, trembling lily of the valley. Mom was frantic—about the state of the house, the state of the guest list, the state of her own life, I think, in seeing her first child married—but she really had everything organized beautifully. The kitchen, however, was pure, glorious chaos.

Seven chefs—Jacques Pépin, Jean Vergnes, Roger Veregne, Maurice Bertrand, Albert Kumin, Pierre Franey, and my dad, wearing every last one of my father's aprons and a couple of my mother's—banged pots and harassed each other in French and Italian. They minced parsley, snapped beans, and drove off to be lost for an hour looking for the grocery store to buy more cream; they chopped garlic and constantly mopped around a case of mussels covered in ice that leaked, insolently, on the floor. And the smells! Simmering veal stock and grilled eggplant; freshly washed berries—strawberries, raspberries, blueberries, blackberries—and sweet boiled carrots; roasted red peppers, which glistened with oil in a glass bowl; and the musky, honeymoon perfume of freshly shaved black truffles. My father was in culinary heaven. I think they all were. It was a jovial, rambunctious scene, a dance of chefs as they slid past each other with dripping colanders and hot skillets.

These chefs, or a slightly different combination of them, had come together before, to cook for Claudia Franey's wedding at Craig Claiborne's house in East Hampton. Craig had adopted, or been adopted by, the families of a few well-known chefs, and he loved to host their events: Jacques and Gloria Pépin's marriage, and Pierre and Betty Franey's 20th anniversary, and all manner of other love/food/wine affairs were conducted at the house on Gardiner's Bay. For Claudia's wedding, the chefs were her dad Pierre; Jacques Pépin; Jean Vergnes; Jean-Jacques Paimblanc, a chef from Boston; Jean Louis Todeschini, the chef from Le Cirque at the time; and Dad. She was married in a simple white cotton dress on a hot day in August, and all the chefs cooked in their bathing suits.

The day of my wedding, the chefs arrived from their bed-and-breakfasts dressed in crisp whites and checkered pants, and, true to the 1980s, I wore a dress with shoulder pads large enough to rival an offensive lineman's, and that rendered me incapable of contributing in the crowded kitchen. But no matter: The chefs were in their own orbit. Pierre Franey eyed the bushel of mussels and decided he was going to invent a new recipe: cold mussel pasta salad with saffron mayonnaise (à la Gena, he called it), with ingredients he had on hand. For 200. The kitchen practically shook with activity, and most everyone of nonculinary import was shooed away. Early in that final cooking session, Dad asked my brother Cham to dig up some wine buried in the dirt floor of the root cellar. He had buried a few gallons from a particularly good homemade vintage about a decade before in anticipation of his daughters' weddings. Dad proudly uncorked the earth-covered bottle and poured Jacques Pépin a glass. The chef sipped, and then passed it back. "Edward," he said, "I think you should bury this again."

Kevin and I were married on the front porch, under a sky full of thick, moody clouds and surrounded by the smell of spring. Twenty or so close friends and family members, and all of the chefs in their tall hats, watched as we exchanged our vows, and my friend Sonja started crying—the only rain that day. As soon as the rings were on, the chefs skedaddled back into the kitchen, to toss and garnish. And moments later, the rest of our friends began pouring down the driveway smiling in their dresses and hats.

They came to wish us well, of course, but I think they really came to eat.

The food was set up buffet-style, but served by the chefs in their whites. The first course consisted of Pierre's pasta salad, which was smooth and cool and rich, and Dad's tangy caponata with roasted peppers, a simple ratatouille of vegetables that is wonderful with a piece of bread. The pasta course was farfalle with smoked trout, which is creamy and smoky and, the way the French chefs served it, loaded with brandy. The main course was filet mignon perigueux, a sauce made with demi-glace, Madeira wine, and truffles, served with a puree of carrots and potatoes, and haricots verts with shallots, all French classics, and the co-operative domain of the chefs. Jacques Pépin made multi-berry compote in red wine to go with Albert Kumin's hazelnut wedding cake with apricot filling, surmounted by two titanic sugar wedding rings. I hear it was a glorious meal. I didn't eat much that day.

When Kevin and I got to the Algonquin Hotel in New York that night, I ate a room service chopped steak with a cold beer. And it was the best thing I ever put in my mouth.

ESSENTIALS OF
MEAL PLANNING

Seasonal eating in Italy may be best summed up by the fresh produce displays in the entrance of restaurants and trattorias. Usually, it's a modest collection: pretty samples to remind the diner of what is in. But occasionally, a restaurant will provide a glorious display of the fish, vegetables, and fruits they are featuring. Our favorite occurs in spring, when some eateries will exhibit three nubbly mounds of fresh-shelled peas: small, medium, and large, from which to choose.

We look forward to spring for the dandelions that start to appear in the yard, and the arugula, which pops up in the cold frame, and the salads we make from them. We gather morels, if luck is on our side, and wild onions for garnishes. The garden fills with new, tender turnip greens, and the last growth of the rape, rapini. We can't wait for our first taste of soft-shell crabs for the year, the shad and its delectable roe. Over and over, we eat baby lamb, spinach, artichokes, spicy fava beans, sugary strawberries, and tangy rhubarb.

Spring meals need to sate hungers for both cold weather and warm weather foods. So while delicate vegetables like peas and asparagus are infinitely pleasing, we still want to eat them in hearty stews and soups. As winter turns to spring, we crave risotto, frittata, rabbit, and lamb shanks. But later, as the days warm up, we eat lighter foods: delicate spaghettini, fish soup, fish with spring vegetables, and scrambled eggs. Although we don't find the abundance of foods that we will see in summer, the foods we do have, when combined, embody the season's sweet duality.

SUNDAY LUNCH

On Sundays when I was a child, we always sat down in the middle of the day to a two-course meal with dessert, and then at night we ate only leftovers: sandwiches made from a piece of meat and a pile of vegetables, like roast veal with a mound of cooked dandelion greens on toasted homemade bread, or roasted chicken with the smashed hearts of leftover baked artichokes. Every Sunday lunch, my parents, even if it is just the two of them, will eat a small pasta course, maybe spaghettini with peas, then split a roasted poussin, and finally a sweet, ricotta pie, washed down with a glass of homemade wine. But more often some combination of family gets together on Sundays. This is the most inviolable of Giobbi traditions, and the same is true for many Italian families.

Sunday lunches in the spring are particularly pleasurable because my parents live in the country, and all of us kids live in the city with our children. One hankers for evidence of new life in the countryside, and so we come out to eat, and sniff the new earth, and hope to find a morel or two. When I was growing up, there was almost always company for Sunday lunch. It was a regular routine to pick up New Yorkers at the train station and bring them straight to the kitchen, where they were promptly handed a glass of wine. Some folks hung around the stove, smelling the roasting meats, chatting and getting in the way, and others stumbled about outdoors, on the brick patio that was buckling from the roots of a giant sugar maple.

Most folks who came were people from the art or food worlds: Frank Sinatra with his wife, gorgeous as a showgirl, and Gregory Peck; Benny Goodman, who liked polenta and blew his nose in the cloth napkins; Hans Hoffman, the great painter who pulled up in the driveway with his beautiful young "niece" in a convertible MG; collectors like Joe Hirshhorn, who tipped $100 to Lisa for clearing the table, and painters like Robert Motherwell, who was partial to tripe, and his wife, Renata. Food pros were always in abundance: Jim Beard, jolly and enthusiastic; the gifted food writer Betty Fussell; Jacques and Gloria Pépin; Nanni Valetto, whose restaurant Nanni's in New York exposed many people to refined Italian food for the first time; a slew of folks connected to Sirio Maccioni and Le Cirque, like Alain Sailhac and Jean Vergnes. And always Craig Claiborne, whom we called Uncle Craig and who sometimes tried to kiss my dad when he'd had too much to drink.

But as time passed, the Giobbi kids began to bring our friends and colleagues. Often hilariously, Lisa's circus friends came. I particularly like Sacha Pavlata, one of the Flying Wallendas, who tends to characterize kids by the circus discipline they would naturally take to—stylish and precise Snow Guilfoyle, Lisa's daughter, is the aerialist; my showy, athletic daughter Carson, the equestrian; and Mo Bone, my loose-limbed, kooky son, the clown.

It seemed Sunday lunches had taken a generational shift, so when we came together a few years ago to honor Pierre Franey, who died in 1996, it was a particularly nostalgic event. Pierre was warm and gregarious and unpretentious. There was, in our household, a feeling for a while that when Pierre died, the good times had gone with him. After his death a big charity event was held at the Tavern on the Green, but my parents, and many of the old crowd, felt the need to remember him in a more personal way. And so one Sunday lunch, Betty Franey and her children and grandchildren, three generations of the Vergnes family, Roger Fessaguet, of Le Caravelle fame, Jacques and Gloria Pépin, and the Giobbis all came together. The chefs cooked: pasta with a sweet tripe sauce, which was one of the dishes Edward regularly served when the chefs came to dine, then a roasted baby lamb, its browned skin smelling of charcoal and rosemary, with a mint pesto, baked asparagus, and roasted potatoes. Jacques made a beautiful galette with rhubarb, which was utterly appetizing in its natural irregularities. Pierre's son Jacques brought a magnum of vintage champagne, and the Franey, Vergnes, and Giobbi grandchildren tumbled on the grass and harassed my mother's flock of aging bantam chickens and never felt the solemnity of the moment, bless them.

As we stood around the laid tables on the bumpy brick patio, the smell of new leaves and the spring water burbling up in the lawn, beside the pond, all over the property, we said a few words of good-bye to Pierre. It was a difficult toast: Sentiments were caught in throats and voices became softer and softer, soft as the crocuses that bobbed brightly around us, until finally Betty, who always says it like it is, pulled the group together. "Pierre would have loved this," she said. "So let's eat." And we did.

Spring
First Courses

Asparagus with Eggs

This is a dish Edward often made for lunch when he was a student in Florence. It works very well as a light entrée, served with a piece of bruschetta and finished with a salad of baby greens.

3 tablespoons olive oil

2 pounds medium asparagus, peeled and cut into 2-inch lengths, tough ends removed (about 4 cups)

2 medium onions, thinly sliced (about 2 cups)

Salt and freshly ground black pepper

8 eggs

⅓ cup grated Parmesan cheese

2 tablespoons finely chopped flat-leaf parsley

Heat the oil in a large skillet over medium heat. Add the asparagus and onions, season with salt and pepper to taste, cover, and cook until the asparagus are fork-tender, about 10 minutes. Create 8 depressions in the vegetables with the back of a spoon. Break each egg individually into a ramekin and slide the eggs, one at a time, into the depressions. Do not break the yolks. Cover and cook until the whites are cooked through, 10 to 15 minutes. Sprinkle with the cheese and parsley and serve immediately.

Serves 4

Bruschetta

Bruschetta (pronounced brew-SKE-ta) is Roman-style garlic bread. It is unlikely you'll see the American version—half-loaves of bread slathered with pasty garlic—served in Italy, and we've never seen it served with pasta. Rather, this lightly seasoned toast is a typical accompaniment for fish salads and stews.

4 slices Italian bread

2 tablespoons extra virgin olive oil

2 garlic cloves, peeled

Salt

Place the bread on a baking tray and dribble the oil all over it. Toast the bread under the broiler, for about 30 seconds on each side. When the bread is browned, remove it and rub the garlic cloves over the toasted bread until they are mashed into the surface of the toast. Season with salt to taste.

Serves 4

Ricotta Balls with Prosciutto

We like to serve these as a first course, or as part of a Spring Vegetable Fritto Misto (see page 77) with a small green salad.

Wet ricotta will be hard to handle in this recipe, so we use Old Chatham Sheepherding Company's fresh sheep milk ricotta (available in most specialty and health food stores), which is drier. Otherwise, drain the ricotta in a colander over the sink for about 20 minutes.

1 cup ricotta

4 slices prosciutto, diced, or ½ cup diced boiled ham

2 tablespoons grated Parmesan or Pecorino cheese

1½ teaspoons finely chopped flat-leaf parsley

Dash of grated nutmeg

Salt and freshly ground black pepper

All-purpose flour for dredging

2 egg whites, lightly beaten

1 cup breadcrumbs

Vegetable oil for frying

1 teaspoon rosemary (fresh or dried; see Note)

2 cups mixed baby salad greens

2 tablespoons extra virgin olive oil

Juice of ½ lemon (about 1½ tablespoons)

In a mixing bowl, combine the ricotta, prosciutto, grated cheese, parsley, nutmeg, and salt and pepper to taste. Mix well and form into 8 to 10 balls about 1½ inches in diameter. Gently roll the balls in the flour, then the egg whites, and then the breadcrumbs.

Heat about 1 inch of vegetable oil in a medium skillet over medium-high heat. Test the heat by throwing a pinch of flour into the oil. If the flour pops, the oil is ready for frying. Add the rosemary. Add the balls and fry until they are golden brown, about 1 minute on each side.

In a small bowl, dress the salad greens with the olive oil and lemon juice. Season with salt and and toss well.

Serve two ricotta balls with about ½ cup of salad on each plate.

Note: We add rosemary to cooking oil not for the flavor, but because it reduces the free radicals by 90 percent when you fry.

Serves 4

Pierre's Salad Gena

This is our best estimation of the recipe that Pierre Franey invented for Gena's wedding.

½ cup dry white wine

½ cup water

¼ teaspoon saffron

5 pounds mussels, scrubbed and debearded

¾ pound farfalle

For the mayonnaise

1 egg yolk

1 teaspoon Dijon mustard

1 teaspoon white wine vinegar or lemon juice

½ cup light olive oil or other vegetable oil

Salt

Freshly ground black pepper

In a large saucepan with a steamer fitted in the bottom, place the wine, water, and saffron. Bring to a boil over medium heat. Add the mussels and steam until they open, 5 to 7 minutes. Shell the mussels and set them aside. Boil the broth until it is reduced to about ¾ cup.

Bring a large pot of salted water to a boil over high heat and add the pasta. Cook until it is al dente. Drain.

For the mayonnaise: In a metal bowl, whisk together the egg yolk, mustard, and vinegar. Add the oil in a very slow dribble, whisking all the while. The mayonnaise should start to thicken right away. Add salt to taste.

Heat the broth over low heat and add the mussels. Allow them to warm thoroughly.

In a serving bowl, combine the pasta with the mussels, broth, and mayonnaise. Season with freshly ground black pepper.

Serves 4

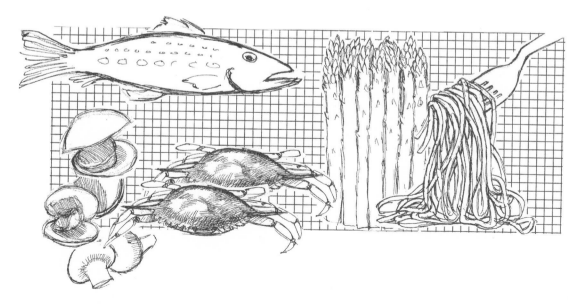

Arctic Char in Aspic

This delicious and elegant dish is convenient because it is best made a day ahead of time; and because it is so light, it is a perfect first course for an evening meal.

1 arctic char (1½ pounds) or other white-fleshed fish such as striped bass, gutted

4 large asparagus spears, peeled

3 cups chicken stock

2 tablespoons unflavored gelatin

3 tablespoons sherry

Dash of nutmeg

Salt

2 tablespoons finely chopped fresh dill

For the green sauce

1 bunch scallions, thinly sliced (about 2 cups)

½ cup finely chopped fresh mint

1 garlic clove, finely chopped

3 tablespoons extra virgin olive oil

2 tablespoons balsamic vinegar

½ cup walnuts

Salt and freshly ground black pepper

Place a rectangular baking dish about 1½ inches deep by 10 inches long (or a 1-quart ring mold) into the freezer and allow it to become very cold.

Place the char in a fish steamer or long covered pot with a rack. Add water to just below the rack. Bring to a boil on top of the stove over medium heat and cook for about 20 minutes, until the fish separates easily from the bone. (You can also use fillets cut by your fishmonger; they will steam more quickly.) Fillet the char and discard the skin and bones.

Place the asparagus in an asparagus steamer or pot with a rack large enough to hold the spears and add water to just below the rack. Add salt. Bring to a boil over high heat and cook until tender, about 6 minutes. Rinse in cold water and cut in half, lengthwise.

In a large pot, bring the stock to a boil over medium-high heat. Strain the stock through fine cheesecloth into a bowl. Add the gelatin in a slow dribble, mixing all the while. Add the sherry and nutmeg and mix well. Add salt to taste. Place the broth in the refrigerator and chill for 10 minutes.

Remove the baking dish from the freezer and pour about ½ inch of the broth into the bottom. Cover with plastic wrap and refrigerate until the gelatin sets, about 15 minutes. Remove the dish from the refrigerator and lay the asparagus across the bottom, with the uncut sides down. You will see the asparagus when you unmold the aspic, so lay them down neatly. Sprinkle the dill over the asparagus. Add the boned fish in an even layer, patching with pieces as necessary. Pour in the rest of the gelatin. Cover the tray with plastic wrap and refrigerate for at least 2 hours, or ideally, overnight.

For the green sauce: In a food processor, combine the scallions, mint, garlic, oil, vinegar, walnuts, and salt and pepper to taste, and pulse to make a smooth puree.

Remove the aspic from the refrigerator about 20 minutes before serving. Carefully flip the aspic over onto a cold serving platter and lift up the baking dish. Serve with the green sauce.

Serves 4 to 6

Soft-Shell Crabs with Avocado Sauce

Elinor loves avocado, so Edward makes this dish for her. This first course is an excellent prelude to shad roe, or serve it as a light dinner with a salad.

4 soft-shell crabs

½ cup all-purpose flour, plus additional for dredging

1 cup beer or white wine

1 egg white, lightly beaten

½ teaspoon baking powder

Salt and freshly ground black pepper

1 ice cube

Vegetable oil for frying

1 teaspoon rosemary (fresh or dried)

For the sauce

1 avocado

2 tablespoons extra virgin olive oil

Juice of ½ lemon (about 1½ tablespoons) or 2 tablespoons balsamic vinegar

1 teaspoon finely chopped flat-leaf parsley

1 scallion, thinly sliced

Salt and freshly ground black pepper

To clean the crabs: Use scissors to snip off the front where the eyes protrude, and lift off the side flaps to remove the gills, or ask your fishmonger to clean the crabs. Wash in cold water and pat dry.

In a large bowl, mix ½ cup flour, the beer, egg white, baking powder, and salt and pepper to taste. Add the ice cube and refrigerate for about 1 hour (longer is okay).

For the sauce: Remove the avocado flesh from the skin with a spoon and place it in a small food processor. Add the olive oil, lemon juice, parsley, scallion, and salt and pepper to taste. Blend to a creamy consistency.

Heat about 1 inch of vegetable oil in a large skillet over medium-high heat. Test the heat by throwing a pinch of flour into the oil. If the flour pops, the oil is ready for frying. Add the rosemary. Dust the crabs in flour. Dunk the crabs in the batter and place them gently in the hot oil. Turn the crabs over after about a minute. Then turn them over again after another minute. Do this four times, until the crabs are golden brown, for a total of about 4 minutes per side. The crabs must be cooked thoroughly or they will be runny inside.

Drain the crabs on paper towels, sprinkle with salt to taste, and serve immediately, with the avocado sauce.

Serves 4

Octopus Salad

Octopus is an excellent, delicate mollusk that is particularly easy on the stomach. We steam it with a wine cork in the pot because the cork tenderizes the octopus. This dish can be made a day ahead of time and stored, covered, in the refrigerator.

1 small octopus, about 1¾ to 2 pounds (have your fishmonger clean the head)

½ cup dry white wine

½ cup sliced scallions

4 garlic cloves, sliced

Salt and hot pepper flakes

1 wine cork

1 cup fresh peas (about 1 pound in the shell)

2 tablespoons chopped cilantro

1 tablespoon chopped mint

2 tablespoons extra virgin olive oil

Juice of 1 lemon
(about 3 tablespoons)

Salt

In a large pot, place the octopus, wine, scallions, garlic, and salt and hot pepper flakes to taste. Add the wine cork. Bring to a boil over medium-high heat, and then lower the heat to medium-low and cook, tightly covered, until the octopus is fork-tender, about 45 minutes. Remove the octopus from the liquid and let it cool. Rub off the dark skin and suction cups from the tentacles. Cut the octopus into 1-inch sections, place in a large bowl, and set aside.

Bring a small pot of water to a boil over medium-high heat and add the peas. Boil the peas until they are tender when tested with a fork, about 10 minutes. Drain and add the peas to the octopus. Add the cilantro, mint, oil, and lemon juice. Season to taste with salt. Allow the salad to rest for 1½ hours. It is best served at room temperature.

Serves 4

Spring Minestrone

We make minestrone, which is simply vegetable soup, all year long: hot varieties in the fall and winter, and room-temperature soups in the spring and summer. You can add chopped spinach or other tender, seasonal greens to this soup as well. Just put them in at the same time as the potato. This makes a terrific first course before any of the entrées in this section.

2 tablespoons olive oil

1 medium onion, finely chopped

2 garlic cloves, finely chopped

1 cup whole canned Italian tomatoes, chopped

3 cups chicken stock

1 cup fresh peas (about 1 pound in the shell)

1 large potato (we prefer Yukon Gold), peeled and diced

1 tablespoon mint chiffonade

Salt and freshly ground black pepper

5 tablespoons raw rice

4 medium asparagus spears, cut into 1-inch lengths

Extra virgin olive oil or grated Parmesan cheese, for garnish

Heat the olive oil in a medium soup pot over medium heat. Add the onion and garlic and cook until the onion becomes translucent, about 5 minutes. Add the tomatoes, cover, and simmer for 5 minutes, until the tomatoes break up. Add the stock and bring to a low boil. Add the peas, cover, and boil for 10 minutes. Add the potato, mint, and salt and pepper to taste. Boil for 5 minutes, then add the rice and allow it to boil in the soup for 5 minutes. Add the asparagus and boil for another 10 minutes, until the rice is cooked and the asparagus are tender. Turn off the heat and allow the soup to come down to room temperature.

Serve the soup at room temperature garnished with either a drizzle of extra virgin olive oil or grated cheese.

Serves 4

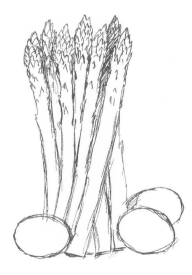

Fresh Pea Soup with Fish

Often, we buy a whole fish, make the fish stock from the bones and head, and finish the soup with pieces of fillet. It is a very economical use of the fish. To do the same, buy a 1-to-2 pound fish, like a black bass, to prepare this dish. Fillet, and reserve the bones for stock.

2 tablespoons olive oil

1 cup chopped leeks (whites only; use the greens in the stock)

2 garlic cloves, sliced (about 1 tablespoon)

4 cups fish stock (recipe follows)

1 cup fresh peas (about 1 pound in the shell)

Juice of 1/2 lemon (about 1 1/2 tablespoons)

1 tablespoon mint chiffonade

Salt

3/4 pound white-fleshed fish such as scrod or striped bass, cut into 1-inch pieces

Extra virgin olive oil, for garnish

4 teaspoons finely chopped flat-leaf parsley, for garnish

Heat the olive oil in a medium soup pot over medium heat. Add the leeks and garlic. Cover and simmer until the leeks are soft, about 5 minutes. Add the stock. Cover and cook for 15 minutes. Add the peas, lemon juice, mint, and salt to taste. Continue cooking, covered, until the peas are tender, about 10 minutes. Pour the soup into a food processor and puree. Return the soup to the pot and bring to a gentle boil. Add the fish and simmer until the fish is cooked, a couple of minutes. Garnish each portion with a drizzle of extra virgin olive oil and a teaspoon of parsley.

Serves 4

Fish Stock

3 tablespoons olive oil

1 medium onion, coarsely chopped

2 small leeks, coarsely chopped

2 garlic cloves, chopped

1 cup whole canned Italian tomatoes, chopped

1 celery rib, chopped

1 tablespoon chopped basil

1 tablespoon chopped flat-leaf parsley

2½ to 3 pounds fish heads (gills removed) and carcasses

8 cups water

½ cup dry white wine

3 bay leaves

Salt and freshly ground black pepper

Heat the oil in a large pot over medium heat. Add the onion, leeks, and garlic and cook until the onion becomes translucent, about 5 minutes. Add the tomatoes, celery, basil, and parsley. Cover and simmer for about 5 minutes, until the tomatoes break up. Add the fish heads and carcasses, the water, wine, bay leaves, and salt and pepper to taste. Bring to a boil, then boil gently for 30 minutes.

Strain the stock and discard all the solids. You can freeze the stock or keep it in the refrigerator and bring it to a boil every third day, in order to kill bacteria (you will lose some volume).

Makes about 6 cups

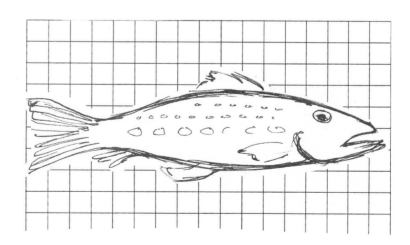

25

Pea and Asparagus Soup

Thin or very fresh asparagus spears are tender enough to eat unpeeled. Thick asparagus are peeled so that the stalks and tips cook more evenly. We use a vegetable peeler. To break off the tough ends of thin spears, we bend them gently until they break naturally. With thick spears, we cut off the ends where the color of the spears changes.

3 tablespoons olive oil

1 medium onion, finely chopped

2 garlic cloves, finely chopped

1 cup whole canned Italian tomatoes, chopped

⅓ cup chopped celery (about half a rib)

1 tablespoon chopped flat-leaf parsley

1 bay leaf

5 cups chicken stock

6 medium asparagus spears, cut into 1-inch lengths

1 cup fresh peas (about 1 pound in shell)

Salt and freshly ground black pepper

¾ cup small cut pasta, like shells or tubetini, or ½ cup raw rice

2 eggs, beaten

6 tablespoons grated Parmesan cheese

Heat the oil in a large soup pot over medium heat. Add the onion and garlic. Cover and cook until the onion becomes translucent, about 5 minutes. Add the tomatoes, cover, and simmer about 5 minutes, until the tomatoes break up. Add the celery, parsley, bay leaf, and stock. Cover and simmer for 15 minutes, then add the asparagus and continue to simmer for 15 minutes more, until the vegetables are soft. Remove the bay leaf. Puree the soup in a food processor or blender. Return the soup to the pot and add the peas and salt and pepper to taste. Cook for 10 minutes over moderate heat, until the peas are tender.

In the meantime, bring a small pot of salted water to a boil over high heat. Add the pasta and cook until it is al dente. If you use rice, cover with salted water, bring to a boil, then turn the heat down to low, cover, and simmer until the rice has absorbed all of the water and is tender, about 10 minutes.

In a small bowl, combine the eggs and 2 tablespoons of the cheese. Bring the pea soup puree to a very gentle boil over medium-low heat. Add the egg mixture and swirl it with a fork through the soup for about 30 seconds, until the eggs are cooked.

To serve, place 2 tablespoons of pasta or rice in the bottom of a soup bowl and pour the soup over. Garnish with the remaining cheese.

Serves 4

Ceci Bean Soup with Shrimp

This intrepid combination of ingredients is fairly common in Italy. We have had it in both Le Marche and Tuscany. You can use any combination of shellfish in this dish.

½ cup dried ceci (garbanzo) beans, soaked overnight and drained

4 cups water

2 garlic cloves, peeled

1 tablespoon chopped fresh rosemary or 1 teaspoon crushed dried

1 bay leaf

Salt and hot pepper flakes

3 tablespoons olive oil

1 medium onion, chopped

2 garlic cloves, finely chopped

1 cup whole canned Italian tomatoes, chopped

2 tablespoons finely chopped flat-leaf parsley

1 medium carrot, chopped

1 celery rib, chopped

½ cup fresh peas (about ½ pound in the shell)

16 shrimp, shelled and deveined, or the equivalent number of mussels, scallops, and/or clams

Extra virgin olive oil, for garnish

In a medium soup pot, combine the ceci beans, water, garlic cloves, rosemary, bay leaf, and salt and hot pepper flakes to taste. Boil gently over medium heat for about 30 minutes.

In the meantime, heat the olive oil in a large skillet over medium heat. Add the onion and chopped garlic and cook until the onion becomes translucent, about 5 minutes. Add the tomatoes and parsley and simmer for 5 minutes, then add the carrot and celery. Cook the vegetables for about 15 minutes, until the carrot is soft. Add the tomato mixture to the ceci bean soup and continue cooking for an hour, covered, until the beans are tender. Add the peas and cook until tender, about 10 minutes. Add the shrimp and continue cooking until they turn pink, about 5 minutes. Remove the bay leaf.

Lace each portion with a drizzle of extra virgin olive oil.

Serves 4

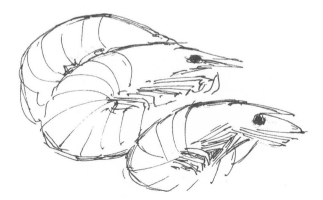

Chicken and Dandelion Soup

We take the chicken out of the pot before the broth is finished so the chicken doesn't overcook, then use the bones to finish the broth. This is an efficient and delightful dish, very light but satisfying. Ask your butcher to grind the beef twice, so it's very fine.

1 chicken (4 to 4½ pounds)

Salt and freshly ground
black pepper

¾ pound lean double-ground beef

1 egg

3 tablespoons finely chopped
flat-leaf parsley

1 teaspoon grated lemon zest

⅓ cup grated Parmesan or
Pecorino cheese, plus 3
tablespoons for garnish

½ cup finely chopped onion

2 large carrots, cut into 3 lengths
each

2 celery ribs, cut into
4 lengths each

1 medium parsnip, scraped

2 bay leaves

5 cups wild dandelions, washed
and coarsely chopped

2 tablespoons fresh lemon juice
(about 1 lemon)

Season the chicken inside and out with salt and pepper.

In a large bowl, make the stuffing by combining the beef, egg, 1 tablespoon of the parsley, the lemon zest, ⅓ cup cheese, onion, and salt and pepper to taste. Set 1 cup of the stuffing aside in the refrigerator. Force the remaining stuffing inside the cavity of the chicken.

Truss the chicken and place it in a large soup pot. Add the carrots, celery, parsnip, bay leaves, the remaining 2 tablespoons of parsley, and salt to taste. Cover with water and cover the pot. Bring to a boil over medium-high heat and allow to boil gently for 15 minutes. Skim off the scum that rises to the top of the pot. Turn off the heat and allow the chicken to rest, covered, in the hot broth for 60 minutes. Remove the chicken from the broth. Bone the chicken and remove the stuffing in one piece, if possible. (It will be cooked solid, like a meatball. If necessary, cut into two pieces and slide stuffing out.) Cover the meat and stuffing and set aside. Toss the bones and skin back in the broth. Partially cover and continue boiling gently over medium heat for about 2 hours.

Strain the broth, discard the solids, and defat the broth. Pour the broth in a medium pot and bring to a boil over medium heat. Add the dandelion greens and boil for about 15 minutes, until the greens are tender. With the remaining 1 cup of stuffing, form 12 small meatballs, no bigger than ¾ inch in diameter. Add the meatballs and lemon juice to the pot and cook about 4 minutes. To serve, place a few pieces of chicken meat in a soup bowl. Add a slice of the stuffing. Ladle the hot dandelion greens and broth over the chicken. Add about 2 meatballs per serving. Garnish with the remaining cheese.

Note: You will have some leftover chicken from this dish. We like to make Boiled Chicken with Asparagus and Peas (page 53).

Serves 6

Spaghettini Salad

We first tasted a version of this recipe on Capri, and nothing embodies that island for us better than this simple, re-freshing pasta dish.

8 cups mixed baby salad greens, such as escarole, endive, water-cress, and wild rugola

5 tablespoons extra virgin olive oil

2 ounces pancetta, cut into ¼-inch cubes (about 4 tablespoons)

¾ pound spaghettini

3 tablespoons white wine vinegar

Salt and freshly ground black pepper

¼ cup Parmesan cheese shavings, for garnish

Wash and dry the lettuce, and tear it into bite-size pieces. Place in a large serving bowl. The lettuce should be room temperature.

Heat 1 tablespoon of the oil in a small skillet over medium heat. Add the pancetta and cook until the fat is rendered, about 5 minutes. Drain the pancetta on paper towels.

Bring a large pot of salted water to a boil over high heat. Add the spaghettini and cook until it is al dente.

While the pasta is cooking, blend the remaining 4 tablespoons of oil and the vinegar in a small bowl.

Drain the pasta and add it to the lettuce. Pour the oil and vinegar over the pasta and lettuce, toss in the pancetta, and season with salt and pepper to taste. Toss well, garnish with the cheese shavings, and serve.

Serves 4

Fried Pasta

This is an unusual dish that Edward first tasted in the home of his longtime friend Principe Giovanni Del Drago, in Rome. The recipe is of southern Italian origin. Italians don't use tinned anchovies for cooking—only salted. Try to get them for this recipe. Fedelini ("little faithful ones") is very thin spaghetti.

4 salted anchovies or 6 fillets packed in olive oil

6 tablespoons extra virgin olive oil, plus additional for pan

12 black olives cured in oil, pitted and sliced

4 garlic cloves, finely chopped

6 tablespoons finely chopped flat-leaf parsley

Hot pepper flakes or freshly ground black pepper

½ pound fedelini

4 tablespoons grated Pecorino or Parmesan cheese

Salt

1 can (6 ounces) Italian tuna fish packed in olive oil, drained

If you are using salted anchovies, gently separate the fillets from the bones. Discard the bones. Rinse the fillets in cold water. Put them in a small bowl, cover them with cold water, and allow to sit for 5 to 15 minutes, until softened. Drain the fillets, pat them dry, and chop. If you're using tinned anchovy fillets, drain off the oil and chop.

Heat 4 tablespoons of the oil in a medium nonstick skillet over medium heat. Add the anchovies, olives, garlic, 4 tablespoons of the parsley, and the hot pepper flakes to taste. Cook until the anchovies dissolve, stirring often, about 3 minutes.

Bring a large pot of salted water to a boil over high heat. Add the fedelini and cook a little more than al dente. Be careful because fedelini overcooks easily. Drain the pasta.

In a mixing bowl, combine the pasta, the anchovy sauce, cheese, the remaining 2 tablespoons of oil, and the remaining 2 tablespoons of parsley. Add salt if you need it (the anchovies and olives are both salty). Add the tuna fish and mix gently.

Cover the bottom of a medium nonstick skillet with a slick of oil. Add the pasta mixture and pat it down so that it is flat and smooth on top. Cook, uncovered, over medium to low heat for about 6 minutes. Place a plate on top of the skillet and flip the pasta over onto the plate. The bottom should be golden brown. Slip the pasta, uncooked side down, back into the skillet. Cook an additional 5 minutes, until golden brown.

Serve the pasta cut in wedges like a pie.

Serves 4

Penne with Asparagus and Shrimp

Before serving this dish, we like to add a thimbleful of additional brandy to each portion. Our friend Jean Vergnes told us that when he was the chef at Le Cirque in New York, he always hit a dish with a little additional booze before sending it out to his customers.

4 tablespoons olive oil

1 pound medium asparagus, cut into 1½-inch lengths

2 garlic cloves, minced

2 cups whole canned Italian tomatoes, chopped

2 tablespoons chopped flat-leaf parsley

1 tablespoon chopped mint

Salt and hot pepper flakes

¾ pound shrimp, shelled and deveined, cut into 1- to 1½-inch pieces

¾ pound penne, ziti, or other tubular pasta

1 jigger brandy

Heat 2 tablespoons of the oil in a large skillet over medium heat. Add the asparagus and cook for about 10 minutes, until they are tender. Remove the asparagus with a slotted spoon and set aside. Add the remaining 2 tablespoons of oil to the skillet and heat. Add the garlic and simmer for about 3 minutes, until the garlic begins to take on color. Add the tomatoes, parsley, mint, and salt and hot pepper flakes to taste. Cover and cook for 10 minutes over low heat, until the tomatoes have broken up. Add the shrimp and simmer about 5 minutes more, until the shrimp turn pink.

In the meantime, bring a large pot of salted water to a boil over high heat. Add the pasta and cook until it is al dente. Drain the pasta and add it to the sauce. Add the reserved asparagus and the brandy and cook several minutes more over high heat, stirring constantly.

Serves 4

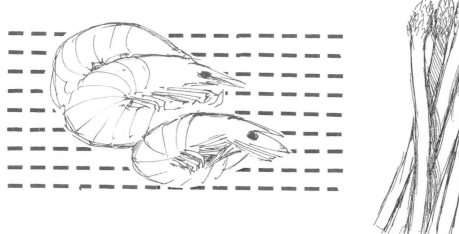

Penne with Peas and Tuna

We make this dish in late spring when the first fresh tomatoes are out, and serve it as a first course before broiled shad and a vegetable like turnip greens. We recommend you use an imported Italian tuna packed in olive oil, with the oil drained off. Our favorite tuna is ventresca, the luscious belly meat; our second choice is jarred tuna imported from Italy, which has a fresher taste than canned; and our final choice is tinned imported Italian tuna. We don't even consider using American-brand tunas packed in water, which taste like cardboard to us.

3 tablespoons extra virgin olive oil

2 medium onions, finely chopped

2 cups fresh tomatoes, pushed through a food mill (or 2 cups whole canned Italian tomatoes, chopped)

1 cup fresh peas (about 1 pound in the shell), blanched

Salt and freshly ground black pepper

1 jar or can (6 ounces) Italian tuna fish packed in olive oil, drained

¾ pound cut pasta, such as penne or fusilli

2 tablespoons finely chopped flat-leaf parsley

2 cups toasted croutons, or extra virgin olive oil, for garnish (see Note)

Heat the oil in a large skillet over medium heat. Add the onions and cook until they become translucent, about 5 minutes. Add the tomatoes, cover, and simmer over medium-low heat until the tomatoes break up, about 10 minutes. Add the peas and salt and pepper to taste. Cover and cook until the peas are tender, about 10 minutes. Add the tuna fish and simmer for several minutes.

Bring a large pot of salted water to a boil over high heat and add the pasta. Cook until it is al dente. Drain the pasta and toss into the sauce. Add the parsley and serve, garnished with the croutons or extra virgin olive oil (or both).

Note: We prefer homemade croutons. To make them, cut day-old bread into cubes about ½-inch square. Toss in olive oil to lightly coat. Then either sauté them in a non-stick skillet over medium heat until lightly browned or toast them on a baking tray in a 400°F oven until lightly browned.

Serves 4

Capellini with Steamed Mussels and Clams

This is a very delicate dish, perfect as a first course or followed by a salad for a late supper. You can substitute other fresh herbs, like dill or tarragon, but avoid dried herbs, which will lend too strong a flavor.

12 littleneck clams, scrubbed

12 mussels, debearded

4 tablespoons extra virgin olive oil

4 garlic cloves, sliced

1 tablespoon basil chiffonade

1 tablespoon finely chopped fresh oregano

1 tablespoon finely chopped flat-leaf parsley

1 cup dry white wine

Salt and hot pepper flakes

1½ cups fish stock or water

¾ pound capellini

In a large shallow pan, place the clams, mussels, oil, garlic, basil, oregano, parsley, wine, and salt and hot pepper flakes to taste. Spread out the seafood so that it doesn't overlap. Cover with foil and allow to rest in the refrigerator for 30 minutes.

Place the covered pan over high heat. As soon as the clams and mussels open (about 5 minutes), remove them from the broth and shell all but 8 mussels. Add the fish stock to the pan, turn down the heat to medium, and bring to a low boil. Add the pasta and cook, stirring often, until the pasta is al dente. Toss in the shelled bivalves. Serve immediately garnished with the unshelled mussels.

Serves 4

Penne with Pork, Asparagus, and Morels

We came up with this dish in Montana, while foraging through forest fire burns for morels with our friend Andrew Geiger. The first spring after a forest fire in the Northwest usually yields a bounty of morels—blacks, blonds, and the valuable grays. We buy commercial licenses, as noncommercial pickers must slice their mushrooms in half, making them very hard to dry.

2 tablespoons unsalted butter

½ pound fresh morels, sliced

½ cup dry Marsala wine

Salt

2 tablespoons olive oil

½ cup minced onion

3 garlic cloves, minced

⅓ pound lean ground pork

12 thin asparagus spears, cut into bite-size pieces

Hot pepper flakes

¾ pound penne or other cut pasta

3 tablespoons finely chopped flat-leaf parsley, for garnish

⅓ cup grated Parmesan cheese, for garnish (optional)

Heat the butter in a small skillet over medium heat and add the morels. Cook them until they release their water, about 5 minutes. Add ¼ cup of the wine and continue cooking for another 3 to 5 minutes, until the mushrooms have absorbed most of the wine. Add salt to taste. Set aside.

Heat the oil in a medium skillet over medium heat and add the onion and garlic. Cook until the onion becomes translucent, about 5 minutes. Add the pork and cook until it is brown, about 10 minutes, stirring constantly. Add the remaining ¼ cup of wine and cook until the pork absorbs the wine, 3 to 5 minutes. Add the asparagus and cook, covered, over medium-low heat, until they are fork-tender, about 10 minutes. Add salt and hot pepper flakes to taste.

Bring a large pot of salted water to a boil over high heat. Add the penne and cook until it is al dente. Drain the penne and pour into a serving bowl. Toss in the pork and asparagus and the morels. Garnish with the parsley, and grated cheese, if you like.

Serves 4

Rigatoni with Tripe

The chefs with whom Edward was (and still is) friends, folks like the late Pierre Franey, Jean Vergnes, and Jacques Pépin, all love simple, hearty country foods like this dish. It became a tradition for him to prepare it for their Sunday potlucks.

1½ pounds honeycomb tripe

Salt

4 tablespoons olive oil

1 large leek, white only, finely chopped (about 1 cup)

3 garlic cloves, finely chopped

1 cup dry white wine

1 tablespoon chopped mint

1 teaspoon crushed dried rosemary

1 bay leaf

Freshly ground black pepper

2 cups whole canned Italian tomatoes, pushed through a food mill

1 large carrot, sliced

1 cup chicken stock

1 tablespoon finely chopped flat-leaf parsley

1 pound asparagus, cut into 2-inch lengths

1½ pounds rigatoni or other cut pasta

½ cup grated Parmesan cheese

Put the tripe in a large pot and add water to cover. Add salt and bring to a boil over high heat. Boil the tripe for 10 minutes, then drain. Allow the tripe to cool, then cut off the fat from the underside of the comb and discard. Cut the tripe into strips about ¼ inch wide and 2 inches long.

Heat 2 tablespoons of the oil in a large saucepan over medium heat. Add the leek and garlic and cook until the leek becomes soft, about 5 minutes. Add the tripe, wine, mint, rosemary, bay leaf, and salt and pepper to taste. Cook until the wine is absorbed, about 10 minutes. Add the tomatoes, carrot, stock, and parsley. Cover and bring the sauce to a boil. Lower the heat slightly and cook the sauce at a low boil for about 90 minutes, until the tripe is fork-tender. If the sauce becomes too dry, add a little more warm chicken stock.

In the meantime, heat the remaining 2 tablespoons of oil in a medium skillet over medium heat. Add the asparagus. Add salt and pepper to taste, and cook the asparagus until they are fork-tender, about 10 minutes.

Bring a large pot of salted water to a boil over high heat. Add the pasta and cook until it is al dente. Drain the pasta and toss it in a serving bowl with the sauce. Remove the bay leaf. Add the cheese and garnish with the sautéed asparagus.

Serves 8

Easter Lasagne

One Easter, Edward dropped this lasagne while removing it from the oven. What was salvageable went directly into a serving bowl. The lasagna noodles were cut into rough papardelle, and we called the dish pasta al pavimento, *or pasta from the floor. It was delicious, but lasagne does look better when you don't drop it.*

For the marinara

¼ cup olive oil

2 medium onions, coarsely chopped

1 medium carrot, sliced

2 garlic cloves, minced

4 cups whole canned Italian tomatoes

Salt and freshly ground black pepper

2 tablespoons unsalted butter

1 teaspoon dried oregano

1 tablespoon chopped fresh basil or 1 teaspoon dried

For the marinara: Heat the oil in a large skillet over medium heat. Add the onions, carrot, and garlic, and cook, stirring, until they are golden, about 8 minutes.

Pour the tomatoes through a food mill or sieve, pushing the pulp through with a spoon. Discard the seeds and skins. Add the tomato puree to the vegetables along with salt and pepper to taste. Simmer for 15 minutes, partially covered.

Pass the sauce through the food mill again, pushing the solids through with a spoon. Return the puree to the skillet. Add the butter, oregano, and basil. Partially cover the sauce and allow it to simmer over medium-low heat for 30 minutes. This will make about 1 quart of sauce.

For the lasagne

2 pounds spinach, washed

2 tablespoons olive oil

1 pound medium asparagus, cut into 1-inch lengths

1 medium onion, finely chopped

1 tablespoon finely chopped flat-leaf parsley

Salt and freshly ground black pepper

¼ cup chicken stock

4 sheets (6½ inches by 7 inches) no-boil lasagna, preferably Delverde, or 12 strips imported Italian lasagna (see Note)

6 cups ricotta

1 cup grated Parmesan cheese, plus additional for garnish

½ cup grated Pecorino cheese (or another ½ cup of Parmesan)

1 teaspoon freshly grated nutmeg

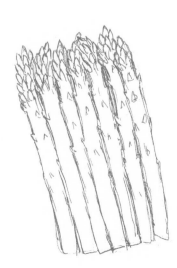

For the lasagne: Bring a large pot of salted water to a boil over high heat. Add the spinach and boil for 5 minutes. Drain and rinse the spinach in cold water. Squeeze it over a bowl, pressing out as much of the liquid as you can. Discard the liquid. Chop the spinach and set aside.

Heat the oven to 400°F.

Heat the oil in a small skillet over medium heat and add the asparagus and onion. Cook until the onion becomes translucent, about 5 minutes. Add the parsley and salt and pepper to taste, cover, and simmer until the asparagus is tender, about 5 minutes more. Place the asparagus and onion into a food processor with the chicken stock and process to a smooth puree. Set aside.

If you are using a lasagna variety other than no-boil, bring a large pot of salted water to a boil over high heat. Add the lasagna and cook until it is al dente. Drain off half the water and set the pot under cold running water to cool the lasagna enough to handle. Lay the lasagna on paper towels. Do not overlap or they will stick together.

In a large mixing bowl, combine the ricotta, Parmesan, Pecorino (if using), spinach, nutmeg, and salt and pepper to taste.

Spoon about ½ cup of marinara sauce into the bottom of the no-boil lasagne baking tray or a 9- × 9-inch baking dish. Place a layer of pasta on top, then a layer of the ricotta and spinach mixture. Add another ½ cup of sauce, and another layer of pasta, and so on. As you reach the top of the dish, add a layer of the asparagus puree between two layers of pasta, and top off with a layer of marinara.

Cover the lasagne with aluminum foil and bake for 30 to 40 minutes, until it is piping hot and bubbling throughout. Allow it to rest for 15 minutes before serving. Garnish with grated Parmesan.

Note: We prefer Delverde instant no-boil lasagna, which is available in some grocery stores. This lasagna doesn't need to be boiled because it is very thin and corrugated for strength. It comes in its own aluminum cooking trays, about 9 by 9 inches, the size we prefer for 8 people as a first course. However, there are 16 or 17 sheets of lasagna in the tray, and as we usually use only 4 sheets, we wash the trays and reuse them.

Serves 8

Risotto with Peas and Asparagus

This is a creamy, sweet risotto, perfect as a first course. We love it for Sunday lunch, followed by Veal Tails with Artichokes and Asparagus (see page 65), a salad, and Zabaglione made with fresh eggs (see page 87).

5 cups warm chicken stock

1 cup fresh peas (about 1 pound in the shell)

4 tablespoons olive oil

½ cup chopped onion

2 garlic cloves, chopped

1 tablespoon finely chopped flat-leaf parsley

1 tablespoon finely chopped mint

2 cups Arborio rice

1 cup dry white wine

2 tablespoons wild garlic or onion grass, finely chopped (optional)

12 medium asparagus spears, cut into 1- or 2-inch lengths

Salt and freshly ground black pepper

½ cup grated Parmesan cheese, for garnish

Bring 2 cups of the stock to a boil in a medium saucepan over medium heat. Add the peas and cook, covered, for 10 minutes, until tender. Remove ¼ cup of the peas with a slotted spoon and set aside. Working in batches, place the remaining ¾ cup of peas with the stock in a blender or food processor and puree until smooth.

Heat the oil in a heavy-bottomed 2-quart saucepan over medium heat. Add the onion, garlic, parsley, and mint. Cook until the onion becomes translucent, about 5 minutes. Add the rice and cook for a few minutes, stirring to coat the rice with the oil. Add the wine and wild garlic (if using), and cook until the wine is absorbed, about 5 minutes.

Warm the remaining 3 cups of stock in a medium pot over medium heat. Add the pea puree and 1 cup of the warm stock to the rice and stir well. The rice will absorb the stock in about 5 minutes. Add another cup of stock, and so on, stirring frequently, until you have used all the stock and have cooked the rice for a total of about 30 minutes, until it is tender. After the first 10 minutes, add the asparagus. After the risotto has cooked for 25 minutes and is almost done, add the whole peas. Season to taste with salt and pepper. Serve garnished with the grated cheese.

Serves 8

Black Rice with Asparagus

Edward first saw black rice in his friend Giancarlo's deli, Tino's, on Arthur Avenue in the Bronx. Commonly used in Northern Italy, black rice is not starchy, but has a delicate, unique flavor. It's easily combined with other ingredients, but we think it is good enough to eat without any additional flavorings at all. Black rice takes a little longer to cook than white rice and doesn't grow to as great a volume.

4 tablespoons olive oil

2 medium onions, finely chopped

4 garlic cloves, finely chopped

2¼ cups chicken stock

1 cup black rice

Salt

8 medium asparagus spears, cut into 1-inch lengths

4 tablespoons mint chiffonade

½ cup thinly sliced scallions

Freshly ground black pepper

Heat 2 tablespoons of the oil in a medium pot over medium heat. Add half the onions and half the garlic, cover, and cook until the onions are translucent, about 5 minutes. Add 2 cups of the stock, the rice, and salt to taste. Cover, bring to a boil, then reduce the heat to low and simmer, covered, for about 30 minutes, until the rice is tender. Allow the rice to rest, covered, for about 15 minutes while you prepare the asparagus.

Heat the remaining 2 tablespoons of oil in a medium skillet over medium heat. Add the asparagus, cover, and cook for about 5 minutes. Add the remaining onion and garlic, 2 tablespoons of the mint, and the scallions and cook until the asparagus are tender, about 5 minutes more. Add the remaining ¼ cup of stock and the rice, and season with salt and pepper to taste. Cover and simmer over medium heat for 5 minutes. Garnish with the remaining 2 tablespoons of mint.

Serves 4

Black Rice with Shrimp

We serve this as a first course, but it can be served as a main course as well, for two. It is a very striking dish. You can find black rice at most gourmet Italian grocery stores (see Sources on page 305).

2 tablespoons olive oil

1 medium onion, finely chopped

4 garlic cloves, finely chopped

2 cups chicken stock

1 cup black rice

Salt

2 tablespoons extra virgin olive oil

6 medium asparagus spears, cut into 1-inch lengths

¾ cup thinly sliced scallions

½ pound medium shrimp, shelled

3 tablespoons mint chiffonade

2 tablespoons fresh lemon juice

Freshly ground black pepper

Heat the 2 tablespoons of olive oil in a medium pot over medium heat. Add the onion and half the garlic, cover, and cook until the onion is translucent, about 5 minutes. Add the stock, rice, and salt to taste. Cover, bring to a boil, then reduce the heat to low and simmer, covered, for about 30 minutes, until the rice is tender. Allow the rice to rest, covered, for about 15 minutes while you prepare the asparagus and shrimp.

Heat the extra virgin olive oil in a medium skillet over medium heat. Add the asparagus, cover, and cook for about 5 minutes. Add the remaining garlic and the scallions and cook until the asparagus are tender, about 5 minutes. Add the shrimp, 1 tablespoon of the mint, the lemon juice, and salt and pepper to taste. Turn the heat up to high and cook, uncovered, until the shrimp turn pink, about 4 minutes.

To serve, place a mound of the rice in the middle of a soup bowl. Add the shrimp and asparagus, and garnish with the remaining 2 tablespoons of mint.

Serves 4

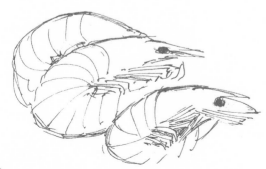

ABOUT EASTER

Food is the great social icebreaker. I've met business contacts in grocery store lines, lovers in cafeterias, like minds in the wine shop. But my dad is the only person I know who has used food to avoid getting arrested.

Every year, on the Friday before Easter Sunday, Edward hits Biancardi's meat store on Arthur Avenue in the Bronx to buy an Italian-style baby lamb. It's about a thirty-minute drive from the Bronx to his house in Katonah, which he shares with my mother. Edward was 77 at the time of this story, and like all the men in his family, he is tough, strong, and intelligent. But maybe his hearing is going a little, and he probably should wear his glasses more often. His car is an incredibly messy SUV, loaded with piles of newspapers and bits of canvas and pieces of wood that the dog dragged in, as well as bird's nests of opera tapes, which I think he plays quite loud.

I don't really love to drive with my father, as he has certain entrenched behaviors that tend to challenge the laws governing the road. For example, for years you used to be able to make a U-turn in Katonah. But as the town filled up with a new generation of city exiles—young families pushing strollers and the ever-bigger-vehicle phenomena—it got pretty crowded, and so a "No U-Turn" sign was installed. But my father predates the sign by decades, and I think he figures he was grandfathered into that U-turn. And so he continues to enjoy the turns he had always made, much to the aggravation of local law enforcement.

Anyway, on the Friday in question, when Dad pulled into the driveway and got out of his car, he was surprised to see that a police vehicle had pulled in behind him, lights swirling. A young officer in a crisp uniform jumped out of his car, highly annoyed.

"Didn't you hear my siren? Didn't you see my lights? I've been following you for miles! You ran through a stop sign. Don't you look in your rearview mirror?"

No, Edward hadn't noticed a thing.

"Well . . . where the hell were you coming from?"

"I was getting my Easter lamb on Arthur Avenue."

"Oh, really? That's where I get my lamb," said the cop, with interest.

It turns out the cop is half-Italian, and, inspired by their mutual interest in eating lambs and goats, he offered to bring over some of his wife's family's olive oil. Edward gave him a tour of the wine cellar and the garden, and then they made a date to exchange various goodies from their respective kitchens. The reason the officer followed Edward in the first place never came up again, and to this day the cop comes around every once in a while to visit and talk food with the old man. "Why not?" asks Dad rhetorically. "Food is the most common experience."

For Italians, Easter is the second biggest holiday of the year after Christmas, and we always get together at the house in Katonah. The menu is usually the same: After a bottle of champagne and a nibble of homemade focaccia bread with a slice of prosciutto, we eat lasagne, then roasted baby lamb with crispy oven-baked potatoes, usually baked asparagus, and a green vegetable, like the last of the winter brocoletti di rape, which we sauté until tender and hot with garlic. Mom's little bantam hens start producing eggs, and she will often make delicate flans with them, or Aunt Mary's no-crust ricotta pie. We drink Dad's white and red wines, and end the meal with espresso and homemade biscotti.

In the afternoon, the children eat the chocolate eggs they found under the sugar maple, and the dog eats the ones they didn't find, including the pastel foil wrappers. Sometimes it snows, often it rains, but when it is sunny, we nap in the new grass, and every so often we roll over to find a clutch of morels that were not there moments before. How and why they resurrect one year and not the next none of us knows. Mushrooms are such a mystery.

SPRING SECOND COURSES

Easter Sunday Frittata

Sal Biancardi, who owns Biancardi Meats on Arthur Avenue in the Bronx, where Edward shops every Friday morning, gave this recipe to us. Sal's family eats this dish for breakfast Easter morning. The Sicilians make this frittata with sufritto, the edible innards of the lamb.

1 tablespoon olive oil

½ pound young spring lamb, fat removed, cut into ½-inch pieces

½ medium onion, finely chopped

1 cup chopped fennel

Salt and freshly ground black pepper

½ cup fresh peas (about ½ pound in the shell)

8 eggs

2 tablespoons milk

1 tablespoon finely chopped flat-leaf parsley

Heat the oven to 450°F. Butter an 8½-inch cast-iron skillet.

Heat the oil in a nonstick skillet over medium heat. Add the lamb and cook, stirring often, until the meat begins to brown, about 5 minutes. Drain off all fat, and add the onion, fennel, and salt and pepper to taste. Cover and simmer for 5 minutes, until the onion becomes translucent.

In the meantime, bring a small pot of salted water to a boil over high heat and add the peas. Cook for 3 minutes, and drain.

Add the peas to the lamb mixture, cover, and simmer for about 7 minutes, until the peas are al dente.

Break the eggs in a small bowl with the milk. Beat until frothy. Add the parsley and salt and pepper to taste. Pour the eggs and the lamb mixture into the cast-iron skillet and place in the oven. Bake, uncovered, for about 15 minutes, until the eggs are set.

Remove the frittata from the oven and let it stand for a few minutes, then place a plate over the skillet and flip the frittata over.

Cut into wedges and serve immediately.

Serves 4

Scrambled Eggs with Scallops and Morels

We made this dish for Lisa's birthday lunch one year: First, lobster bisque with tarragon, then this egg dish, followed by a green salad. With champagne, of course.

12 sea scallops (dry pack)

2 tablespoons breadcrumbs

4 tablespoons unsalted butter

⅓ pound fresh morels, soaked in warm water to remove all sand, and sliced

Salt

12 eggs

Tabasco sauce

4 teaspoons minced chives, or another fresh herb like tarragon or flat-leaf parsley, for garnish

Heat the broiler. Place the scallops on a sizzle plate. Dust the scallops with the breadcrumbs and broil until they are brown, about 3 minutes on the first side and 2 minutes on the other side. Remove and set aside.

Heat 2 tablespoons of the butter in a small nonstick skillet over medium-low heat. Add the morels and cook until their liquid cooks out, about 5 minutes, then cook for an additional 5 minutes, until they are dry and beginning to caramelize. Add salt to taste and set aside. Slice the scallops.

Heat the remaining 2 tablespoons of butter in a large nonstick skillet over medium-low heat. Beat the eggs with salt and Tabasco to taste. Pour the eggs into the skillet. Allow to set for a minute, and then start scrambling gently. Cook until the eggs are firm but soft, about 5 minutes, then add the morels and scallops, and combine gently.

Serve immediately garnished with the minced chives.

Serves 4

Soft-Shell Crabs with Asparagus

The arrival of soft-shell crabs in the markets is a sure sign of spring, and we eat them a number of ways. When you buy soft-shells, be sure they are alive. We like to serve these crabs on a piece of bruschetta. With a salad, it makes a lovely late-night dinner or a light lunch.

4 large soft-shell crabs (about ½ pound each)

1 cup milk

Salt and freshly ground black pepper

All-purpose flour for dredging

1 tablespoon unsalted butter

4 tablespoons olive oil

4 large asparagus spears, trimmed and cut into 2-inch lengths

4 garlic cloves, chopped

2 tablespoons chopped mint

½ cup port wine or sherry

Clean the crabs according to the instructions on page 21. Pour the milk into a shallow bowl. Dip the crabs in the milk. Salt and pepper the crabs to taste, then dredge them in flour.

In a large skillet over medium heat, heat the butter and 2 tablespoons of the oil. (A nonstick skillet is best.) Add the crabs, cover, and cook, turning often, for about 10 minutes, until the crabs are golden brown on both sides.

In the meantime, heat the remaining 2 tablespoons of oil in a small skillet over medium heat. Add the asparagus, garlic, and salt and pepper to taste. Cover and cook, turning often, for about 10 minutes, until the asparagus are tender. Add 1 tablespoon of the mint and cook for an additional 5 minutes.

Add the wine, asparagus, and remaining 1 tablespoon of mint to the crabs and cover. Cook an additional 5 minutes, turning the crabs over several times.

Serves 4

Monkfish with Asparagus

Monkfish is a reasonably priced fish that you rarely find in supermarkets. The taste is rich and the meat is dense, almost like lobster. It is well worth asking for or making a trip to a fishmonger.

2 tablespoons olive oil

1 medium onion, coarsely chopped

½ pound sliced mushrooms

4 medium asparagus spears, cut into 1-inch lengths

Salt and freshly ground black pepper

1 cup whole canned Italian tomatoes, chopped

2 tablespoons extra virgin olive oil

4 garlic cloves, thinly sliced

2 monkfish fillets (about 1 pound each)

Heat the oven to 450°F.

Heat the olive oil in a medium skillet over medium heat. Add the onion, cover, and cook until it is translucent, about 5 minutes. Add the mushrooms and continue cooking for 5 minutes, until the mushrooms release their liquid, then add the asparagus and salt and pepper to taste. Cover and cook another 5 minutes. Add the tomatoes, cover, and simmer for 5 minutes, until the tomatoes break up.

Place the extra virgin olive oil and the garlic in a baking dish. Season the monkfish fillets with salt and pepper and place them in the baking dish. Cover with aluminum foil and bake for 10 minutes. Pour the sauce over the monkfish and cook for an additional 10 minutes.

Serve half of each fillet per person, with a few tablespoons of sauce spooned over it.

Serves 4

Shad with Green Sauce

Shad is strictly a spring fish in the Northeast, luxurious and moist, with a high oil content. At one time great quantities were caught in the Hudson River, and after years of decline, the population is finally recovering due to the Clean Water Act. We hope future environmental policies will continue to nurture the resurgence of Hudson River shad.

It is hard to find someone who knows how to bone shad—there are three attached fillets. Shad is the only fish boned this way, which is why it costs more than most fish. Shad is very easy to stuff, because you can just fold the fillets over like a sandwich. The roe is excellent as a first course, but we find an all-shad meal to be quite rich.

4 tablespoons extra virgin olive oil

1 boned fresh shad (about 1¼ pounds)

4 garlic cloves, chopped (about 2 tablespoons)

Salt and freshly ground black pepper

1 lemon, cut into wedges, for garnish

For the Sauce

6 tablespoons extra virgin olive oil

2 tablespoons chopped flat-leaf parsley

2 garlic cloves, chopped

2 celery ribs, chopped

4 tablespoons chopped mint

2 teaspoons mustard (we like Coleman's)

4 tablespoons wild garlic, wild onions, or scallions, chopped

Salt

Heat the broiler. Pour 4 tablespoons of oil into a baking tray and lay the fish on top of it. Open the shad (the fillets will be attached to the skin), sprinkle it with the garlic, and season with salt and pepper. Cook the shad close to the heat for about 10 minutes, until the flesh is white and flaky.

For the sauce: In a food processor, place the oil, parsley, garlic, celery, mint, mustard, wild garlic, and salt to taste and puree to the consistency of pesto.

Serve the fish with the sauce and a lemon wedge.

Serves 4

Shad Roe with Tarragon

Our family has had this many times on Elinor's birthday, which is April 18th and smack in the middle of shad roe season. It is a very delicate dish, and quite reasonable. It makes for a fantastic luncheon, served with champagne. Boiling keeps the roe from splitting or popping out of the membrane. The recipe is easily doubled.

1 quart water

1 teaspoon salt

1 pair very fresh shad roe

2 tablespoons olive oil

1 tablespoon unsalted butter

Salt and freshly ground
black pepper

3 tablespoons sherry

1 tablespoon chopped tarragon

1 tablespoon fresh lemon juice

In a large pot over high heat, bring the water and salt to a boil. Add the roe and boil for 2 minutes. Carefully drain the roe.

In a large nonstick skillet, heat the oil and butter over medium heat. When the butter is melted, add the roe and season with salt and pepper. Cover and cook for 3 minutes, then turn the roe over, being careful not to puncture the membrane covering the roe. Add the sherry, tarragon, and lemon juice. Cover and cook over moderate heat for 5 minutes more.

Serves 2

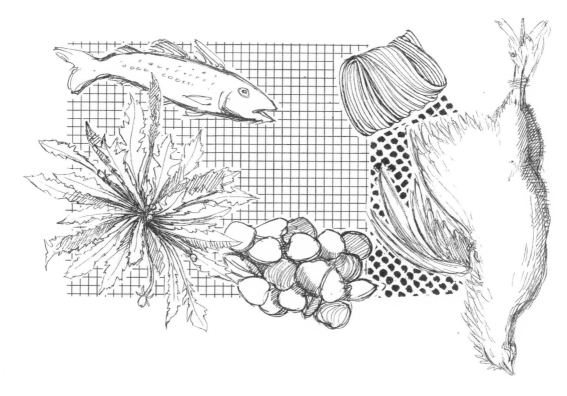

Fillet of Sole with Spinach Sauce

We like to serve this elegant dish with roasted asparagus and boiled potatoes, following risotto with peas, or a simple appetizer of warm boiled fava beans with a slice of Pecorino cheese.

10 tablespoons olive oil

1 pound fresh spinach, well washed (about 2 bunches)

6 garlic cloves, finely chopped

3 tablespoons chopped walnuts

Salt and freshly ground black pepper

4 sole fillets or other white-fleshed fish

Juice of ½ lemon

Heat the oven to 450°F.

Pour 6 tablespoons of the oil in an ovenproof pan. Add the spinach and garlic. Toss. Cover and bake in the oven for 10 minutes, stirring occasionally, until the spinach is wilted.

Put the spinach and walnuts into a food processor and pulse to puree. Add the pan juices in small amounts until the puree is a smooth consistency. Add salt and pepper to taste.

Pour the remaining 4 tablespoons of oil into a baking dish. Place the fillets in the dish; season with salt and pepper and the lemon juice. Cover and bake for about 10 minutes, until the fish flakes easily.

Spoon the sauce onto plates or a platter. You may need to add about 4 tablespoons of warm water to the sauce so that it spreads easily. Place the fish on the sauce and serve.

Serves 4

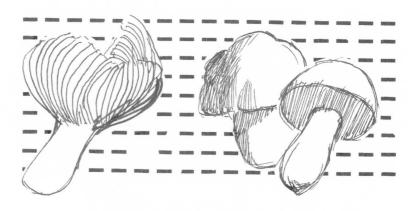

Swordfish with Peas

We didn't eat swordfish for many years due to the mercury content, but occasionally Edward's fishmonger in Mount Kisco, New York, has some very fresh, seasonal swordfish that is available only in the spring.

This dish is excellent preceded by Spaghettini Salad (page 29), or Black Rice with Asparagus (see page 39).

4 tablespoons olive oil

1 medium onion, thinly sliced

4 garlic cloves, chopped

Hot pepper flakes

2 tablespoons chopped
flat-leaf parsley

2 tablespoons white wine vinegar

1 cup fresh peas (about 1 pound
in the shell)

1 to 1½ cups warm chicken stock

1 pound swordfish, cut into
2-inch chunks

Salt and freshly ground
black pepper

2 tablespoons chopped mint or
flat-leaf parsley, for garnish

Heat 2 tablespoons of the oil in a large skillet over medium heat. Add the onion, garlic, and hot pepper flakes to taste and cook until the onion becomes translucent, about 5 minutes. Add the parsley and vinegar and cook until the vinegar cooks out, about 3 minutes. Add the peas and 1 cup of the stock. Cover and simmer until the peas are tender, about 10 minutes. Add more stock if needed to keep the peas wet.

In the meantime, heat the remaining 2 tablespoons of oil in a medium skillet over medium heat. Add the swordfish, salt and pepper to taste, and gently turn the fish until all sides are cooked, about 3 minutes. Add the pea and onion mixture to the fish and continue cooking over medium heat for another 5 minutes, until the fish separates easily when prodded with a fork. Do not overcook.

Garnish with the mint or parsley.

Serves 4

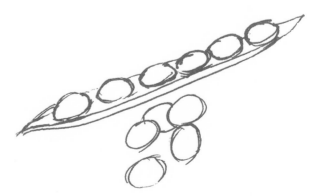

Chicken with Peas and Shrimp

This is a typical second course that the Giobbis eat for Sunday lunch, following Risotto with Peas and Asparagus (see page 38) or Penne with Peas and Tuna (see page 32). It's a variation of a dish we love to eat in the late summer, chicken with mussels.

3 tablespoons olive oil

1 chicken (about 4 pounds), cut into 8 pieces

Salt and freshly ground black pepper

1 tablespoon dried rosemary

6 garlic cloves, with skins on

1 cup dry white wine

1 teaspoon dried basil

2 bay leaves

24 pearl onions, peeled

6 slices prosciutto, chopped (about ¾ cup)

1½ cups warm chicken stock

1 cup fresh peas (about 1 pound in the shell)

2 tablespoons mint chiffonade

1 pound large shrimp, shelled, deveined, and butterflied

Heat the oil in a large skillet over medium heat. Add the chicken, salt and pepper to taste, and the rosemary. Cook, uncovered and turning often, until the chicken is browned, about 30 minutes. Remove the chicken and drain and discard the fat. Return the chicken to the skillet and add the garlic, wine, basil, and bay leaves. Cover and cook over medium heat until the alcohol cooks out of the wine, about 5 minutes. Add the onions, prosciutto, and stock. Cover and cook over medium heat for 10 minutes. Add the peas and mint. Cover and cook for 10 minutes, until the peas are tender. Add the shrimp. Cover and cook for about 4 minutes, until the shrimp are pink. Remove the bay leaves before serving.

Serves 6

ng

Boiled Chicken with Asparagus and Peas

This is a wonderful dish with the chicken leftover from making Chicken and Dandelion Soup (see page 28). You can make this dish with leftover roasted chicken or turkey as well. We like to serve it with sliced boiled potatoes or rice.

3 tablespoons olive oil

1 medium onion, sliced

2 garlic cloves, sliced

2 cups whole canned Italian tomatoes, chopped

1 tablespoon chopped flat-leaf parsley

1 tablespoon chopped mint

Salt and hot pepper flakes

1 cup fresh peas (about 1 pound in the shell)

6 medium asparagus spears, cut into 1½-inch lengths

2 cups sliced boiled chicken

Heat the oil in a large skillet over medium heat. Add the onion and garlic, cover, and cook until the onion becomes translucent, about 5 minutes. Add the tomatoes, parsley, mint, and salt and hot pepper flakes to taste. Cover and simmer for 10 minutes, until the tomatoes break up.

In the meantime, boil the peas in a pot of salted water over high heat for about 5 minutes. Drain the peas. Add the peas and asparagus to the tomato sauce. Cover and simmer for about 10 minutes, until the asparagus are tender. Add the chicken, cover, and simmer for an additional couple of minutes to meld the flavors.

Serves 4

Stuffed Chicken Legs

This is a very savory second course, one we love to serve at our Sunday lunches, following a pasta or soup course.

8 chicken legs with thighs

5 tablespoons olive oil

1 medium onion, finely chopped

2 medium asparagus spears, cut into ½-inch lengths

1 tablespoon finely chopped flat-leaf parsley

Salt and freshly ground black pepper

4 slices prosciutto, chopped (about ½ cup)

1 cup ricotta

3 tablespoons grated Parmesan or Pecorino cheese

2 tablespoons dried rosemary

1 cup dry white wine

2 tablespoons mint chiffonade

Heat the oven to 500°F.

Bone each chicken leg but leave the thighbone in. To do so, cut the meat around the leg bone and push the meat up above the knee, like a sock. Separate the leg bone from the thighbone and chop the leg bone just above the ankle, leaving the bottom fragment still attached to the skin. This will anchor the stuffing and make the leg look like it is intact. Now pull the meat back down.

Heat 3 tablespoons of the oil in a medium skillet over medium heat. Add the onion, asparagus, parsley, and salt and pepper to taste. Cook, uncovered, for about 10 minutes, until the asparagus become tender. Add the prosciutto and cook for a couple of minutes more.

In a large bowl, combine the ricotta with the onion and asparagus mixture. Add the Parmesan and mix well. Stuff 2 tablespoons of ricotta into the cavity of each chicken leg and thigh. Close the opening with a toothpick or with culinary string.

Place the remaining 2 tablespoons of oil in a baking tray large enough to hold all of the chicken legs and thighs without overlapping. Add the chicken legs and thighs and sprinkle them with the rosemary and salt and pepper to taste. Bake the chicken, uncovered, in the oven for about 45 minutes, until golden brown. Drain off the fat and oil and add the wine and mint. Cover and continue baking until the wine is reduced, about 10 minutes.

Serves 8

Rabbit with Fennel and Fava Beans

We brine the rabbit in order to retain the meat's moisture. Because it is very lean, rabbit can become dry if over-cooked, so if the sauce becomes too tight, just add a little water. We love to serve this dish with soft polenta.

1 gallon water

1 cup salt

⅓ cup sugar

Half a rabbit, cut lengthwise (about 1¾ pounds)

Salt and freshly ground black pepper

6 garlic cloves, with skins on

1 tablespoon crushed dried rosemary

5 tablespoons olive oil

1 medium onion, coarsely chopped

2 cups sliced wild mushrooms

½ cup dry white wine

1 cup whole canned Italian tomatoes, chopped

1 teaspoon dried marjoram

½ medium fennel bulb, cored and sliced (about 1 cup)

1 pound fresh fava beans, shelled

In a large pot, pour the water, 1 cup of salt, and the sugar. Add the rabbit and place in a cool spot for 24 hours. Drain and cut into 6 pieces, and dry each piece with a kitchen cloth. Salt and pepper the rabbit to taste.

Heat a cast-iron or nonstick skillet over medium heat and add the rabbit, garlic, and rosemary. Cook, uncovered and dry, until the rabbit begins to take on color. Add the oil, onion, and mushrooms. Cook until the onion becomes translucent, about 5 minutes. Add the wine, cover, and lower the heat to medium-low. Cook until the alcohol cooks out of the wine, about 5 minutes. Add the tomatoes and marjoram and bring to a boil. Add the fennel, cover, and simmer over medium heat for 20 minutes.

In the meantime, bring a medium pot of salted water to a boil over high heat and add the favas. Blanch the fava beans for about 1 minute. Drain, and then run cold water over the beans to stop the cooking. Remove the tough outer skin by pinching off the end of the skin and squeezing the bean out. Add the beans to the rabbit. Continue cooking for another 10 to 15 minutes, until the fennel is tender.

Allow the dish to rest for about 15 minutes before serving.

Serves 4

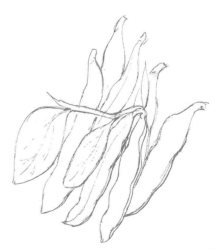

Butterflied Leg of Lamb with Mint Pesto

For one of Craig Claiborne's parties in the mid-1970s, Edward prepared a whole grilled lamb. He hit upon an ingenious sauce to serve beside it—mint pesto. Martha Stewart, who attended and tasted the sauce, published a similar recipe as her own innovation. Edward has been annoyed with her ever since. Indeed, when the now-defunct Martha Stewart Living television show asked him to be a guest, he declined. "But don't you want the exposure?" asked an incredulous coordinator for the show. "At my age," responded Edward, "it would be indecent to expose myself."

1 leg of spring lamb, boned (about 8 pounds bone-in, and about 4½ pounds without bones)

6 garlic cloves, slivered

1 cup dry white wine

2 tablespoons crushed dried rosemary

Salt and freshly ground black pepper

For the pesto

2 cups packed mint leaves (preferably spearmint)

⅓ cup warm chicken stock

¼ cup extra virgin olive oil

¼ cup walnuts

2 tablespoons grated Parmesan or Pecorino cheese

2 garlic cloves, sliced

Salt

Cut the meat into two sections for easier handling. Cut thin gashes in the meat and insert the garlic slivers. Place the meat in a large nonreactive pan. Pour the wine over the meat, rub in the rosemary, and season with salt and pepper to taste. Marinate the meat for 2 hours. In the meantime, prepare your grill.

Remove the meat from the marinade and grill it on a hot grill for about 15 minutes on each side, turning often. Remove the meat from the grill and allow it to rest for at least 15 minutes. Slice the lamb on a bias, against the grain of the meat.

For the pesto: In a food processor, combine the mint, stock, oil, walnuts, cheese, garlic, and salt to taste. Pulse to create a smooth puree.

Serve the pesto beside the sliced grilled lamb.

Serves 8

Lamb Shanks with Artichokes

This is a typical second course for a Giobbi Sunday lunch, following a dish like Pea and Asparagus Soup (see page 26). It is rare we'd eat a dish like this at night, when we prefer fish and lighter fare. You can substitute 1½ cups of fresh shelled peas for the artichokes, if you like.

2 lamb shanks, with bone, trimmed of excess fat (about 3½ pounds)

Salt and freshly ground black pepper

2 tablespoons vegetable oil

1 branch rosemary

6 garlic cloves, with skins on

12 pearl onions, peeled

1 celery rib, chopped

1 red or green bell pepper, seeded and chopped

1 cup dry red wine

2 tablespoons chopped flat-leaf parsley

Hot pepper flakes (optional)

2 bay leaves

4 cups warm chicken stock

4 medium artichokes, cleaned and cut in half, or 10 small artichokes

2 scallions, thinly sliced

2 tablespoons chopped fresh mint, for garnish

Heat the oven to 500°F.

Season the shanks with salt and pepper and place them in a deep oven-proof pot. Add the oil and rosemary and place the lamb in the oven. Cook the shanks, uncovered, turning occasionally, for about 30 minutes. Add the garlic. Continue roasting the shanks until they are well browned, about 20 minutes more. Remove the shanks and garlic and set aside. Drain the oil and fat from the pot and discard. Return the shanks and garlic to the pot and add the onions, celery, bell pepper, wine, parsley, hot pepper flakes to taste (if using), and bay leaves. Cover and return the shanks to the oven.

Cook until the wine evaporates, about 10 minutes. Add the stock. When the stock boils (about 5 minutes), lower the heat to 375°F and roast for 30 minutes. Add the artichokes and scallions and continue roasting for another 40 minutes.

Allow the shanks to rest before serving. Remove the bay leaves. Garnish with the mint.

Note: To simplify peeling pearl onions, soak them for 15 minutes in warm water first.

Serves 4

Spring Lamb with Peas and Mint

In the early 1970s, Edward decided to do something about the fact that the white mushrooms available in our markets are not as tasty as wild mushrooms. His solution was to combine them with soaked imported porcini mushrooms. Indeed, dried porcini have an excellent taste, but the texture leaves something to be desired. However, when the flavorful porcini is combined with the meaty texture of the domestic white mushroom, the results are excellent.

1¼ pounds lean spring lamb (leg or shoulder), cut into stew pieces

Salt and freshly ground black pepper

All-purpose flour for dredging

6 tablespoons olive oil

6 garlic cloves, with skins on

½ cup dry white wine

2 bay leaves

1 tablespoon crushed dried rosemary

2 cups chicken stock

2 cups sliced white mushrooms (about ½ pound)

¾ ounce dried porcini mushrooms, soaked in 1 cup of warm chicken stock

1 cup whole canned Italian tomatoes, chopped

16 pearl onions, peeled

2 tablespoons mint chiffonade

2 cups fresh peas (about 2 pounds in the shell)

1 tablespoon finely chopped flat-leaf parsley, for garnish

Season the lamb with salt and pepper and dust it lightly with flour.

Heat 3 tablespoons of the oil in a large skillet over medium heat and add the lamb. Cook, stirring frequently, for a few minutes, then add the garlic. Continue cooking, stirring often, until the lamb is seared all over, about 10 minutes. Add the wine, bay leaves, and rosemary. Cover and lower the heat to medium-low. Cook until most of the wine has been absorbed, about 5 minutes. Add the stock, cover, and simmer for about 30 minutes.

In the meantime, heat the remaining 3 tablespoons of oil in a large skillet over medium heat. Add the white mushrooms and cook, uncovered, for 5 minutes, until the mushrooms begin to release their liquid. Add the dried porcinis with their soaking liquid and cook for an additional 5 minutes. Add the tomatoes, cover, and cook for 5 minutes more, until the tomatoes break up.

Add the lamb and its juices to the mushroom and tomato sauce, then add the onions and mint. Reduce the heat to medium-low, cover, and simmer for 45 minutes.

In the meantime, bring a medium pot of salted water to a boil over high heat. Add the peas and boil until they are tender, about 10 minutes. Drain and add to the lamb. Cook for several minutes more so that all the flavors meld, then turn off the heat. Allow to sit for 10 minutes. Remove the bay leaves. Sprinkle with the parsley to garnish.

Serves 4

Lamb with Potatoes

The potatoes in this recipe are prepared in one of our favorite ways, and we serve them with many other dishes. This lamb dish is excellent after a first course of Asparagus with Eggs (see page 17).

2 pounds baby lamb, cut into 1½- to 3-inch pieces, including the bony parts, such as the ribs, leg, and shoulder

Salt and freshly ground black pepper

4 tablespoons olive oil

8 large garlic cloves, with skins on

1 tablespoon plus 1 teaspoon crushed dried rosemary

1 cup dry white wine

1 tablespoon tomato paste

Hot pepper flakes (optional)

3 bay leaves

¼ cup warm chicken stock or water

1 teaspoon dried oregano

1 tablespoon chopped mint

1 tablespoon finely chopped flat-leaf parsley

2 medium potatoes (we prefer Yukon Gold)

Season the lamb with salt and pepper. Heat 2 tablespoons of the oil in a large stew pot over medium heat. Add the lamb—be sure the pieces do not overlap—and the garlic. Cook, uncovered and turning often, for 5 minutes. Add 1 tablespoon of the rosemary and continue cooking until the meat is browned, about 25 minutes. Remove the meat and garlic and set aside. Drain the fat from the pot and discard. Return the lamb to the pot. (Save the garlic to smear on bruschetta.) Add the wine, tomato paste, hot pepper flakes to taste (if using), and bay leaves. Mix the tomato paste into the wine. Cover and cook for about 15 minutes over medium heat until the wine evaporates. Add the stock, oregano, mint, and parsley. Cover, reduce the heat to medium-low, and simmer for 20 minutes more.

Heat the oven to 450°F.

In the meantime, bring a medium pot of water to a boil over high heat. Add the potatoes and cook for 10 minutes, until they are al dente. Drain and peel the potatoes, then cut into slices ½ inch thick.

Pour the remaining 2 tablespoons of oil in a baking pan. Add the potatoes, being careful not to overlap. Add salt to taste and the remaining 1 teaspoon of rosemary. Place the potatoes in the oven and roast them for about 10 minutes, turning them over with a spatula periodically, until they are brown all over.

Remove the bay leaves from the lamb, combine the lamb and the potatoes on a large platter, and serve.

Serves 4

Sufritto

Whenever we buy a whole baby lamb, we ask the butcher to give us the innards. While we understand that American tastes generally disdain offal, it is very much a part of Italian cooking. Sufritto is a stew of tasty innards, which we like to serve on top of soft polenta.

3 tablespoons olive oil

1 medium onion, coarsely chopped

2 garlic cloves, finely chopped

The innards of a baby lamb or goat (the liver, heart, sweetbreads, and kidneys), cut into bite-size pieces

Salt and hot pepper flakes

½ cup dry white wine

1 tablespoon finely chopped flat-leaf parsley

1 teaspoon crushed dried rosemary

1 teaspoon dried marjoram

2 cups chopped white or wild mushrooms, or a combination of the two

2 tablespoons tomato paste diluted in ½ cup warm chicken stock or water

1½ cups fresh peas, (about 1½ pounds in the shell) blanched and drained

1 tablespoon chopped mint, for garnish

Heat the oil in a medium skillet over medium heat. Add the onion and cook, uncovered, until it becomes translucent, about 5 minutes. Add the garlic, innards, and salt and hot pepper flakes to taste, and continue cooking, mixing often, until the onion begins to brown and the innards take on color, about 10 minutes. Add the wine, parsley, rosemary, and marjoram. Cover and simmer over medium-low heat until the wine has been absorbed, about 5 minutes. Add the mushrooms and cook until they give up their liquid, about 10 minutes, and then add the tomato paste mixture, peas, and salt to taste. Cover and continue cooking for about 45 minutes. If the sufritto looks dry, add another ½ cup of warm chicken stock.

Serve immediately, garnished with the mint.

Serves 4

Skirt Steak with Asparagus

We love skirt steak because it is very flavorful, adaptable (we use it many different ways), and fairly inexpensive. It is wonderful grilled or cooked on top of the stove. Don't judge a skirt steak by the weight: One steak will generally feed 4 people, when served in addition to vegetables.

4 tablespoons extra virgin olive oil

1 whole skirt steak, cut into ½-inch wide strips

6 garlic cloves, sliced

Salt and freshly ground black pepper

4 tablespoons balsamic vinegar

2 cups sliced white or wild mushrooms, or a combination of the two

1 pound asparagus, cut into 2-inch lengths, tough ends removed

2 scallions, sliced

1 tablespoon chopped cilantro

Heat the oil in a medium skillet over high heat and add the steak. Add the garlic and season with salt and pepper to taste. Cook, uncovered, stirring frequently, for about 10 minutes, until the meat is browned. Add the vinegar and cook for a minute or so. Remove the meat with a slotted spoon.

Add the mushrooms to the skillet and cook over high heat for about 5 minutes, until the mushrooms release their liquid. Add the asparagus and scallions and salt and pepper to taste. Cook for a minute or so, and then add the cilantro. Cook until the asparagus are fork-tender, about 10 minutes. Add the meat and toss with the vegetables for a minute more to meld the flavors.

Serves 4

Meat Loaf with Ricotta

You must let this meat loaf rest for at least 15 minutes after cooking or the ricotta will run. Once it holds together, be sure to place the sliced meat loaf on top of the sauce so the diner can see the sliced egg inside.

2 tablespoons olive oil

1 medium onion, finely chopped

2 garlic cloves, finely chopped

1 pound lean ground beef

1/2 pound lean ground pork

1 egg, beaten

1/3 cup grated Parmesan cheese

2 tablespoons finely chopped flat-leaf parsley

Salt and freshly ground black pepper

2 cups marinara sauce (see page 258), for serving

For the filling

3/4 pound ricotta

1 egg, beaten

2 tablespoons finely chopped flat-leaf parsley

1/3 cup grated Parmesan cheese

1/3 teaspoon grated nutmeg

Salt and freshly ground black pepper

2 eggs, hard-cooked and shelled

Heat the oven to 400°F. Butter a 9- × 5- × 3-inch loaf pan.

Heat the oil in a small skillet over medium heat. Add the onion and garlic. Cook until the onion is translucent, about 5 minutes.

In a large mixing bowl, combine the beef, pork, egg, cheese, parsley, salt and pepper to taste, and the cooked onions and garlic. Mix well and set aside.

For the filling: In a separate bowl, combine the ricotta, egg, parsley, Parmesan, nutmeg, and salt and pepper to taste and mix well.

Line the bottom of the loaf pan with about 3/4 inch of the meat mixture. Build up walls on the inside of the pan that are the same thickness. Fill the center cavity with the ricotta mixture. Force the whole boiled eggs end to end into the ricotta mixture so that the eggs are completely covered by ricotta. Add the remaining meat on top of the ricotta so that the filling is completely covered by the meat.

Place the meat loaf, uncovered, in the hot oven and bake for 50 to 60 minutes, until the top is golden brown. Remove the meat loaf and allow it to rest about 15 to 20 minutes.

In the meantime, heat the marinara sauce.

Slice the meat loaf and serve it on a puddle of sauce.

Serves 6

Stuffed Veal Breast

We often make this dish for parties in the spring. Served at room temperature, it is perfect for a buffet. It is also very easy to make, but plan ahead, since the roast must rest for 3 hours before serving. It's even better when served the day after you make it.

Ask your butcher to bone the veal breast for you. There will be about 6 pounds of bones, which you should save to make stock.

1 whole breast of veal (about 11 pounds), boned and trimmed

Salt and freshly ground black pepper

½ pound ground veal

1 pound ricotta

1 egg

½ teaspoon grated nutmeg

1 cup grated Parmesan or Pecorino cheese

½ cup pistachios

2 tablespoons golden raisins

2 tablespoons finely chopped flat-leaf parsley

6 slices pancetta or Canadian bacon

4 branches fresh rosemary

About 5 cups dry white wine

1 cup dry Marsala wine or other sweet wine

Heat the oven to 500°F.

Lay a cheesecloth about 22 inches long down on a work surface. Place the veal breast on the cloth, long end toward you, and season the meat with salt and pepper.

In a large bowl, combine the ground veal, ricotta, egg, nutmeg, 1 tablespoon of salt, the Parmesan, pistachios, raisins, parsley, and black pepper to taste. Mix well. Spread the ricotta mixture over the veal breast, leaving about ¾ inch free of stuffing around the edges of the meat.

Gently roll the veal as you would a jellyroll, toward one end of the cheesecloth, leaving the cheesecloth flat on the counter. Roll the cheesecloth over and around the veal breast. Twist one end of the cheesecloth and tie it, then tighten the other end by twisting, and tie it off as well. Tie the entire roll with kitchen string at 1-inch intervals, as you would a roast. Slide the pancetta slices and the rosemary branches under the string against the cheesecloth.

Place the veal breast in a large roasting pan. Add 2 cups of the white wine and bake, uncovered, for 2 hours in the oven. Baste the roast often, turning it over periodically. Add white wine as needed to keep the roast moist.

Remove the veal breast from the oven. Remove the veal from the roasting pan and defat the pan drippings. Heat the pan over medium-high heat on top of the stove. Add the Marsala and scrape away at the clinging bits as the drippings boil. When the drippings have reduced by about one-third, pour them into a small saucepan and set aside.

Let the veal rest at least 3 hours before serving. To serve, untie the string and remove the cheesecloth. Using a very long, sharp knife, slice the breast. Heat the drippings and spoon them over the meat.

Serves 12

Veal with Peas and Potatoes

Veal breast is a wonderful cut, with lots of bony parts and fat, which adds to the flavor.

2 pounds veal breast, cut into
1-inch sections (your butcher will
need to do this)

Salt and freshly ground
black pepper

2 tablespoons dried rosemary

10 garlic cloves, with skins on

12 pearl onions, peeled

1 cup dry white wine

1 tablespoon dried basil

4 bay leaves

2 cups chicken stock

2 cups fresh peas (about 2 pounds
in the shell)

3 medium potatoes, peeled and
cut into quarters (we prefer Yukon
Gold)

4 scallions, sliced

2 tablespoons mint chiffonade

Heat the oven to 400°F.

Season the veal with salt and pepper and put the veal pieces into a shallow ovenproof pot so that the meat sections do not overlap. Add the rosemary and garlic and roast, uncovered, in the hot oven for 1 hour, stirring often, until the meat browns. Drain off the fat. Add the onions, wine, basil, and bay leaves. Cover and return the pot to the oven. Roast until the wine reduces, about 5 minutes.

In the meantime, heat the stock in a small pot over medium heat. Add the peas to the stock and cook until they are halfway cooked, about 5 minutes. Remove the pot from the oven and add the chicken stock and peas to the veal. Add the potatoes, scallions, mint, and salt to taste. Reduce the oven temperature to 350°F. Return the pot to the oven and bake for about 30 minutes more, until the veal and potatoes are fork-tender. Remove the bay leaves before serving.

Serves 6

Veal Tails with Artichokes and Asparagus

This is Italian comfort food, savory and straightforward. It is excellent served after Risotto with Peas and Asparagus (page 38). It also marries well with both red and white wines. You can substitute oxtails for the veal tails in this dish.

1 pound veal tails

Salt and freshly ground black pepper

All-purpose flour for dredging

6 tablespoons olive oil

4 garlic cloves, with skins on

1 medium onion, finely chopped

1 medium red bell pepper, seeded and chopped

1 tablespoon dried rosemary

4 bay leaves

1 cup dry white wine

2 cups chicken stock

¾ ounce dried porcini mushrooms soaked in 1 cup warm chicken stock

½ pound white mushrooms, sliced

12 small artichokes, about 1½ inches in diameter, tough outer leaves removed (a little over a pound)

Half a lemon

12 medium asparagus spears, cut into 2-inch lengths

Heat the oven to 400°F.

Season the veal tails with salt and pepper. Lightly dust them with flour.

Heat 4 tablespoons of the oil in a heavy Dutch oven or casserole with a fitted top over medium heat. Add the veal and garlic. Cook, stirring constantly, until the veal is lightly browned all over, about 10 minutes. Add the onion, bell pepper, rosemary, and bay leaves. Cover and cook until the onion becomes translucent, about 5 minutes. Add the wine, turn up the heat to medium-high, and mix well. Once the wine is boiling, reduce the heat to medium and simmer until the wine reduces, about 5 minutes. Add the stock, the porcini mushrooms (with their soaking liquid), and the white mushrooms. Cover and place in the oven. Bake for 1 hour.

In the meantime, cut ¾ inch off the tops of the artichokes and discard. Rub the cut edges with the lemon half and place in a bowl of cold water. Squeeze the juice from the lemon into the water.

Heat the remaining 2 tablespoons of oil in a small skillet over medium heat. Add the asparagus and cook until tender, about 10 minutes. Set aside.

After the veal has baked for 1 hour, add the artichokes. Cover and reduce the heat to 375°F. Bake for 1 hour more, for a total of 2 hours. Check periodically to be sure the stew is moist. If not, add a little more warm stock. Remove the bay leaves before serving.

Garnish each portion with the cooked asparagus.

Serves 4

ASPARAGUS,
ARTICHOKES,
AND
DANDELION GREENS

"[Dr. Urbino] enjoyed the immediate pleasure of smelling a secret garden in his urine that had been purified by lukewarm asparagus." I have remembered that line since Gabriel Garcia Marquez's *Love in the Time of Cholera* was published, not only because of its wonderful outrageousness, but because it reminds me of how specialized our bodies' relationships with particular foods are. To be keenly aware of those nuances — and many are not as obvious as asparagus — is a kind of state of gastronomical grace. I think the way to get there is to eat the freshest and most pristine foods you can find. And that means eating seasonally.

Asparagus, artichokes, spinach, and peas are the quintessential spring vegetables, and we Giobbis rarely eat them out of season. Indeed, we gorge on them to such an extent that it takes a year before we start craving them again.

According to Alan Davidson's marvelous *Oxford Companion to Food,* the eating of artichokes, one leaf at a time, is the source of the Italian phrase "la politica del carciofo," or the art of settling with one opponent at a time. Children love to eat artichokes this way, dipped into mayonnaise or some other creamy dressing. The Romans ate them with dips made from fish pickle, hard-boiled eggs, mint, and spices, but we prefer artichokes cooked in stews or *al forno* ("from the oven").

When Edward was a student in Italy in 1951, he often visited his Zio Quintillio's farm in Offida. During one spring visit by the fireplace, Zio Q prepared several freshly picked fist-size artichokes. He gently opened the outer leaves, slid in a few slivers of garlic, drizzled some olive oil on them, and placed them in the hot, gray ashes. After about ten to fifteen minutes, he removed the artichokes, peeled off the charred outer leaves, and handed an artichoke to Edward, who ate the soft, perfumey vegetable like an apple. We bake artichokes in an oven version of this dish and throw them into rich lamb shank or veal tail stews. Choose artichokes that have tightly packed leaves and feel heavy in your hand. Once you have removed the outer leaves, soak the artichokes in cold water with lemon juice, as the leaves tend to discolor when exposed to air.

We use peas in many dishes, like a quick, unusual pea soup with fish, and creamy risotto with peas and asparagus; for the second course, a refined sauté of swordfish and peas, a rich saucy veal stew with peas or another, with chicken, and delicate baby lamb cooked with peas and mint. We harvest or buy our peas in the pod when they are young and crisp, although frozen peas really are a decent substitute in a pinch. We avoid canned peas, as the heating involved in the canning process destroys the flavor, color, and texture. (Remember those pale, mushy cafeteria peas? Canned.)

Of the wild edibles, we gather fiddlehead ferns, watercress, red root, purslane, lamb's-quarters, and onion grass, but dandelion greens are the real prize. Picking dandelion greens requires little more than kicking open the back door. And there they are, all over the yard, handsome young *Taraxacum officiale.* The earliest greens are the best, before the plant flowers. We choose the ones growing in looser earth away from the direct sunlight, which toughens the leaves. With a sharp knife, cut around the plant at the root, so you can pull the plant up intact. (Picking individual leaves is very time consuming.) Wash the entire plant, then cut off the leaves. Discard the root (although it is edible). We eat the leaves in a number of ways: chopped and thrown into vegetable and bean soups, sautéed in a skillet with turnip greens, or cooked with chestnuts. However they are prepared, dandelions have a sassy, nutty taste that is quite elegant.

It would be impossible for a Giobbi to poison weeds in a lawn for many reasons, but I guess the biggest one is: How else would we get our dandelion greens? Dandelion greens can be found in many markets these days—commercially produced greens are quite large compared to the smaller, wild greens—but if you don't live in a city, and you find these excruciatingly fresh greens popping up all over your yard, why deny yourself? It's a pleasure worth sharing.

SPRING VEGETABLES AND SALADS

Baked Artichokes

This is a variation of a dish Edward ate on his family farm in Italy decades ago. Rubbing the artichoke with the lemon keeps the leaves from discoloring.

4 medium artichokes (about the size of a fist)

1 lemon, halved

4 garlic cloves, slivered

2 tablespoons chopped mint

4 teaspoons olive oil

Salt

Heat the oven to 400°F.

Remove the tough outer leaves of one of the artichokes and cut off the stem. Rub the artichoke with the lemon. Open the artichoke leaves and stuff the slivers from 1 garlic clove inside the artichoke. Place the artichoke on a piece of aluminum foil and sprinkle a pinch of the mint, 1 teaspoon of the oil, and a pinch of salt inside the leaves. Wrap the artichoke in the foil. Place the wrapped artichoke on a baking tray. Repeat for the remaining 3 artichokes. Bake for about 1 hour, until the leaves are crisp and brown. (After about 45 minutes, open one foil package to check if the leaves are crisp and brown.)

Note: You can also cook these artichokes by throwing them into the embers in the fireplace. Just be careful they don't burn, because they will cook faster in the hot embers.

Serves 4

Fried Artichokes

The trick to preparing this recipe is the olive oil, which does not get as hot as other oils. If you use an oil like canola, the artichokes will burn before they are tender. This is a simple recipe—really, more of a technique.

4 medium artichokes (about the size of a fist)

Olive oil for frying

1 teaspoon fresh or dried rosemary

Salt

1 lemon, cut into 4 wedges, for garnish

Prepare the artichokes: Remove the tough outer leaves. Cut the base of the artichokes flat, so that they will sit upright. Turn the artichokes upside down and press down gently but firmly. The intention is to loosen the leaves slightly, so they will separate easily as the artichokes cook.

Pour about 1 inch of oil into a pot about 6 inches wide and 3 inches deep. Add the rosemary. Heat the oil over medium-high heat until it is very hot, on the verge of smoking. Gently place the first artichoke into the oil with a pair of metal tongs. The oil will spatter. Cover the pot. As the artichoke fries, the leaves will open like a flower. Cook for about 5 minutes, until the artichoke is brown on the bottom. Carefully turn the artichoke over with the tongs. Press the artichoke down into the oil with the back of a metal ladle. Cook for about 4 minutes, pressing down repeatedly, until the top of the artichoke is browned. Remove the artichoke from the oil with the tongs and drain on paper towels. The artichoke should be about 1 inch thick, and look like a dried flower. Repeat for the remaining artichokes.

Sprinkle with salt to taste and serve with a lemon wedge.

Serves 4

Artichokes Stuffed with Spinach

We like to serve these artichokes with Meat Loaf with Ricotta (see page 62), with Lamb with Potatoes (see page 59), or as a light vegetarian entrée.

4 large artichokes, tough outer leaves removed

1 lemon, halved

2 tablespoons olive oil

2 garlic cloves, finely chopped

2 pounds spinach, well washed

4 tablespoons pignoli nuts

4 tablespoons diced ricotta salata

2 tablespoons extra virgin olive oil

2 tablespoons chopped mint

Salt and freshly ground black pepper

½ cup dry white wine

½ cup water

Heat the oven to 400°F.

Prepare the artichokes: Cut the base of the artichokes flat, so that they will sit upright. Cut the leaves down to about 2 inches above the base. Open each artichoke gently, separating the leaves to give you access to the choke. Using a spoon or knife, scrape out the choke. Rub the surface of the artichokes with the lemon halves. Squeeze the remaining juice out of the lemon into a bowl large enough to hold all 4 artichokes. Place the artichokes in the bowl, add cold water to cover, and set aside while you prepare the stuffing.

Heat 2 tablespoons of olive oil in a large nonstick skillet over medium heat. Add 1 teaspoon of the garlic and sauté for a minute. Add the spinach, cover, and cook, stirring periodically, for about 5 minutes, until the spinach wilts. Allow the spinach to cool, and then squeeze as much of the moisture out of it as you can. You can do this by pressing the spinach in your hands, or placing it in a piece of cheesecloth and twisting the cloth around the spinach until the moisture comes out.

In a medium bowl, combine the spinach, pignoli nuts, ricotta salata, the remaining garlic, the extra virgin olive oil, mint, and salt and pepper to taste. Mash together until the stuffing is well blended.

Drain the artichokes. Stuff the stuffing into the cavities. Place them in a 9- × 9-inch baking dish. They should fit snugly. Add the wine and water to the bottom of the baking dish and cover the dish with aluminum foil. Place in the oven and cook for about 1 hour, until the artichokes are tender.

Serves 4

Artichokes with Peas and Prosciutto

Peas cooked with prosciutto is an Italian classic. The addition of artichokes and lettuce makes this dish more substantial. The lettuce practically dissolves when cooked and acts as a very delicate binder.

8 small artichokes

Juice of 1 lemon

3 tablespoons olive oil

1 medium onion, finely chopped

2 thick slices prosciutto (about 2 ounces), cut into thin strips

Salt and freshly ground black pepper

2 cups fresh peas (about 2 pounds in the shell)

2 tablespoons chopped mint

2 cups shredded lettuce (romaine, Bibb, or iceberg)

½ cup chicken stock

Clean the artichokes by removing the tough outer leaves. Go down to the pale green leaves. Trim the bottoms and tips, and cut in half. Place in a bowl of cold water with the lemon juice.

Heat the oil in a large skillet over medium heat. Drain, dry, and add the artichokes and onion; cover, and simmer until the onion becomes translucent, about 5 minutes. Add the prosciutto, salt and pepper to taste, the peas, mint, lettuce, and chicken stock. Cover and cook over medium to low heat for about 30 minutes, until the artichokes are tender. If the dish looks dry, add a little more stock or water.

Serves 4

Roasted Asparagus

Edward has published this recipe many times, and for good reason. It is one of the best recipes we know for asparagus. The buds get rather crunchy, and the garlic browns, lending a nutty flavor. The stems, however, can easily become overcooked, so watch them closely. You can also place the asparagus under the broiler.

16 medium asparagus spears (about 1½ pounds)

3 garlic cloves, thinly sliced

2 tablespoons finely chopped flat-leaf parsley

4 tablespoons olive oil

Salt and freshly ground black pepper

Heat the oven to 500°F.

Cut the tough ends of the asparagus off, or snap them off where they break naturally, and discard. Wash the asparagus well. Place the asparagus on a baking tray so that they don't overlap. Sprinkle the garlic and parsley over the asparagus. Sprinkle the oil over the asparagus and add salt and pepper to taste.

Place the asparagus in the oven and roast, uncovered, until the asparagus are tender, about 10 minutes.

Serves 4

Sautéed White Asparagus

White asparagus are very expensive, as dirt must be mounded around the asparagus as they grow, keeping the vegetable continuously hidden from the sun until they are mature. We eat them as a special treat. They are wonderful served beside a piece of fish or soft-shell crabs. They are also wonderful with fresh sautéed morels mounded on top.

2 tablespoons olive oil

1 tablespoon unsalted butter

1 medium onion, finely chopped

1 pound white asparagus, cut into 2-inch lengths, tough ends removed

Salt and freshly ground black pepper

½ cup warm chicken stock or water

2 tablespoons finely chopped flat-leaf parsley, for garnish

In a small skillet over medium heat, heat the oil and butter. Add the onion and cook for several minutes, until it begins to soften. Add the asparagus and salt and pepper to taste. Cover and simmer over medium-low heat for 10 minutes, until the asparagus are tender. Add the stock and continue cooking an additional 4 minutes, until the stock reduces. Serve garnished with parsley.

Serves 4

Wild Dandelion Greens with Chestnuts

One Friday when he was food shopping, Edward met a friend from Arthur Avenue who told him that greens cooked with chestnuts were excellent. Edward went home and made it. The next week he told her the combination of greens and chestnuts was indeed delicious. "What chestnuts?" she asked. "I said greens and beans!"

1 tablespoon olive oil

1 small onion, chopped

2 garlic cloves, minced

4 cups wild dandelion greens, washed and blanched

½ cup dried chestnuts (see Note), soaked overnight in water and drained, or ½ cup dried cannellini beans soaked overnight and drained

2 cups water

Salt and hot pepper flakes

Heat the oil in a medium skillet over medium heat. Add the onion and garlic and cook until the onion becomes translucent, about 5 minutes.

Transfer the onion and garlic to a Dutch oven or medium soup pot and add the greens, chestnuts, water, and salt and hot pepper flakes to taste. Bring to a boil over high heat, and then lower the heat, cover, and simmer for 30 minutes, until the chestnuts are tender. If using beans, cook for about 1 hour.

Note: Dried chestnuts can be found in most specialty markets.

Serves 4

Pearl Onions with Marjoram

Marjoram is often used in Marchigiana cooking. It marries very well with onions, and perks up this classic caramelized onion dish. Soak pearl onions in water for about 15 minutes to make the skins easier to remove.

20 large or 40 small pearl onions, peeled

1½ cups water

1 tablespoon unsalted butter

1 tablespoon sugar

Salt and freshly ground black pepper

¼ to ½ teaspoon dried marjoram

Place the onions in a shallow saucepan or skillet so they are in one layer. Add the water, butter, sugar, and salt and pepper to taste. Heat over medium heat until the water begins to boil. Partially cover and cook until the water has just about cooked away, about 20 minutes. Remove the cover and jiggle the pan so the onions roll around. They will begin to take on a brown color within a minute or two. Keep jiggling the pan until the onions are evenly browned and shiny. Take off the heat, stir in the marjoram, and serve.

Serves 4

Peas with Prosciutto

This dish is one of the most popular ways to serve peas in Italy. When ordering prosciutto for this dish, ask for it to be cut in double thickness, not the thin slices you would use when eating prosciutto plain. Canadian bacon is a decent substitute for prosciutto because it is not smoked.

2 tablespoons extra virgin olive oil, plus additional for garnish

4 thick slices prosciutto, cut into ½-inch cubes, or Canadian bacon (about ¾ cup or a little over ¼ pound)

2 cups fresh peas (about 2 pounds in the shell)

3 tablespoons mint chiffonade

Salt and freshly ground black pepper

Heat the oil in a medium skillet over medium heat. Add the prosciutto and cook for several minutes to release the flavor.

Bring a medium pot of salted water to a boil over high heat. Add the peas and cook, uncovered, for several minutes, until the peas are partially cooked. Drain and reserve about 1 cup of the water. Add the partially cooked peas and reserved water to the prosciutto. Cook for several minutes, and then add the mint and salt and pepper to taste. Cover and cook until the peas are tender, about 7 minutes. Garnish each portion with a dribble of extra virgin olive oil.

Serves 4

Potatoes with Garlic

We always mash potatoes and other root vegetables by hand or push them through a ricer. This ensures a light, fluffy mash. Using a food processor will get you a gluey mess.

1½ pounds potatoes, preferably Yukon Gold, peeled (about 6 medium potatoes)

Salt

4 tablespoons extra virgin olive oil

8 garlic cloves, minced

Freshly ground black pepper

Place the potatoes in a large pot. Cover with water, season with salt, and bring to a boil over high heat. Cook the potatoes until they are tender, about 20 minutes. Drain the potatoes and push them through a ricer into a medium bowl.

Heat the oil in a small pot over medium heat and add the garlic. Cook for about 3 minutes, until the garlic begins to take on color. Do not brown.

Pour the garlic and oil mixture into the riced potatoes, add salt and pepper to taste, and mix well.

Serves 6

Green Rice

This is a wonderful dish, very easy to make, and terrific as a side dish or as a first course.

3 tablespoons extra virgin olive oil, plus additional for garnish

2 leeks, whites only, finely chopped

2 cups chicken stock

2 carrots, finely chopped

1 tablespoon finely chopped flat-leaf parsley

Salt and freshly ground black pepper

½ cup rice (we like Uncle Ben's or basmati)

½ pound fresh spinach, chopped

Grated ricotta salata, for garnish

Heat the oil in a medium pot over medium heat. Add the leeks, cover, and cook until the leeks are soft, about 5 minutes. Add the stock, carrots, parsley, and salt and pepper to taste. Cover and simmer for 30 minutes. Add the rice and cook for 5 minutes. Add the spinach, cover, and simmer until the rice is tender, about 20 minutes.

Serve each portion garnished with extra virgin olive oil or grated ricotta salata.

Serves 4

Turnip Greens

In our garden, we let the turnips and rape go to seed in the fall. In the spring, sweet-tasting greens appear. We look forward to our spring harvest from March until June. In June, we allow five or six plants to go to seed: Nature then broadcasts the seeds about and the process continues. Spring greens anointed by evening frost taste best.

3 tablespoons olive oil

1 medium onion, coarsely chopped

½ cup chopped pancetta or Canadian bacon

2 garlic cloves, chopped

Hot pepper flakes

12 packed cups turnip and other spring greens (about 1½ pounds), washed

2 cups water

Salt

Extra virgin olive oil, for garnish

Heat the olive oil in a large saucepan over medium heat. Add the onion, pancetta, garlic, and hot pepper flakes to taste. Cover and cook until the onion becomes translucent, about 5 minutes. Add the greens, water, and salt to taste and boil gently for about 1 hour and 15 minutes, until the greens are tender.

Garnish each serving with a dribble of extra virgin olive oil.

Serves 4

Spring Vegetable Fritto Misto

While we eat this mixed vegetable fry with a second course, it is also a lovely first course. Either way, be sure you serve a salad with oil and vinegar dressing, as the acid cuts the fat in fried foods nicely. A glass of white wine will also go well with this dish, which consists of fried artichokes, zucchini flowers, leeks, and onion blossoms. The artichokes and leeks can be prepped a day in advance.

For the batter

3 cups all-purpose flour

3 teaspoons baking powder

3½ cups dry white wine

Salt

For the vegetables

6 small artichokes

3 tablespoons fresh lemon juice

½ cup white wine

½ cup water

2 tablespoons olive oil

2 garlic cloves, chopped

1 tablespoon chopped mint

Salt

6 zucchini with flowers attached (each about 3 inches long), or just the zucchini, or just the flowers

6 leeks, about 1 inch in diameter, greens removed (but retained for stock)

6 onion blossoms with stems, about 3 inches long, rinsed and dried

Vegetable oil for frying (we like canola)

For the batter: In a wide bowl, whisk together the flour, baking powder, wine, and a pinch of salt. Allow it to rest for about 30 minutes. More is okay.

For the vegetables: Heat the oven to 450°F.

Wash the artichokes and remove the tough outer leaves. Trim the stem end and cut off about ½ to ¾ inch from the top. Cut in half and soak in cold water with the lemon juice for 30 minutes.

In an ovenproof pot, combine ½ cup wine, water, olive oil, garlic, mint, and salt to taste. Add the artichokes, cover, and bake for 30 minutes. Remove the pot and set aside. Allow it to cool.

Clean the zucchini flowers by checking inside the blossoms for any insects and shaking them out. Do not wash.

Prepare the leeks. Cut a slit along the leek on each side and wash well. Do not cut all the way through—the leek should remain whole. Bring a large pot of salted water to a boil over high heat and boil the leeks for about 10 minutes, until they are tender. Drain and shock in cold water to stop the cooking. Drain and allow the leeks to cool and dry.

Heat 1½ inches of vegetable oil in a large, deep skillet over medium-high heat until it is hot. You can test how hot the oil is by throwing a pinch of flour into the oil; if the flour pops, the oil is ready for frying. Dip the vegetables in the batter and fry until they are golden brown all over. The artichokes and leeks will take about 6 minutes, and the zucchini with blossoms and onion blossoms will take about 4 minutes. Drain the vegetables on paper towels and season with salt.

Serves 6

ABOUT RICOTTA

For years it seemed as if the only ricotta we could find was Polly-O, a heavy, creamy supermarket brand that wasn't at all like the light, aerated version of the cheese we'd eaten in Italy. And then Edward started shopping on Arthur Avenue in the Bronx.

Salvatore Calandra Cheese has been making ricotta and mozzarella for more than 50 years, since the days when sheep used to be herded along Arthur Avenue to graze the Botanical Garden. It is a minimalist's heaven: white Formica counters, clean white tiles, and soft white mounds of cheese, cut with a long knife onto pieces of white, waxy paper. Calandra's ricotta, like all ricotta, is made from whey, the liquid left over from cow or sheep's milk when the curds are removed for a cheese like Pecorino. It is delicate and mildly flavored, with a hint of saltiness.

We also find good ricotta at DiPalo's Fine Foods. Located in what is left of Little Italy in lower Manhattan, DiPalo's is where the Italian expatriates shop. Women in thick gold necklaces and men in soft cashmere suits line up, often four rows deep, to be served by Luigi, Sal, or Marie DiPalo, who have carried on the family business started by their grandparents in 1925. It doesn't matter how crowded they are: If you are unsure of which fresh Pecorino to buy, the DiPalos provide commentary and samples on bits of butcher's paper, oblivious to any grumbling in the crowd. The store, which has changed location once in 94 years, and then only across the street, has become more and more like a cheese store you would encounter in Rome or Florence. The DiPalos are obsessed with preserving traditional cheese recipes and stock their shelves with an array of imported goods. But while we sometimes buy mini Amaretto cookies to crush and sprinkle on poached pears, and other times Italian quince paste to eat with nuts for dessert, we always buy one of the three types of ricotta DiPalo's sells: imported sheep's milk, imported whole milk (which they call Tipo Romano), or their own whole milk ricotta. The imported ricottas are sold within 3 days, and of the DiPalo variety, they sell only what they make that day.

Whey is rich in water-soluble proteins. It is a sweet, greenish liquid that Luigi DiPalo says was consumed 2,000 years ago. Even a generation ago, pregnant women used to come by the store for a jar of whey to ease their constipation, as it is a natural laxative. Ricotta, which translates as "cooked twice," or "cooked again," is made when whey is heated to about 180°F. Tiny white particles rise to the top of the liquid. Those particles—the proteins—are then strained off using very fine cheesecloth. The ricotta is then hung to drain any last bits of liquid. Ricotta made with the whey exclusively is a little dry, tasteless, and gritty, and sours quickly. When fresh milk is added during the heating process, the results are a smoother texture, more flavor, and a higher yield. Luigi tells me that pretty much all ricotta has milk of some sort added these days.

We use ricotta in many ways, but we love it in desserts, like Aunt Mary's no-crust ricotta pie, which is light and lemony, a recipe she got from her Italian women's club, Coronas, in Waterbury, Connecticut, and fried ricotta fritters washed in a lemon sugar glaze. When preparing these dishes with supermarket ricotta, place it in cheesecloth over a colander and refrigerate the ricotta for an hour or so. The more liquid that drains out, the lighter the ricotta will be. Ricotta can also be whipped to a cream. With sugar and a sweet wine like Marsala added, it makes a rich, indulgent complement to berries in season—in spring, it's especially good with the tiny Long Island strawberry. Indeed, our spring desserts are limited to those ingredients that are seasonal. We make Jacques Pépin's free-form rhubarb galette, cool, creamy panna cotta with a layer of strawberry puree, and strawberry-rhubarb coffee cake, which is one of those baked goods that is scrumptious when eaten fresh out of the oven, and so soft and sweet it never lasts around the house for long. But then, that's true for most family desserts: They are a treat, not an entitlement.

When I was a child, we had only homemade sweets in the house. There are many parenting traditions that I have carried on from my own childhood: I insist my children not waste paper, I value individuality over the pack mentality, and I tell my kids that if they want sweets, they have to make them.

SPRING DESSERTS

Jacques' Rhubarb Galette

Jacques Pépin made this country-style dessert for a chef's lunch honoring the late Pierre Franey. It is a surprisingly dainty dish, despite its loose, relaxed presentation. We often substitute other fruits for the rhubarb, depending on the season.

For the pastry

1 cup all-purpose flour, plus additional for dusting the board

¼ teaspoon salt

½ cup unsalted butter, very cold, cut into pieces

1 tablespoon cold water

For the bottom mixture

3 tablespoons ground almonds

2 tablespoons all-purpose flour

¼ cup sugar

For the filling

1½ pounds rhubarb

⅓ cup sugar

2 tablespoons unsalted butter, cut into little bits

¾ cup apricot, raspberry, and/or plum preserves, heated and strained

For the pastry: In a large bowl, combine the flour and salt. Cut in the butter until the mixture has a sandy texture. Work quickly so the butter doesn't get soft. Add the cold water and combine. Do not form into a ball.

You will need to work on a marble countertop or other very smooth surface. Grab a walnut-size piece of the dough (it will be loose and crumbly, but that's okay) and smear it with the heel of your hand against the work surface. The process causes the butter to integrate with the flour in long streaks. Gather the smear and set aside. Repeat with the remaining dough.

Form the dough into a patty, cover with plastic wrap, and refrigerate for at least 30 minutes.

In the meantime, heat the oven to 400°F.

For the bottom mixture: In a small bowl, combine the almonds, flour, and sugar. Set aside.

For the filling: Cut off and discard any leaves from the rhubarb and split the rhubarb in half if the stalks are thick. Cut the stalks into 2-inch lengths.

Line a baking tray with a piece of parchment.

Remove the pastry from the refrigerator and place on a floured surface. Pat out the dough with a floured rolling pin until the butter has softened enough to roll out. Try to roll the dough out in an oval about ⅛-inch thick and about 12 inches wide by 14 inches long. Roll the dough up on the pin and transfer it to the baking tray, rolling it out on top of the parchment.

Sprinkle the almond mixture over the dough to within 2 inches of the edge. Place the rhubarb pieces on the dough. Fold the edges of the dough up and around the fruit, to create an edge. Sprinkle the fruit with the sugar and dot with the butter.

Bake for about 1 hour, until the galette is brown and crunchy. Remove and paint the preserves all over the top. Allow to cool to room temperature before serving.

Serves 8

Lemon-Glazed Ricotta Balls

In some parts of Italy, ricotta balls are not cooked all the way through, so they have slightly gooey insides, something like a molten cake. We prefer them cooked through, however, and more like a doughnut.

3 large eggs

2 tablespoons plus ⅓ cup sugar

1 cup all-purpose flour

4 teaspoons baking powder

5 tablespoons brandy

2 teaspoons lemon zest

1 pound ricotta

Salt

Corn oil or other light vegetable oil for frying

⅓ cup fresh lemon juice

In a medium bowl, combine the eggs, 2 tablespoons of sugar, the flour, baking powder, brandy, lemon zest, ricotta, and a pinch of salt. Mix well, cover the bowl, and refrigerate the batter for 1 hour.

Heat 1½ to 2 inches of oil in a large saucepan over medium-high heat. Test to make sure the oil is hot by dropping a bit of the batter in the oil. If the oil boils violently, it's ready. Drop rounded teaspoonfuls of the batter into the hot oil and fry, a few at a time, until golden, about 5 minutes. Ricotta balls brown quickly, but that doesn't mean they are done inside. Let them cook 1 minute after they have turned golden, and they will be dry and fluffy inside.

Drain the ricotta balls on paper towels.

In a small bowl, dissolve the remaining ⅓ cup of sugar in the lemon juice. Using a pastry brush, paint the lemon glaze over the hot ricotta balls. Allow the glaze to harden for a couple of minutes, and then serve immediately, while the ricotta balls are still warm.

Makes about 30 balls

Lucy's Pound Cake

This is the nicest pound cake recipe we've ever used, and the simplest, one made often by our late friend Lucille Shannon. You can substitute any flavoring for the coconut extract, like vanilla, orange, lemon, or almond. All are delicious. For the glaze, we generally prefer lemon juice, but you can also replace the lemon juice with orange juice or grapefruit juice. Both work well. Sometimes we scatter chopped almonds, orange zest, or coconut over the top of the glaze as well.

½ cup (1 stick) unsalted butter, softened

1½ cups sugar

3 large eggs

1 cup all-purpose flour

1 teaspoon baking powder

2 teaspoons coconut extract

¼ cup fresh lemon juice

Heat the oven to 350°F, with a rack positioned in the upper third. Butter a 9- × 5- × 3-inch loaf pan and dust it with flour.

In a large bowl, cream the butter and 1 cup of the sugar. Add the eggs, one at a time. Don't worry if the batter looks like it is separating. It is okay.

In a small bowl, sift the flour and baking powder together. Add the flour to the batter, beating all the while. Mix in the coconut extract.

Pour the batter into the pan and bake in the upper third of the oven for about 45 minutes, until a straw inserted in the middle of the cake comes out clean.

In the meantime, in a small bowl, combine the lemon juice and the remaining ½ cup of sugar to make a glaze.

Allow the cake to rest for a few minutes, and then flip it over onto a cooling rack. Allow the cake to cool for about 10 minutes, and then flip it over onto a piece of wax paper. Using a pastry brush, brush the glaze all over the top of the cake. Allow the glaze to harden a bit before serving.

Serves 6

Ricotta Pie

Our Aunt Mary Mancinelli has made a variation of this sweet lemony pie for decades, from a recipe published in her Italian women's club book, Sweet Things. *It is much like a cheesecake, only lighter. You can serve it with fresh or cooked berries on the side, if you like.*

4 large eggs

1 cup sugar

1½ pounds ricotta

1 tablespoon lemon extract

1 teaspoon lemon zest

¾ cup milk

1 tablespoon ground cinnamon

Heat the oven to 300°F.

Break the eggs into a large bowl and blend with an electric mixer. Add the sugar and ricotta and beat until the mixture is smooth. Add the lemon extract and zest and stir well. Add the milk and stir well.

Pour the batter into a 9-inch glass pie plate. Sprinkle the cinnamon on top. Place the pie in the center of the oven. Bake for about 1 hour and 15 minutes, until the pie is set and the edges are golden.

Allow to cool to room temperature.

Note: The pie will collapse some as it cools, but the slow cooking ensures a steadier center. If the pie puffs up, it will really sink when it cools.

Serves 8

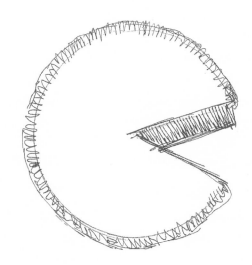

Strawberry Panna Cotta

We make this very simple dessert a day ahead of time, as the panna cotta needs to set for about 8 hours or overnight in the refrigerator. It is very cool and refreshing. Panna cotta means cooked cream, which this isn't. But the taste is panna cotta–like: rich, smooth, and creamy.

3 teaspoons powdered gelatin

3 tablespoons boiling water

1 cup heavy cream

1 cup milk

¼ cup plus 1 tablespoon sugar

¼ teaspoon vanilla extract

1 tablespoon unsalted butter

8 large strawberries, washed, hulled, and sliced, plus additional for garnish

¼ teaspoon ground cinnamon

In a small bowl, dissolve 2 teaspoons of the gelatin in 2 tablespoons of boiling water. Be sure the gelatin is completely dissolved.

In a medium saucepan, place the cream, milk, ¼ cup of sugar, the vanilla extract, and the dissolved gelatin and cook over medium-low heat for about 10 minutes, stirring to help the sugar dissolve, until the mixture is just about to boil.

Remove from the heat and pour into 4 ramekins. Refrigerate for 2 hours.

In the meantime, heat the butter in a small skillet over medium heat. Add the strawberries, the remaining 1 tablespoon of sugar, and the cinnamon and cook for about 7 minutes, until the strawberries are soft and the juice is thick.

In a small bowl, dissolve the remaining 1 teaspoon of gelatin with the remaining 1 tablespoon of boiling water. Be sure the gelatin is completely dissolved. Add the gelatin to the hot strawberries. Put the cooked strawberries and gelatin into a blender and blend to a puree.

Check to see if the cream has set—the top will be solid, although the cream will wiggle underneath. Carefully spoon the strawberry puree on top of each ramekin, dividing it evenly.

Return the ramekins to the refrigerator and allow to chill for an additional 6 hours or overnight.

To serve, run a sharp knife around the perimeter of the panna cotta. Turn the ramekin over and tap abruptly onto a plate. The panna cotta should pop right out.

Garnish with a fresh strawberry.

Note: You can experiment with the layering of the strawberries in this dish. For example, you may want to prepare twice as much of the strawberry puree, and pour one layer in the bottom of the ramekin, allow to set, pour a layer of cream, allow to set, then another layer of strawberries, and so on.

Serves 4

Strawberry-Rhubarb Coffee Cake

We love the way the fruit drops down into the cakey part of this seasonal version of a classic sour cream coffee cake.

1 large egg

¾ cup granulated sugar

1 tablespoon unsalted butter, melted

1 cup sour cream

1 teaspoon vanilla extract

1½ cups sifted all-purpose flour

2 teaspoons baking powder

¼ teaspoon baking soda

¾ teaspoon salt

For the topping

½ cup packed brown sugar

2 tablespoons all-purpose flour

2 tablespoons unsalted butter, softened

½ teaspoon ground cinnamon

1 cup small-diced rhubarb

1 cup small-diced strawberries

Heat the oven to 375°F. Butter an 8- × 8-inch baking pan.

In a large bowl, beat the egg until it is frothy. Add the sugar and melted butter and continue beating until the mixture is light and fluffy. Add the sour cream and vanilla extract and blend well. In a medium bowl, sift the flour, baking powder, baking soda, and salt together. Add the flour mixture to the sour cream mixture and blend well.

For the topping: In a small bowl, combine the brown sugar, flour, butter, and cinnamon. We find it is easiest just to mash it up with our fingers. It should be crumbly. If it is very wet and greasy, add an additional teaspoon of flour.

Pour the batter into the pan. Sprinkle the rhubarb over the top of the batter. Then sprinkle the strawberries over the rhubarb. Sprinkle the topping over the strawberries.

Bake the cake for 40 to 45 minutes, until the top is golden brown and a knife slipped into the cake comes out clean.

Serves 8

Zabaglione with Cream

We make this dish with fresh eggs from Elinor's bantam chickens. They start to lay like crazy in early April. You can make zabaglione in a double boiler, but our best results are with a round-bottomed copper bowl placed over a pot of boiling water.

4 large egg yolks, at room temperature

¼ cup sugar

4 tablespoons Marsala wine (or other sweet wine)

¾ cup heavy cream

Strawberries, for garnish

In a small bowl, whisk together the yolks, sugar, and wine.

Fill the lower portion of a double boiler with water and bring it to a boil over medium heat. Pour the egg mixture into the upper portion of the double boiler and start whisking. The egg mixture will become frothy, and then, in about 45 seconds, it will begin to thicken. Keep whisking about 10 to 15 seconds more. Zabaglione is supposed to be foamy and light, not thick like pudding, so take it off the heat immediately if you see any custard forming in the corners of the pot.

Whip the heavy cream and carefully fold into the zabaglione.

Pour the zabaglione into dessert glasses and garnish each with a strawberry.

Serves 4

Variations:
Reduce the Marsala wine by 1 tablespoon and substitute 1 tablespoon of shaved semisweet chocolate or 1 tablespoon of strong espresso (or a combination of espresso and chocolate).

SUMMER

LE MARCHE

For as long as I can remember I've come to Le Marche, or the Marches, the eastern seaboard region of central Italy, to visit my dad's kin, particularly my grandmother, Teresa Gasparetti Giobbi, a sassy little woman with cat-eye sunglasses and a sharp tongue, and my Zia Ada, always elegant in her brown silk and gold chains. We visited when I was a very young child, hardly aware of the difference between my little brother and a cat, and infatuated with Gorgonzola cheese. We visited every couple of weeks over the year, and we lived in a spiffy apartment near the Piazza di Spagna in Rome, from which we took family outings in our orange Volvo station wagon with New York plates (always getting stolen), the back seat stuffed with prepubescent children, a large Labrador retriever, and our tiny, polite southern grandmother (from my mother's side), who would thank waiters in her southern accent, "*Per pia cherry, sen your eh,*" and demurely take another sip of wine, unaware of her hilarity. I came as a teenager and gorged on Nonna's delicate *spaghetti alla vongole* and went to discos prowled by horny bravos, and again later in life, with a husband, then a husband and a baby, then two babies. We ate with family on farms in Offida, Monsampolo, Centobuchi, and other little towns scattered along the Tronto River valley and its adjacent hills, and my memories of those country meals are among my most precious.

But the farm life is a hard life, and now most of the old folks are dead, including Nonna, and few people from my generation have stayed on. Aside from the wonderful Verdicchio grape, there has been an overall decline in regional agricultural production, and the valley, once patterned with tomato arbors as far as the eye could see, now sports factories and truck parking. My father warned me of as much when we planned a recent Giobbi family trip along the Via Salaria, the imperial Roman road that spans the peninsula, from the Villa Borghese, east over the Apennines, past Ascoli Piceno, down the Tronto River to San Benedetto and my grandmother's little apartment by the sea.

The Marches is about 100,000 kilometers square, flanked by Emilia-Romagna to the north and Abruzzi to the south. The land rises up from narrow coastal plains to the Apennines, which forms a boundary with Umbria and Tuscany to the west. The Tronto valley is in Piceno, the southern quarter of the Marches. The surrounding hills are rounded by thousands of years under the plow, and most are surmounted by a farm, church, or ancient fortified town. The landscape looks like a rumpled patchwork quilt with spindly cypress trees reaching toward the blue, blue sky.

At the head of the Tronto valley is Ascoli, an ancient Italic city that was co-opted by the Romans, and the provincial and cultural capital of the Marches. Ascoli is where we went to eat in a nice restaurant, or visit a museum, and once, in one of those weird culture warps (which were less common then), to see James Brown take it to the bridge. What a relief to find it was exactly the same: still a mid-size bourgeois city built from travertine marble, untouched by tourism, with graceful medieval towers and a beautiful 13th-century piazza. It even smelled the same: of lavender and vinegar. We dined at Gallo D'Oro—for decades a family favorite—which specializes in Marchigiana cuisine. I can remember falling asleep on those banquettes while the grown-ups lingered over their espressi. My daughter napped here years ago, and on this trip my neice Snow clocked some time drooling on the upholstery, too.

Our first meal in the Marches was one that restored to memory the foods I enjoyed on the farms: *Vincisgrassi,* a delectable lasagne made with a ragu of chicken giblets and a *Fritti Ascolani,* which consists of tiny fried lamb chops, fluffy lamb brains ("Brains?" asked my daughter skeptically. "I don't think so"), crunchy fried zucchini, eggy fried *creme* (creams), and probably the signature taste of Piceno, stuffed Ascoli olives, which are very mild, in part because they are cured in lime. We drank one of the best local wines, the Rosso Piceno Superior from nearby Offida. The Marchigiane, like most Italians, don't eat many sweets. Fruit ends a meal, sometimes cheese. At Gallo D'Oro we had a wonderful piece of Pecorino di Fossa, a sheep cheese from northern Marche that is aged in limestone caves or ditches, and a glass of Meletti, Ascoli's anise-flavored liquor, which is served *alle mosce,* or "with flies" (they're actually coffee beans, but we don't tell the kids).

The next stop on our trip toward the sea was Offida, near the farm where my grandfather Achille and his brothers were raised (and where my great grandfather dug up an Italic skeleton draped in bronze jewelry). The family spread throughout the region, but the Offida farm remained ground zero. Unfortunately, the Giobbis who stayed on the land had a feud: They split the farm and house down the middle and now live in a kind of Italianized Hatfield and McCoy scenario—we figured they wouldn't appreciate two *cinque centi* full of grinning American relatives descending on them. (Occasionally we see members of that branch in New York. On one such visit our cousin Cesarina asked why Americans didn't use bidets. Dad didn't want to remind her that he remembers when she didn't have indoor plumbing, and so told her that there was a button on one side of the toilet, didn't she see it? When pressed, a hand came up and wiped your bottom clean. Cesarina's eyes widened with awe at American ingenuity.)

But I remember the farmhouse: the boxy, sienna-colored house with bougainvillea growing in luxurious heaps over the iron stair. There were flies everywhere, and it smelled earthy and barny. The farmers would come in from the field, their faces deeply lined, their hands tough as baseball gloves, and their wives, with forearms big as prosciuttos, would administer bone-crunching hugs. And then the dining would begin.

At each place sat a pile of plates, and as you finished a course, the plate would be whipped away and the next filled: first, succulent homemade *lonza,* from the pork tenderloin, and pieces of their own Pecorino—white and pure, it tasted sweet and sour, like a baby smells; then pasta. Always two, always made at home: hand-cut fettucine with chicken giblet sauce, and light little lumps of gnocchi—I remember the tongue-lashing Nonna once gave a cousin because her gnocchi were of inconsistent size. We were also served two meat dishes: their own farmyard chickens, tough and flavorful, cooked with green olives and the family Verdicchio until the skin was crispy and the flesh saturated with wine, and rabbit cooked with cognac and black olives. The meal ended with peppery salad greens, fresh peaches sliced into our glasses of wine, and bitter black espresso. I'd eat beyond full, and after lunch my sister and I would explore the haystacks, looking for fresh eggs and kittens.

"They had kittens?" asked my daughter wishfully. Oh yes. Struggling, hissing feral fluff balls that we tried, unsuccessfully, to smuggle home in our pockets.

The town of Offida sits on the crest of a hill dividing the Tesino River from the Tronto.

It is built of pale tufo brick, silent, with many closed doors. Since we couldn't go to the farm, we hit the streets, just to feel the medieval stones under our feet again. We parked near what used to be the hospital where my great uncle Attilio Gasparetti had his appendix removed. While we tried to squeeze our car into a coffin-size parking place, inch-by-inch, Dad recounted the tale. Zio Attilio was taken to the hospital in one of his construction trucks, along with his wife Zia Ada, my dad, a driver, a mechanic who always rode in the truck to service it on the road, and various muddy construction workers. He checked into a room at the hospital, and the whole crew went in to wait with him, smoking cigarettes, and assuring Zio he was going to be fine. Shortly after he was rolled away to the operating room, the doctor, a tiny man with a big mustache and bloody apron, came running in holding a small red piece of red meat in his surgical scissors. "*Questo il diavolo!*" ("This is the devil!") he announced, and all the workers took a look, nodding solemnly in grubby agreement. "It was like a Fellini movie," Dad said as he eased the car into its spot. "But then, they're a little crazy in the country."

Offida is famous for its manufacture of lace—I still have pieces made by my cousins—and on a sunny lane we encountered five ladies sitting outside their doorways at work. With thick red fingers they rattled their spindles into spidery patterns that they pinned to their cushions like butterflies. We stopped for a coffee and a taste of *funghetti,* a dry anise-scented sweet at the Centro Sociale, a bar near the old city wall, where an Offidano grandpa launched into a story about a hunchback with a tremendous wiener. After a scolding by the bartender, he dropped the topic, and then revealed he was a cousin of Pipo, my father's uncle.

Pipo was a Giobbi. Zio Attilio was a Gasparetti, my grandmother's brother, and mayor of Centobuchi (meaning, a hundred holes, probably because local salt dealers used to sell salt from depressions in the ground). Zio Attilio was an awesome man, and not only because of his barrel chest and big square head. When I was young, we would ask permission to stand by his chair and watch him eat chicken bones. *All* of the bone, with huge, tooth-shattering crunches and lots of scary winks. It was a freaky demonstration. But he has been long dead and Zia Ada long on her own. My father is the son Ada never had, though they are both too old to tell who is the eldest. When we visited her cool house—with its terrazzo tiles and old lady bric-a-brac, a house smelling of flower sachets and sun-dried tomatoes—Ada prepared Edward's favorite foods: Ascoli olives stuffed with fish—a creation of the San Benedetto chefs — *Vongole all Marchigiana* — tiny clams boiled briefly in hot pepper, white vinegar, and garlic — and a *Brodetto* — a tangy fish stew made of at least 10 different fin fish and prickly crustaceans. Ada says the dish was created by the fishermen's wives, who used the small, bony fish their husbands couldn't sell.

After lunch she cranked an old Victrola and played a scratchy 78 rpm recording of *Madama Butterfly.* She closed her eyes as the faraway voice of Licia Albenese rose through the static, singing along in her own aged warble, tender and sentimental as a virgin. As the Victrola wound down and Licia's singing slowed, so did Ada's, until she realized what was happening and cranked the thing up again.

It's only a 15-minute drive from Centobuchi to the sea. At 17, my grandmother traded in her small-town existence in Centobuchi for marriage and 35 years in a sweatshop in Connecticut. She retired to San Benedetto, a middle-class beach resort, in 1966, a year after my grandfather died, with a Chihuahua named Pepita who snarled at the world from her perch on Nonna's lap. She lived across the street from a beach promenade lined with bushy palm trees, sweet-smelling oleander, and scruffy little pines. There is something about the smell of those pines . . . but it reaches too far back into my childhood.

Still, the beach is the main attraction here: 6 kilometers of white sand fine as sugar, with salty, warm water that is like swimming in spit, or tears. There are more bathers than I remembered, but the Italians are as forgiving of their bodies as ever: bow-legged and big-tummied men in Speedo bathing suits; swarthy blades standing a quarter mile out (and still the water only comes to their waists), smoking a cigarette or talking into their *telefonini.* Teenage girls with big beautiful butts and bouncing bosoms still hug their boyfriends, whose backs are so tan their gold chains look white in the sun. Grandmas inspect the shore as they walk, looking for anything edible; and dark, slender gypsy men ply the beach, selling fresh coconut. Countless lounge chairs line the sand, and the clubs to which they are attached provide ice cream, open air showers, and the loud thump of peppy disco music. For 30 years I've had one of those songs stuck in my head: "*Sta sera mi butto, sta sera me butto, mi butto con te.*"

Thirty years.

We lunched at Il Pescatore, a low-key fish joint and maybe the best on the beach, which has been serving for decades. We ordered family-style: platters of fried baby eel, delicate as thread; cool salads of baby shrimp and squid; a carpaccio made of swordfish dressed with intense extra virgin olive oil. We ate mussels stuffed with fine breadcrumbs and parsley, and mussels cooked in wine; sardines with roasted red peppers, and a white shrimp and cold poached whitefish salad, and a salmon salad, both served with fine oil and minced green peppers. Then, a platter of grilled fish, including chop-size scampi in the shell, and a whole fish with a head and teeth like a cat, and shrimp and squid on a skewer. We ate a platter of fried fish: small back halves of little triglia, and shrimp and squid served with wedges of glistening lemon, and finally, a simple green salad, followed by what the owners call a sorbetto, but is actually lemon sorbet combined with spumanti in a champagne glass. And then, back to the beach, to watch the children play in the sand, and promise ourselves to swim the equivalent of a mile . . . but after a nap.

Twenty years ago, as the sun reached its zenith at noon, it was time to go in, where Nonna had prepared lunch for me. I'd eat while she tore apart pieces of bread and gossiped about the tailor, who labored over a tiny garden outside her window. It is a testament to the Italian passion for freshness that every little strip of available land is gardened. For us, summer dining *is* the garden, and we enjoy its fruits in many ways: zucchini flower soup followed by fish-stuffed cabbage; tomato frittata before chicken sausages with pole beans, and maybe a ramekin of cherry crisp; tomatoes stuffed with ricotta and tuna, then a vegetable plate of eggplant with ricotta salata, and a scoop of lively beet granita.

"His wife practices witchcraft and drinks his blood to keep him faithful," Nonna told me many times, as she nodded toward the old man hoeing his row of basil plants. I'd never egg her on, but she'd go ahead and tell me anyway that boys who eat industrialized chickens will grow breasts like a woman, and the Pope, if I didn't know it already, was a crook.

But she's not there.

The apartment, now my father's, is rented to tourists in the summer. I wandered around, looking for some connection to the past, but most signs of my grandmother are gone. It seemed like much of the Marches I knew had washed out to sea. I entered her tiny storeroom, once stocked with home-canned tomatoes and wheels of Pecorino cheese separated by clean, worn dishtowels. I leaned my forehead against the empty shelves and closed my eyes. And then I smelled something, something familiar. This time, I recognized what it was. Rosemary and ironed napkins—the faint scent of my grandmother. And then I wept.

ESSENTIALS OF MEAL PLANNING

We eat copious amounts of whatever is in the garden: zucchini flowers, then zucchini; eggplant; peppers for roasting, stuffing, sautéing; tomatoes of all sorts; green beans; beets and their delicious greens; yellow squash and herbs in abundance; oregano, parsley, cilantro, basil, rosemary, mint—which by summer has spread all over—and marjoram. We make cool salads with thin sliced cucumbers and sweet onions, dressed with olive oil and lemon juice, but once the cucumber harvest spins out of control, we serve a platter of them peeled, sliced, and seasoned with salt at every meal. There are always lettuce salads and the fresh greens are so satiating we even prepare them in pasta. We often eat the weeds in the garden: the purslane and lamb's-quarters that come up between the rows. Many vegetable dishes are turned into a supper with the addition of a couple of eggs poached on top.

By summer our home-canned tuna is perfectly aged, and we throw the pink chunks into vegetable salads, toss it into pasta, or combine it with ricotta to make a delicious dip or stuffing. Because of the hot weather, we tend to eat more fish. We love cheap fish like sperling, whiting, and monkfish, as much as the dearer ones, the lobsters, clams, and snappers. We can get Maine sardines year-round (they are fished by helicopter, so weather determines the catch—particularly wind), but we prefer them in summer, charred on the grill.

During the summer we eat more desserts, primarily of the fruits that are in season: cherries, peaches, and apricots. All of our desserts, however, are very simple. With seasonal fruits, one doesn't need to fuss much at all, and often all that's really needed is a peach, a sharp knife, and a little wine left in your glass.

ABOUT WILD FOODS

Many of our favorite meals come straight from the wild. Fresh food is the primary element of fine cuisine, and one cannot find fresher food than that which one harvests oneself. But beyond the joys of super-fresh foods, there is an even more intense experience to be found in what the great mushroomer Jack Czarnecki calls the "unbroken chain of sensual pleasures," from the hunting, fishing, or gathering to the preparation in the kitchen to the dining. We Giobbis have gathered all kinds of delightful foods outdoors, and always, it's the dual joy of foraging and eating that makes wild edibles so engaging.

Most of the wild edibles we collect are from the sea and are primarily used as first-course dishes. Seafood is light enough to discourage diners from filling up, and is easily followed by most dishes. But ultimately, we love pairing seafood with seafood: farfalle with zucchini flowers and shrimp followed by broiled mackerel with peppers; spaghettini with Maine sardines followed by fish stew with almond pesto; whitebait frittata followed by chicken with shellfish.

Edward's father was an inveterate hunter/gatherer. During the Depression, foraging helped sustain the family. In the summer he gathered mussels and clams along the Connecticut shoreline. We summered as a family on Cape Cod during the 1960s and 70s. Sailing? Waterskiing? Snorkeling? Forget about it. Giobbi family sports consisted of hunting for blueberries in the sand dunes to eat with great dollops of whipped cream and pulling mussels off the rocks and wooden piles of fishing piers that appeared at low tide, to stuff with breadcrumbs and herbs, or steam with wine and garlic. We seined for sperling—the 2- to 3-inch silver fish that swim in schools around your legs at high tide—with a 12-foot net, which we then fried until they were golden, sprinkled with kosher salt, and ate like potato chips with big goblets of cold white wine, or rolled into eggy frittatas redolent with tarragon. We followed the convoluted trails of moon snails, and at the end of their path we would flip the large, pearly mollusk out of the sand with our feet, its thick slimy pad deliciously encasing our toes before we chucked them in a bucket, to cook in a savory pot of garlic and parsley. Once a year we would travel to Cumberland Island, Georgia, where we owned a small piece of wetland. It was a private island at the time, but not in an exclusive, golf-coursey way. Cumberland was wild and jungley, with feral pigs and cows and horses, chiggers that fed on children's bare legs, eccentric aristocrats who lived in moldering, moss-covered mansions, and melancholy ghosts who haunted a burnt ruin called Dungeness in search of their lost children. We caught bouncy pompano in nets we threw into the surf, and oysters, small and frilly, which the adults would gather by the hundreds and cook on fireplaces in a field of chimneys, the heartbreaking remnants of an old slave community.

These days, with my own family, and any Giobbi who is around and willing, we slosh through Long Island's low tide in search of big burly New England oysters, which we open and swallow down on the beach, or throw into a bowl of hot linguine fini flavored with garlic, salt, and their own liquor. Or we boat out to a neighbor's clam bed and jump into the muck, to paw at the warm mud for clams. We follow the Greek grandmas swathed in black, who gather limpets at waterline, and we gather them too, cooking the tiny chunks of meat in a ragu of tomato and garlic and herbs, and savor their luscious taste, although it takes forever to chew them up. One July day we stumbled across a patch of sea grass and disturbed a colony of scallops, which snapped at us furiously and shot away between our legs before we could capture more than a handful, which we broiled and ate with a few drops of melted butter. We even ate the vicious mantis shrimp—a large, centipede-looking thing not even closely related to the shrimp family, which can supposedly flip its tail with such speed it can break your finger. My son Mo found a couple thrown up on the beach in a storm, and we cooked them in a pan with white wine and garlic. They were well armored, and much pulling apart and sucking was necessary to extract their wonderful lobsterlike flavor.

These pleasures are small and grand at the same time. For me, the art of hunting, gathering, and preparing wild foods is a conduit to the good life. It brings us closer to nature; it provides wonderful, real tastes; and it fulfills a particular pleasure that all independent-minded people can appreciate. I think Dad used to call it beating the system.

SUMMER
FIRST COURSES

Eggs and Tomatoes

This is a Marchigiana specialty that Edward's mother used to make. For a light dinner, we like to serve this dish with Italian bread and a green salad.

3 tablespoons extra virgin olive oil

1 large onion, thinly sliced

2 medium tomatoes, chopped

1 teaspoon chopped marjoram

8 eggs

Salt and freshly ground black pepper

Heat the oil in a medium nonstick skillet over medium heat. Add the onion, reduce the heat to medium-low, and simmer until the onion becomes translucent, about 5 minutes. Add the tomatoes and marjoram, cover, and simmer for about 8 minutes, until the tomatoes break up.

Whisk the eggs in a bowl and season with salt and pepper. Pour the eggs into the simmering tomatoes. Cover and cook, stirring occasionally, until the eggs are cooked, about 5 minutes. The eggs should be soft, like scrambled eggs.

Serves 4

Whitebait Frittata

We like to serve this dish as part of an antipasto plate, with maybe a stuffed tomato and a few slices of roasted peppers.

Whitebait are about ¾ inch long and an ivory white color. They look like small worms with black eyes. But don't be put off by this description. They are rapturously delicious. We find them in better fish markets, like those on Arthur Avenue.

1 pound whitebait, washed and drained

3 tablespoons milk

Salt and freshly ground black pepper

1 tablespoon finely chopped tarragon

¼ cup grated ricotta salata

6 eggs, lightly beaten

1 teaspoon grated lemon zest

2 tablespoons olive oil

In a mixing bowl, combine the whitebait, milk, salt and pepper to taste, tarragon, ricotta salata, eggs, and lemon zest. Warm the oil in a 12-inch nonstick skillet over medium-low heat. Pour the egg mixture into the skillet. Cover and cook over low heat for about 20 minutes, until the eggs have set.

Let the frittata rest for 15 to 30 minutes. Place a large serving plate over the skillet and flip the frittata over onto the plate. Cut into wedges.

Serves 12

Zucchini Flower Frittata

Edward and Eugenia developed this recipe in Colorado. As mentioned earlier, we use rosemary in frying oil because it cuts down the free radicals in the oil by 90 percent.

18 large zucchini flowers

1½ cups all-purpose flour

2 cups dry white wine

2 teaspoons baking powder

Salt

3 tablespoons olive oil

1 medium onion, thinly sliced

10 eggs

¼ cup milk

1 tablespoon finely chopped
flat-leaf parsley

Freshly ground black pepper

Vegetable oil for frying

1 teaspoon fresh rosemary leaves

½ cup grated ricotta salata

Check the insides of the zucchini flowers for insects and shake them out. Brush any dirt off the flowers, but do not wash them or the flowers won't be crisp when you fry them. Chop 6 of the flowers and set aside.

In a bowl, combine the flour, wine, baking powder, and a pinch of salt and refrigerate for 1 hour (a little more or less is okay). Heat the olive oil in a medium skillet over medium heat. Add the onion and chopped zucchini flowers and cook until the onion becomes translucent, about 5 minutes. Scrape the onion and zucchini flowers into a mixing bowl. Add the eggs, milk, parsley, and salt and pepper to taste and mix well.

Heat the oven to 300°F.

Place ¾ inch of vegetable oil in a large nonstick skillet with the rosemary. Heat the oil over high heat. The oil must be very hot. You can test it by throwing a dash of flour into the oil. If the flour pops, the oil is ready for frying. Dunk the zucchini flowers into the batter and place them gently in the hot oil. Don't put too many flowers in at once or it will bring down the temperature of the oil, and they mustn't touch sides or they will stick together. Do not flip the flowers over until you can see that the lower edges have turned golden brown, about 2 minutes. If you are using an iron skillet and the flowers stick, let them cook 30 seconds more. Turn the flowers over with tongs and fry for an additional minute, then remove and drain on paper towels. Do not add more battered flowers until you are sure the oil has come up in temperature again. Sprinkle with salt and set aside.

Place half of the fried flowers on the bottom of an ovenproof nonstick pan in a pinwheel pattern. Pour half of the egg mixture on top. Add the ricotta salata, then another layer of fried zucchini flowers. Add the remaining egg mixture, cover, and bake for 30 minutes, until a knife plunged into the center comes out clean. Allow to rest for 15 minutes, and then flip the frittata over onto a serving platter. Cut into wedges.

Serves 8

Mozzarella with Brioche

Edward first tasted this dish at the home of Giovanni Del Drago, an Italian aristocrat whose cook is a master of simple Italian fare. For this recipe to succeed, only the best ingredients can be used: very fresh homemade or imported mozzarella, garden fresh tomatoes, and fine imported prosciutto. The simple brioche recipe calls for letting the dough rest overnight in the refrigerator, so plan accordingly.

For the brioche

1 tablespoon sugar

¼ cup milk, at room temperature

½ package active dry yeast
(we use Fleischmann's)

2 cups all-purpose flour, sifted

8 tablespoons (1 stick) unsalted
butter, softened

4 eggs

½ teaspoon salt

For the filling

2 tablespoons olive oil

1 pound mozzarella, sliced
¼-inch thick

3 medium tomatoes, sliced
¼-inch thick

1 cup fresh basil, loosely packed

¼ pound prosciutto, thinly sliced

1 egg white whisked with 1 tablespoon water for an egg wash

For the brioche: Add ½ tablespoon of the sugar to the tepid milk. Add the yeast and dissolve. Add ½ cup of the flour and mix well. Cover and allow to rise in a warm place until fluffy, about 30 minutes.

In a bowl, combine the remaining 1½ cups of flour with the remaining ½ tablespoon of sugar. Beat in the butter, 2 eggs, and the salt. Add the yeast mixture and beat again. Add the remaining 2 eggs, one at a time, beating thoroughly. Cover and let rise until fluffy, about 3 to 4 hours. Beat the dough again and refrigerate overnight.

Heat the oven to 400°F.

For the filling: Pour the oil into a 10-inch round, deep-dish pie plate. Place in a layer of sliced mozzarella, then a layer of sliced tomatoes, then a layer of basil leaves (about 8), then a layer of prosciutto. Repeat the layering until the pie plate is filled.

Remove the dough from the refrigerator and punch it into a disk roughly 10 inches in diameter. Place the dough on top of the filling. Allow some dough to fall over the lip. With scissors, snip an × into the top of the dough. Using a pastry brush, brush the egg white wash on the dough.

Bake for 20 to 25 minutes, until the brioche is brown. Using a sharp knife, cut off any dough that has fallen over the edge of the plate. Allow to rest about 10 minutes, and serve.

Note: For a more elegant presentation, prepare this dish in individual ramekins.

Serves 8

Tomatoes Stuffed with Ricotta and Tuna

This is a perfect summer appetizer: light and fresh tasting. A variation on this dish is to prepare the ricotta/tuna combination as a spread topped with diced fresh tomatoes and served in a ramekin with a piece of thinly sliced, toasted Italian bread on the side.

4 medium firm tomatoes

½ pound ricotta

1 can (6 ounces) Italian tuna fish packed in oil, drained

Salt and freshly ground black pepper

2 teaspoons chopped flat-leaf parsley, for garnish

Slice off the stem ends of the tomatoes and hollow out the centers. Cut a little flat slice on the bottom of each tomato so that it will sit straight on the plate. (If you use plum tomatoes, cut them lengthwise.)

In a small bowl, combine the ricotta, tuna fish, and salt and pepper to taste. Stuff the tomatoes with the ricotta and tuna mixture. Garnish with a sprinkle of parsley.

Note: This is an excellent stuffing for fried zucchini flowers. Pipe the stuffing into 12 flowers and fry according to the recipe for Zucchini Flower Frittata, page 101.

Serves 4

Cuttlefish Salad

Cuttlefish are shipped to the United States from Spain and Italy, where they are highly prized. Similar but superior to a squid, the cuttlefish has thick, sweet white flesh. It can be steamed, broiled, grilled, stewed, and fried. This is one of our favorite ways to prepare it. For a fall variation, we add boiled fresh cranberry beans to this salad.

1 large cuttlefish (1½ to 2 pounds), cleaned and with head and tentacles intact (see Note)

Olive oil

Salt and freshly ground black pepper or hot pepper flakes

1 tablespoon chopped rosemary

2 large red bell peppers, roasted, peeled, cored, and cut into ½-inch slices (see page 119)

4 tablespoons extra virgin olive oil

Juice of 1 lemon

4 garlic cloves, sliced

1 tablespoon chopped flat-leaf parsley

2 bay leaves

Prepare a grill.

Rub the cuttlefish with some oil, salt, pepper, and the rosemary. Place the cuttlefish on a piece of aluminum foil that is a couple of inches larger than the fish. Place on the grill and cook for about 20 minutes. Turn the cuttlefish over and cook for another 5 minutes. Remove the cuttlefish, discard the foil, and continue to grill the cuttlefish for about 2 minutes on each side—this will create browned grill marks on the fish.

Remove the cuttlefish and cut the body into strips about ½ inch wide and 2 inches long. Cut the head and tentacles into thin slices.

In a large serving bowl, combine the cuttlefish with the bell peppers, extra virgin olive oil, lemon juice, garlic, parsley, bay leaves, and salt to taste. Allow the salad to rest for at least 2 hours before serving. Remove the bay leaves before serving.

Note: Clean the cuttlefish head by cutting off the beak and eyes, and remove the skin. Remove the innards and bone and discard. Or, ask your fishmonger to clean the cuttlefish.

Serves 4 to 6

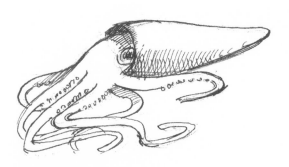

104

Fish Soup with Zucchini and Green Beans

This soup is light but substantial. It is excellent before Red Snapper with Zucchini Flowers (see page 129).

For the stock

3 tablespoons extra virgin olive oil

1 medium onion, coarsely chopped

2 small leeks, rinsed and coarsely chopped

2 garlic cloves, chopped

1 large tomato, chopped

1 celery rib, chopped

1 tablespoon basil chiffonade

1 tablespoon finely chopped flat-leaf parsley

2½ to 3 pounds fish head (gills removed), collar, and carcass

8 cups water

½ cup dry white wine

3 bay leaves

Salt and freshly ground black pepper

For the soup

4 cups fish stock

⅓ pound green beans, cut into 1-inch lengths

1 pound zucchini, diced

¼ pound capellini

¾ pound fillet of sole or other white-fleshed fish such as red snapper or black bass, cut into bite-size pieces

1 tablespoon finely chopped tarragon

Grated Parmesan cheese, for garnish

For the stock: Heat the oil in a medium pot over medium heat. Add the onion, leeks, and garlic and cook until the onion becomes translucent, about 5 minutes. Add the tomato, celery, basil, and parsley. Cover and simmer for about 10 minutes, until the tomato breaks up. Add the fish bones, water, wine, bay leaves, and salt and pepper to taste. Cover and boil gently for 30 minutes.

Strain the stock and discard the bones and vegetables. Reserve 4 cups for the soup and freeze the rest.

For the soup: Bring the fish stock to a boil in a large soup pot over high heat. Add the beans and cook for about 5 minutes. Add the zucchini and pasta and cook for 3 minutes. Add the fish. When the soup returns to a boil, add the tarragon. Reduce the heat to medium-low and simmer, covered, for about 5 minutes, until the fish is cooked.

Garnish each portion with grated cheese and serve with a spoon and fork.

Serves 4

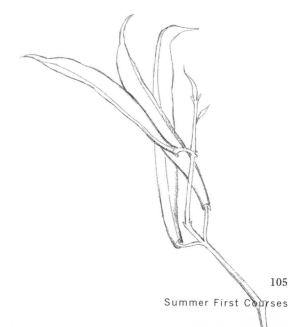

Summer Minestrone alla Genovese

This was Edward's favorite minestrone as a child. It is served at room temperature, which is particularly refreshing in the summer. For small amounts of pesto like that called for in this recipe, we find a mini food processor is most effective.

6 cups water

2 large carrots, diced

2 cups chopped Savoy cabbage

1 medium onion, chopped

¼ pound Swiss chard, chopped

1 pound zucchini, chopped

1 large red-skinned potato, peeled and diced

1 cup fresh peas (about 1 pound in the shell)

¼ pound green beans, cut into 2-inch lengths

Salt and freshly ground black pepper

1 cup fresh basil leaves

½ cup grated Parmesan cheese

5 tablespoons extra virgin olive oil

3 tablespoons pignoli nuts

2 garlic cloves, chopped

1 cup tubettini pasta

Pour the water into a medium soup pot. Add the carrots, cabbage, onion, and Swiss chard. Cover and boil gently over medium heat for 30 minutes. Add the zucchini, potato, peas, and green beans. Cover and cook another 30 minutes. Remove the pot from the stove and allow to cool, uncovered. Add salt and pepper to taste.

In the meantime, make the pesto. In a food processor, combine the basil, ¼ cup of the cheese, the oil, pignoli nuts, garlic, and salt to taste. Puree and set aside.

Once the soup is cool, stir in the pesto.

Bring a small pot of salted water to a boil over high heat and add the tubettini. Cook until it is al dente. Drain and rinse the pasta in cold water. Add a portion of pasta to the bottom of each bowl and ladle the minestrone over it. Garnish with the remaining ¼ cup of cheese.

Serves 6

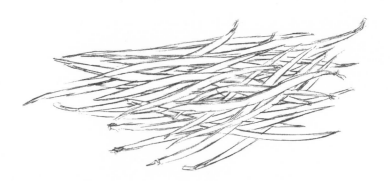

Zucchini Flower Soup

This is a light soup that we like to serve before Chicken with Ascoli Olives (see page 132) or Marinated Grilled Rabbit (see page 136). You can prepare this recipe well ahead of time—the rice retains its integrity nicely and the taste just gets more intense.

3 tablespoons olive oil

1 medium onion, coarsely chopped

3 cups zucchini flowers, chopped (about 15 large flowers)

1 tablespoon chopped flat-leaf parsley

Salt and freshly ground black pepper

4 cups chicken stock

4 tablespoons rice

2 small zucchini (about 6 inches long), diced

Grated Parmesan cheese or extra virgin olive oil, for garnish

Heat the olive oil in a medium soup pot over medium heat. Add the onion and cook until it becomes translucent, about 5 minutes. Add the zucchini flowers, parsley, and salt and pepper to taste. Cover and simmer for 10 minutes. Add 2 cups of the stock, cover, and simmer for 10 minutes. Puree in a food processor or blender. Return to the soup pot. Add the remaining 2 cups of stock and cook for 10 minutes. Add the rice and cook until it is tender, about 20 minutes. Add the zucchini, cover, and simmer for 5 minutes, until the zucchini are tender when prodded with a fork.

Garnish each serving with grated cheese or a drizzle of extra virgin olive oil.

Serves 4

Pasta Primavera

This is the authentic Italian recipe for Pasta Primavera, which is called spring pasta because it utilizes the first tomatoes that come in. Edward introduced this dish to Le Cirque restaurant in 1973. The chef, Jean Vergnes, adapted it, and it became a national favorite. The original recipe called for all the ingredients to be hand chopped, but we prefer them blended in a food processor or blender.

4 cups coarsely chopped fresh, garden-ripe, never-been-refrigerated plum tomatoes

4 tablespoons extra virgin olive oil

4 tablespoons fresh basil, chopped

1 tablespoon chopped flat-leaf parsley

2 garlic cloves, chopped, or more if you like

Salt and freshly ground black pepper

1 pound spaghetti

Extra virgin olive oil, for garnish

In a food processor, combine the tomatoes, oil, basil, parsley, garlic, and salt and pepper to taste and pulse to blend.

Bring a large pot of salted water to a boil over high heat. Add the pasta and cook until it is al dente. Drain the pasta and toss it in a serving bowl with the raw sauce. Garnish each portion with a dribble of extra virgin olive oil and serve immediately.

Serves 6

Tagliolini with Pesto di Trapano

This recipe is perfect before a fish, meat, or poultry second course. Add a can of Italian tuna fish (with oil drained), and the dish becomes more robust.

4 large fresh ripe tomatoes, chopped

⅓ pound blanched almonds

3 tablespoons extra virgin olive oil

2 tablespoons chopped basil

2 garlic cloves, chopped

Salt and freshly ground black pepper

¾ pound egg pasta, such as tagliolini or fettucine

4 tablespoons toasted bread-crumbs, for garnish

In a food processor, puree the tomatoes, almonds, oil, basil, garlic, and salt and pepper to taste.

Bring a large pot of salted water to a boil over high heat and add the pasta. Cook until al dente. Drain and toss the pasta with the sauce in a large serving bowl. Garnish with breadcrumbs.

Serves 4

Farfalle with Zucchini and Eggs

The heat from the pasta will cook the eggs, making a rich sauce for the pasta.

4 tablespoons extra virgin olive oil

1 large onion, thinly sliced

4 garlic cloves, sliced

2 pounds zucchini, sliced

2 tablespoons basil chiffonade

2 tablespoons finely chopped flat-leaf parsley

Salt and freshly ground black pepper

¾ pound cut pasta such as farfalle or penne

2 eggs, lightly beaten

4 tablespoons grated Parmesan cheese, for garnish

Heat the oil in a medium skillet over medium heat. Add the onion and garlic and cook until the onion becomes translucent, about 5 minutes. Add the zucchini, cover, and cook until the zucchini are tender, about 10 minutes. Add the basil and parsley, and season with salt and pepper.

Bring a large pot of salted water to a boil over high heat. Add the pasta and cook until it is al dente. Drain the pasta and pour into a serving bowl. Immediately toss in the eggs and mix well. Add freshly ground black pepper, then the zucchini sauce. Mix well, and garnish each serving with a tablespoon of grated cheese.

Serves 4

Spaghettini with Clams

We have a problem with most pasta with clam dishes that we eat in this country. Italians use a very small, tender clam, which is not available here. We've made this pasta with Maine clams, trawled from deep waters, which are tiny and excellent, but they are very hard to find. American restaurants will use cockles from New Zealand, which are often tough, and there is little marriage between the clam and the pasta. We think this recipe solves the problem.

4 tablespoons olive oil

4 to 6 garlic cloves, coarsely chopped, plus 1 peeled garlic clove

3 tablespoons finely chopped flat-leaf parsley

1 tablespoon chopped oregano, or 1 teaspoon dried

½ cup dry white wine

Hot pepper flakes

1 dozen fresh littleneck clams

1 large tomato, seeded and chopped

1 tablespoon chopped basil

3 tablespoons extra virgin olive oil

Salt and freshly ground black pepper

¾ pound spaghettini

Heat the olive oil in a large skillet over medium heat. Add the chopped garlic and cook until it begins to take on color, about 2 minutes. Add 2 tablespoons of parsley, the oregano, wine, and hot pepper flakes to taste. Bring to a boil and add the clams. Cover and cook over medium heat until the clams open. Remove the clams immediately and remove the meat. Return the clam meat to the sauce and simmer for about 5 minutes over low heat. Pour the sauce into a food processor and pulse to chop. The pieces of clam should be quite small but not pureed.

In a food processor, combine the tomato, basil, garlic clove, 1 tablespoon of extra virgin olive oil, and salt and pepper to taste and blend to a puree. Set aside.

Bring a large pot of salted water to a boil over high heat. Add the spaghettini and cook until it is almost al dente. Reserve 1 cup of the cooking water, then drain the pasta.

Heat the remaining 2 tablespoons of extra virgin olive oil in a large skillet. Add the chopped clams and the tomato puree. When warm, add the pasta. Stir the pasta constantly until it is finished cooking, 2 to 4 minutes. Add some of the reserved water if the pasta looks dry. Garnish with the remaining 1 tablespoon of parsley.

Serves 4

Farfalle with Zucchini Flowers and Shrimp

In general, it is our rule to cook shrimp separately, as they tend to overcook quickly. You can substitute scallops for the shrimp, or use both to make a richer dish. This is an early summer dish, as we have asparagus in our garden through June.

For the zucchini flower sauce

3 tablespoons extra virgin olive oil

1 medium onion, coarsely chopped

10 large zucchini flowers, chopped (see Note)

1 tablespoon unsalted butter

1 tablespoon basil chiffonade

Salt and freshly ground black pepper

1½ cups chicken stock

¼ teaspoon saffron

¾ pound cut pasta such as farfalle or penne

2 tablespooons extra virgin olive oil

1 pound asparagus, cut into 1-inch lengths

2 garlic cloves, finely chopped

¾ pound shrimp, shelled, deveined, and butterflied

Salt and freshly ground black pepper

2 tablespoons finely chopped flat-leaf parsley, for garnish

For the zucchini flower sauce: Heat 3 tablespoons of oil in a medium skillet over medium heat. Add the onion and cook until it becomes translucent, about 5 minutes. Add the zucchini flowers, the butter, basil, and salt and pepper to taste. Cover and simmer for 10 minutes, until the flowers are soft.

In the meantime, heat the chicken stock in a small pot over medium heat. Add the saffron, cover, and simmer for about 5 minutes, until the saffron dissolves. Add 1 cup of the stock to the zucchini flower mixture, cover, and simmer for 10 minutes, until the flavors meld.

Put the sauce into a food processor and puree. The sauce should be the consistency of light cream, so if it is too thick, add a little more warm chicken stock.

Bring a large pot of salted water to a boil over high heat and add the pasta. Cook until it is al dente. Drain.

In the meantime, heat 2 tablespoons of oil in a medium skillet. Add the asparagus and cook, uncovered, for about 10 minutes, until they are fork-tender. Add the garlic and cook several minutes more. Add the shrimp, season with salt and pepper to taste, and turn up the heat. Cook until the shrimp turn pink, about 4 minutes.

Toss the zucchini flower sauce and the pasta in a large serving bowl. Garnish each serving with parsley, then a portion of the asparagus and shrimp.

Note: Large zucchini flowers are about 5 inches long. If you pick or purchase smaller ones, increase the number of flowers you use in the recipe.

Serves 4

Spaghettini with Maine Sardines

This quick dish is rich and luxurious. Edward ate it as a child on Good Friday. "You were supposed to suffer on Good Friday," he says, "but I thought it was the best thing I ever tasted."

We like to serve this recipe followed by a salad and a grown-up dessert like Cherries in Wine (see page 151) or Espresso Granita (see page 154). You can substitute small Tinker mackerel or fresh anchovies for the sardines.

¾ pound fresh Maine sardines

4 tablespoons extra virgin olive oil

2 salted anchovies, rinsed, boned, and chopped, or 4 canned fillets

4 garlic cloves, finely chopped

Freshly ground black pepper or hot pepper flakes

1 teaspoon chopped fresh rosemary

2 tablespoons tomato paste dissolved in 2 cups water

1 tablespoon finely chopped flat-leaf parsley

¾ pound spaghettini

Salt

For the garnish

1 cup fresh breadcrumbs

2 tablespoons olive oil

1 tablespoon finely chopped flat-leaf parsley

Prepare the sardines: Cut off the heads and split the fish from the anus to the gills with a sharp knife. Remove the guts. Flatten the sardine out so the flesh fillets open. With your thumb and forefinger, pull out the spine. Rinse in cold water and cut into bite-size pieces.

Heat 4 tablespoons of extra virgin olive oil in a medium skillet over medium heat. Add the anchovies, garlic, and pepper to taste and cook until the anchovies dissolve, about 2 minutes. Add the sardines and rosemary. Cover and cook for 5 minutes, mixing often. Add the tomato paste with water and the parsley. Cover and cook for 10 minutes, until the tomato and the fish flavors are well melded.

For the garnish: Heat the broiler. In a small bowl, combine the breadcrumbs, olive oil, and parsley. Spread the garnish on a baking tray and toast under the broiler until the breadcrumbs are golden brown, about 2 minutes.

Bring a large pot of salted water to a boil over high heat. Add the pasta and cook until almost al dente. Drain.

In the meantime, pour the sauce into a large skillet and bring it to a boil over medium-high heat. Add the drained pasta and, mixing constantly, cook for about 2 minutes, until the pasta is al dente. Add salt to taste.

Serve immediately garnished with the breadcrumbs.

Serves 4

Capellini with Whiting

Edward created this delicious pasta dish for a summer weekday lunch. With it we drank a cold glass of homemade white wine, and afterward we ate a salad picked fresh from the garden, dressed simply with lemon, oil, and salt. Dessert was a Giobbi family staple: fresh peaches peeled and sliced into our wine glasses, with a little more white wine poured over them.

Whiting is inexpensive and finely flavored.

4 tablespoons olive oil

4 garlic cloves, coarsely chopped

2 large fresh tomatoes, coarsely chopped

½ cup dry white wine

1 tablespoon chopped flat-leaf parsley

1 tablespoon basil chiffonade

Salt and hot pepper flakes

4 medium whiting (about 10 inches long) or other white-fleshed fish, with heads and gills removed (reserve the fish heads), cut into 2-inch thick steaks (you can also make this with fillet, cut into sections)

¾ pound capellini

Extra virgin olive oil, for garnish

Heat the olive oil in a deep saucepan over moderate heat. Add the garlic and cook until the garlic begins to color, about 2 minutes. Add the tomatoes, wine, parsley, basil, salt and hot pepper flakes to taste, and the fish heads. Cover and simmer over moderate heat for about 10 minutes.

Add the fish pieces and poach the fish in the sauce. Add a little water if it is too dry. Cook about 5 minutes, until the flesh is cooked through. Remove the fish and the heads. Keep the meat warm and discard the heads. Place the capellini, raw, into the sauce. Add a little water if the sauce is dry, but you won't need much. Mix often. The pasta will be al dente in about 5 minutes.

Serve the pasta with a few pieces of the fish and a dribble of extra virgin olive oil.

Serves 4

113

Zucchini Flower Lasagne

This dish is composed of three zucchini recipes layered with ricotta into a lasagne. It is a rather time-consuming but exceptional dish. All of the elements except for the fried flowers can be made a day ahead of time. Edward created this dish for his 78th birthday.

For the fried zucchini flowers

16 large zucchini flowers

1½ cups all-purpose flour

2 cups dry white wine

2 teaspoons baking powder

Salt

Vegetable oil for frying

1 teaspoon fresh rosemary leaves

For the baked zucchini

2 tablespoons olive oil

4 large zucchini (about 12 inches each), cut into slices ½ inch thick and 3 inches long

For the fried zucchini flowers: Check the insides of the zucchini flowers for insects and shake them out. Brush any dirt off the flowers, but do not wash them or your flowers won't be crisp when you fry them.

In a bowl, combine the flour, wine, baking powder, and a pinch of salt, stirring until smooth, and refrigerate for 1 hour (a little more or less is okay).

Place ¾ inch of vegetable oil in a large nonstick skillet with the rosemary. Heat the oil over high heat. The oil must be very hot. You can test it by throwing a dash of flour into the oil. If the flour pops, the oil is ready for frying. Dunk the flowers in the batter and place them gently in the hot oil. Don't put too many flowers in at once or it will bring down the temperature of the oil, and they mustn't touch sides or they will stick together. Do not flip the flowers over until you can see that the lower edges have turned golden brown, about 2 minutes. If you are using an iron skillet and the flowers stick, let them cook 30 seconds more. Turn the flowers over with tongs and fry for an additional minute, then remove them and drain them on paper towels. Do not add more battered flowers until you are sure the oil has come up in temperature again.

Sprinkle with salt and set aside.

For the baked zucchini: Heat the oven to 500°F.

Rub the oil onto two baking trays and place the zucchini slices on it. Turn them over so they become coated with oil. Bake for about 15 minutes, until the zucchini turn golden brown, then flip them over and cook for about 5 minutes more, until brown. Remove from the oven and set aside.

For the zucchini flower sauce

4 tablespoons olive oil

1 medium onion, finely chopped

8 cups zucchini flowers, coarsely chopped (about 40 flowers)

4 tablespoons basil chiffonade

Salt and freshly ground
black pepper

3 cups chicken stock

½ teaspoon saffron

1 tablespoon butter

For the ricotta stuffing

4 pounds ricotta

4 tablespoons finely chopped flat-leaf parsley

½ teaspoon grated nutmeg

Salt and freshly ground black pepper

8 sheets Delverde instant lasagna, or 24 strips imported (see Note, page 37)

1 cup grated ricotta salata or 1 cup grated Parmesan

For the zucchini flower sauce: Heat the oil in a large skillet over medium heat. Add the onion and cook until it becomes translucent, about 5 minutes. Add the zucchini flowers, basil, and salt and pepper to taste. Cover and simmer for 5 minutes.

In the meantime, bring the stock to a boil in a small pot. Add the saffron, reduce the heat to medium-low, and simmer for 5 minutes, until the saffron dissolves. Add the broth to the zucchini mixture and simmer for 5 minutes over medium-low heat.

Puree the sauce to a smooth consistency in a food processor or blender. Return to the pan and swirl in the butter. Keep warm.

For the ricotta stuffing: In a medium bowl, combine the ricotta, parsley, nutmeg, and salt and pepper to taste and set aside.

Assemble the lasagne: Heat the oven to 450°F.

If you are using a lasagna variety other than no-boil, bring a large pot of salted water to a boil over high heat and cook the lasagna until it is al dente. Drain off half the water and set the pot under cold running water to cool the lasagna enough to handle. Lay the lasagna on paper towels. Do not overlap or they will stick together.

Pour about ⅓ cup of the zucchini flower sauce in the bottom of each of two 8-inch square baking dishes. Add a sheet of pasta, and then spread a layer of ricotta, then a layer of fried zucchini flowers, and some more sauce. Add another layer of pasta, a layer of baked zucchini, some grated cheese, a layer of sauce, another layer of pasta, etc. Build up the lasagne in any way you see fit, but end with a layer of sauce and a sprinkle of grated cheese.

Cover the lasagne with aluminum foil and bake for about 45 minutes. Allow the lasagne to rest for 15 minutes before serving.

Serves 16

Zia Ada's Gnocchi with Chicken Giblet Sauce

This is a country dish from the town of Offida, in Le Marche. Typically, the ragu is made with chicken head, feet, and cockscombs. We've adapted it for the more readily available giblets. We never buy commercial gnocchi. Making it by hand is not difficult—just a little messy.

For the chicken giblet sauce

1 pound chicken bones (backs, wing tips, necks), cut up

½ pound chicken giblets (gizzards, livers, hearts)

1 small carrot, peeled

1 celery rib, cut into thirds

1 small onion, peeled and studded with 2 whole cloves

2 garlic cloves, smashed

2 tablespoons finely chopped pancetta

½ cup dry white wine

8 large tomatoes, peeled, seeded, and chopped

1 2-inch piece Parmesan cheese rind (optional)

1 tablespoon unsalted butter

Salt and freshly ground black pepper

For the gnocchi

4 Idaho potatoes

1 teaspoon salt

1 large egg, beaten

2 cups all-purpose flour

Grated Parmesan cheese, for garnish

For the chicken giblet sauce: In a large wide pan, combine the chicken bones, giblets, carrot, celery, onion, garlic, and pancetta and cook over medium-low heat, stirring occasionally, until the bones become dark brown and the vegetables are soft, about 1 to 1½ hours.

Add the wine, scraping the thick layer of browned bits stuck on the bottom of the pan with a wooden spoon, and cook for 3 to 4 minutes. Add the tomatoes and cheese rind, if using, and cook, partially covered, until the sauce thickens, about 30 minutes. Remove and discard the bones, giblets, onion, garlic, and cheese rind and transfer sauce to a food processor. Pulse to blend. Return sauce to pan, add the butter, and season with salt and pepper. Keep sauce warm over low heat.

For the gnocchi: Place the potatoes in a saucepan, cover with cold water, and bring to a boil over high heat. Reduce the heat to medium-high and cook the potatoes at a gentle boil until tender. Drain, and when cool enough to handle, peel and work potatoes through a ricer or food mill. Spread the mashed potatoes on a flat surface and let cool to room temperature.

Add the salt and egg to the potato mixture, working it in with your hands. Sprinkle 1½ cups of flour over the potato mixture and knead as for bread. When smooth and doughlike, set aside.

Sprinkle a flat surface with the remaining ½ cup of flour. Cut a piece of the dough about 3 inches in diameter. Roll it on the board with your palms to create a long sausage about ½-inch thick. Cut into 1-inch lengths. Continue this process until all the dough is used.

Bring a large pot of salted water to a gentle boil over medium heat and add the gnocchi. Cook, stirring often, until the gnocchi rise to the surface and are tender, about 2 to 3 minutes. Drain, transfer to a serving platter, toss with the sauce, and serve with grated cheese.

Serves 8

Vincisgrassi

This is a specialty of Le Marche. Sometimes black summer truffles are layered into this dish, which supposedly gets its name from an Austrian prince, Alfred zu Windischgratz, who may have eaten it in the early 1800s.

4 cups all-purpose flour

¾ cup semolina

½ teaspoon salt

9 tablespoons unsalted butter, at room temperature

6 eggs

6 tablespoons Marsala wine or vin santo

Double recipe chicken giblet sauce (see opposite page)

1 pound fresh mozzarella

2 cups freshly grated Parmesan cheese

In a large bowl, place the flour, semolina, and salt. Work 6 tablespoons of the butter into the flour until it resembles coarse meal. Work the eggs and Marsala into the dough until it holds together. Transfer to a lightly floured surface and knead until smooth, about 10 minutes. Cut the dough into 6 pieces, shape each into a rectangle, cover with plastic wrap, and set aside for 1 hour.

Feed the wide side of one piece of dough through the smooth cylinders of a pasta machine on the widest setting. Repeat rolling, decreasing the setting by one notch and feeding the narrow end of the pasta through the machine, until all pasta sheets have gone through all settings. Cut the sheets into thirds crosswise. Then lay them on a floured surface, not touching, to dry for 1 hour.

Cook several sheets of pasta at a time in a large pot of boiling water over high heat until tender, 25 to 30 seconds, then dip in a bowl of cold water. Lay the sheets out, not touching, between damp kitchen towels.

Butter a 10-inch springform pan. Completely line the bottom and sides of the pan with some of the pasta sheets, allowing the pasta to overhang the rim. Spread 1 cup of chicken giblet sauce over the pasta, scatter with ⅔ cup of the mozzarella and ¼ cup of the Parmesan, and cover with more pasta sheets. Repeat layers, ending with pasta. Fold overhanging pasta over the top, wrapping pie completely. Refrigerate for 1 hour.

Heat the oven to 350°F.

Melt the remaining 3 tablespoons of butter, then brush it over the top of the pasta. Bake until heated through, about 1 hour. Sprinkle with Parmesan. Allow the vincisgrassi to rest for about 15 minutes. Cut in wedges to serve.

Serves 6 to 8

Risotto with Pork and Zucchini Flowers

Arborio rice, which Italians use in risotto, is a variety of short-grained rice. It is an almost round grain that has a higher starch content than long-grain varieties, hence the creamy texture of finished risotto.

5 tablespoons olive oil

2 garlic cloves, finely chopped

2 medium onions, finely chopped

½ pound lean double-ground pork

Salt and freshly ground
black pepper

1 cup Arborio rice

½ cup dry white wine

2 to 3 cups warm chicken stock
(or more)

1 cup zucchini flower sauce
(see page 115)

1 tablespoon finely chopped
flat-leaf parsley

1 tablespoon finely chopped basil

4 tablespoons grated Parmesan
or Pecorino cheese

⅓ pound string beans, cut into
1-inch lengths, for garnish

Heat 2 tablespoons of the oil in a small nonstick skillet over medium heat. Add the garlic and half the onion and cook until the onion becomes translucent, about 5 minutes. Add the pork and season with salt and pepper. Cook, uncovered, mixing with a wooden spoon to break up the chunks of meat, for about 10 minutes, until the pork is cooked through. Set aside.

Heat the remaining 3 tablespoons of oil in a medium pot over medium heat. Add the rest of the onion and cook until it becomes translucent, about 5 minutes. Add the rice and cook for about 1 minute, stirring to coat the rice with the oil. Add the wine, cover, and cook until the rice absorbs the wine, about 5 minutes. Add about half the chicken stock a ladle at a time, stirring with a wooden spoon, for about 15 minutes, making sure the rice absorbs the stock before adding more. Add the ground pork mixture and the zucchini flower sauce. Continue mixing, adding stock by the ladleful as the rice absorbs the liquid. Add the parsley and basil. Cook for 10 minutes more, until the rice is al dente but still creamy. Add salt and pepper to taste. Add the cheese and stir in well.

In the meantime, bring a small pot of salted water to a boil over high heat. Add the beans and cook until they are tender, about 5 minutes. Drain. Serve the risotto garnished with the string beans.

Serves 4

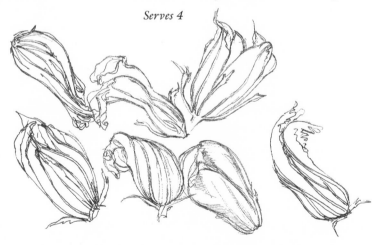

Tripe and Roasted Red Pepper Salad

Tripe, the stomach lining of an animal, is a delicious and economical food. It is a shame many Americans are prejudiced against it. This recipe is a good introduction.

Note that the salad must rest several hours to overnight before serving, so plan ahead. Any broth left over from boiling the tripe may be used in a soup or stock.

½ pound honeycomb tripe

3 cups chicken or beef stock

1 celery rib, cut into 3 sections

1 carrot, peeled and cut into 3 sections

1 small onion, halved

4 or 5 large fresh basil leaves

2 bay leaves

2 large red bell peppers

3 tablespoons extra virgin olive oil

2 tablespoons finely chopped flat-leaf parsley

1 tablespoon finely chopped chives

Salt and freshly ground black pepper

Bring a large pot of water to a boil over high heat. Add the tripe and boil it for 5 minutes. Drain and rinse the tripe in cold water. Turn the tripe comb-side down, and with a sharp knife, cut off the excess fat. Cut the tripe into strips ½ inch wide and 1½ inches long.

In a large stockpot, add the stock, celery, carrot, onion, basil, bay leaves, and tripe. Cover and bring to a boil over high heat. Reduce the heat to medium and continue to boil gently for about 2 hours, until the tripe is fork-tender. Drain the tripe but retain the broth. Remove the bay leaves. Allow the tripe to cool.

In the meantime, broil the bell peppers over an open flame or under the broiler until the entire exterior of the peppers has blackened and blistered. As soon as you can handle the peppers, remove the skins. Do not put the peppers in a bag prior to peeling, as they will steam and overcook. Remove the stems and seeds and cut the peppers into strips about ½ inch wide and 2 inches long.

In a serving bowl, combine the tripe and roasted peppers with the oil, parsley, chives, 3 tablespoons of the tripe broth, and salt and pepper to taste. Allow the salad to rest for several hours before serving.

Serves 4

EATING AL FRESCO

Italians love to eat outdoors. In fact, one of the most popular places to eat in Italy is at the *frasca,* a vineyard eatery. *Frasca* means branch, and the name comes from the tradition of hanging a laurel branch at an intersection of roads to point the way to a vineyard that has new wine to sell. At an outdoor table, under something deliciously flowering or fruiting or budding, the vineyard will serve a little homemade prosciutto and a piece of bread to ease the transition from one wine tasting to another. This is the kind of meal—absolutely simple and utterly satisfying—that one remembers for a lifetime.

Although this kind of *frasca* flourishes in the spring, when the white wines are ready, and in late fall, when the red wines are ready, many *frascas* have evolved into what are called *agritourismi.* These are like *frascas,* only you get more food, and they are open more often, and they are particularly popular during the warm months of summer, when the children can inhale a plate of gnocchi before taking off to torment the farmyard chickens. By definition, *frascas* serve only what is produced on the premises. In contrast, *agritourismi* produce only 50 percent of what they serve; 40 percent is produced in the immediate area, and 10 percent is purchased from elsewhere. The locations for *frascas* and *agritourismi* are the same—vineyards and family farms in the middle of nowhere—and famously hard to find.

Eating at a *frasca* or *agritourismo* is a casual affair: paper napkins, wooden serving boards, wildflowers, and you recycle your fork into the second course. Your table will usually have to be cleared of freshly picked plums, or zucchini blossoms, or whatever produce is in season, and the bees and bits of earth swept onto the ground. Most of the farms are real, working farms. For example, Zaro in Piano delle Farcadizze in Fruili is a bosky spot tortuously difficult to get to and found only after traveling endless ribbons of winding road, but once there, you are offered the most special reward: homemade Pecorino and caprino (goat milk cheese), fresh, achingly rich salami on homemade bread, pickled baby zucchini with cipolini and basil, and a liter jug of scarlet merlot with pink fizz on top. We snacked while the fat dogs lounged in the sun and a charming little girl named Martina flirted.

The Giobbis have always eaten outdoors when we could. During the 1960s and 70s, when we spent the summer months in Provincetown, Massachusetts, we often ate outside the tiny, wooden village house my parents owned. Brightly painted inside, it had a small courtyard of sandy brick, surrounded by thick, dark privet hedges. A heavy grapevine curled around an arbor overhead. It was a shady spot, somewhat damp, and smelled mightily of the sea. A long time ago, Dad used to prepare pasta with fish sauces for the painter Hans Hoffman and serve it to him under the inedible grapes, which hung in rich bundles at their ears. I remember sharing those Provincetown meals with bowls of yet-to-be-washed blueberries, and big plastic buckets of moon snails—the fat critters would slide up the sides of the pail until they reached the lip, and then I would reach out my toe and knock them back to the bottom. The buckling wood picnic table was decorated with a variety of shells, mainly big chowder clamshells that we painted with poster paints, and always a stinking starfish or two. We ate outside for all the years we owned the house.

We eat on the front porch of the house in Katonah when the weather allows, and certainly all summer long. Indeed, my mother starts asking if we think it is warm enough to eat outside in April. By July, the atmosphere is thick with humidity, and the leaves of the trees are so puffed up with water and sun they flap like birds' wings from their branches. The porch is situated sensibly for this climate: What summer breezes there are seem to be tunneled past our table. We eat as formally outside as in: with the good silver and proper dishes and cloth napkins, wine glasses and beautiful pitchers full of cool water or fresh mint. There are always vases of fresh mint on the table as mint keeps the flies away.

We usually gather for Sunday lunch, kids wet from swimming, dogs lying around under the table with muddy paws and lolling tongues. Although Dad will trudge out in the winter to work on his gas grill, melting the snow for two feet all around him, summer is when he enjoys it most—when we all do. We often have a pasta with a summer garden vegetable: tomatoes, zucchini flowers, or broccoli, followed by grilled rabbit or eel, or broiled mackerel, shrimp, and scallops. Grilled meats and fish, with herbs fresh from the garden, served warm or at room temperature, make the perfect summer meal. Eating al fresco just makes it summer.

SUMMER SECOND COURSES

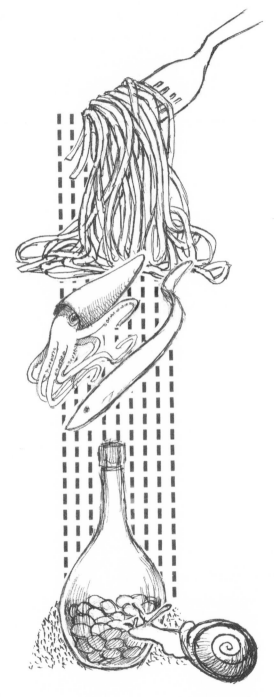

Brodetto alla San Benedetto del Tronto

Brodetto is a great example of regional cuisine: As you travel up the Adriatic coastline, the brodetto recipes change significantly every 20 miles or so. In San Benedetto, brodetto is made with green tomatoes and vinegar. In Civitanova, it is made with fish stock and saffron, and so on. Brodetto is a fish stew, not a fish soup. The semi-ripe tomatoes this recipe calls for are green on the outside and pink on the inside.

½ cup olive oil

1 pound squid, cleaned and sliced into rounds

1 large red bell pepper, seeded and chopped

2 scallions, chopped

4 tablespoons chopped onion

6 tablespoons finely chopped flat-leaf parsley

⅓ cup wine vinegar

2 large semi-ripe tomatoes, chopped

Salt and hot pepper flakes

1 pound monkfish, cut into 3-inch chunks

16 mussels, scrubbed and debearded

3 medium whiting, with heads on (about 10 inches long), cut into 3-inch pieces

½ pound medium shrimp, shelled and deveined

½ cup dry white wine

Bruschetta (see page 17), for serving

Heat the oil in a large wide saucepan over medium heat. Add the squid and cook for 8 minutes. Add the bell pepper, scallions, onion, and 3 tablespoons of the parsley. Turn the heat up to high and cook for several minutes, until the onion begins to soften, then add the vinegar. Cook for several minutes, then add the tomatoes and salt and hot pepper flakes to taste and continue cooking, uncovered, for 5 minutes. Lower the heat to medium and add the monkfish and cook for 5 minutes. Add the mussels and cook until they begin to open, a few minutes. Add the whiting and cook for several minutes more. Add the shrimp and as soon as they begin to change color, add the wine. Cover and simmer for about 5 minutes. Add the remaining 3 tablespoons of parsley and simmer a few minutes more. Serve over bruschetta.

Serves 8

Fish Stew with Almond Pesto

This recipe is of southern Italian origin. It is a real crowd-pleaser and infinitely variable. Add or subtract fish as you see fit. Because it is so light, your guests won't feel overfull if you serve a pasta first (we like Spaghettini with Clams, see page 110), a salad afterwards, and a dessert after that (we love Broiled Apricots with Lavender Syrup, see page 150).

2 tablespoons olive oil

1 pound cuttlefish, cleaned (see page 104) and cut into 1-inch strips, or squid

1 large onion, finely chopped

1 tablespoon finely chopped tarragon

¼ cup white wine vinegar

2 large fresh tomatoes, peeled, seeded, and chopped

2 tablespoons mint chiffonade

Salt and freshly ground black pepper

1 skate wing (about 2 pounds), skinned and cut into 8 sections

1 pound monkfish fillet, sliced

½ pound fresh eel, cut into 1-inch sections

16 littleneck clams, scrubbed

½ pound medium shrimp, shelled and deveined

For the pesto:

½ cup blanched almonds

1 tablespoon finely chopped tarragon

2 garlic cloves, finely chopped

Half a medium green tomato, chopped

2 tablespoons extra virgin olive oil

Salt and freshly ground black pepper

Heat the olive oil in a medium skillet over medium heat. Add the cuttlefish, onion, and tarragon and cook until the onion becomes translucent, about 5 minutes. Add the vinegar, cover, and reduce the heat to medium-low. Cook until the vinegar evaporates, about 5 minutes. Add the tomatoes and mint. Cover and cook for 10 minutes, until the tomatoes begin to break up. Add salt and pepper to taste.

Transfer the cuttlefish and sauce to a large skillet or braising pan over medium heat. Add the skate wing sections, season them with salt and pepper, cover, and cook for 5 minutes. Turn the wings over occasionally. Add the monkfish and eel and cook for 10 minutes. Add the clams and shrimp to the stew. Cover and cook until the clams open, about 5 minutes.

For the pesto: In a food processor, blend the almonds, tarragon, garlic, tomato, and extra virgin olive oil. The consistency should be about like heavy cream. If it is not, add some broth from the stew. Add salt and pepper to taste.

Add the pesto to the fish stew and blend. Adjust the seasoning.

Serves 8

Polpette di Pesce

We use whiting in this recipe, but any white-fleshed fish will do when making polpette *or fish balls. We like to serve this dish with baked zucchini, after a first course of Pasta Primavera (see page 108). Follow up with Cherry Almond Sorbet (see page 153) for a very light, elegant meal.*

For the stock

2 tablespoons extra virgin olive oil

1 small onion, chopped

2 tablespoons finely chopped red bell pepper

2 tablespoons basil chiffonade

2 garlic cloves, chopped

1 tablespoon finely chopped flat-leaf parsley

Hot pepper flakes (optional)

Heads and bones from 2½ pounds whole whiting (gills removed)

½ cup dry white wine

1 cup water

Salt

For the polpette

Fillets from 2½ pounds whole whiting

3 tablespoons fresh breadcrumbs

2 tablespoons grated Parmesan cheese

1 tablespoon finely chopped flat-leaf parsley

1 tablespoon basil chiffonade

2 garlic cloves, finely chopped

1 tablespoon finely chopped tarragon

1 egg white, lightly beaten

Salt and freshly ground black pepper

For the stock: Heat the oil in a medium soup pot over medium heat. Add the onion, bell pepper, basil, garlic, parsley, and hot pepper flakes to taste (if using). Cover and cook until the onion becomes translucent, about 5 minutes. Add the fish bones and heads and the wine. Cover and simmer for about 10 minutes. Add the water and simmer for 25 minutes. Add salt to taste.

Strain the stock through a fine sieve, and set the stock aside.

For the polpette: Finely chop the fillets and add to a bowl with the breadcrumbs, cheese, parsley, basil, garlic, tarragon, egg white, and salt and pepper to taste. Mix well and form into 12 balls, each about 1½ inches in diameter.

Bring the stock to a boil in a medium, shallow pot over medium heat. Add the fish balls, cover, and cook about 8 minutes. Remove the balls with a slotted spoon and place in shallow soup bowls. Spoon a couple of tablespoons of stock over the balls to serve.

Serves 4

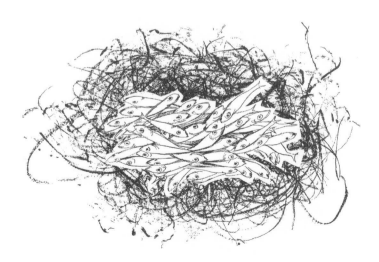

Cabbage Stuffed with Fish

We make this elegant dish when the summer cabbage comes in. It is much like a meat-stuffed cabbage; however, the combination of fish and basil pesto makes for a much lighter variation. We love to serve it with rice. You can also serve this as a first course for 8.

For the sauce

3 tablespoons olive oil

1 large onion, coarsely chopped

2 garlic cloves, finely chopped

2 large fresh tomatoes, coarsely chopped

2 tablespoons basil chiffonade

1 tablespoon finely chopped flat-leaf parsley

Salt and freshly ground black pepper or hot pepper flakes

8 large cabbage leaves

1½ pounds white-fleshed fish fillets such as cod, striped bass, or flounder, coarsely chopped

2 tablespoons basil pesto (see page 106)

2 tablespoons breadcrumbs

1 egg white

2 tablespoons grated Parmesan cheese

Salt and freshly ground black pepper

Extra virgin olive oil, for garnish

4 teaspoons chopped flat-leaf parsley, for garnish

Heat the oven to 450°F.

For the sauce: Heat the olive oil in a medium saucepot over medium heat. Add the onion and garlic and cook until the onion becomes translucent, about 5 minutes. Add the tomatoes, basil, parsley, and salt and pepper to taste. Cover and cook gently for 10 minutes, until the tomatoes break up. Puree the sauce in a food processor and set aside.

In the meantime, bring a medium pot of salted water to a boil over high heat. Add the cabbage leaves and cook for a couple of minutes, until they are tender. Drain and carefully rinse. Do not tear the leaves. If the center rib is very tough, shave it down a little. Set aside.

In a medium bowl, combine the fish, pesto, breadcrumbs, egg white, cheese, and salt and pepper to taste.

Lay a cabbage leaf out on your work counter and place about ¼ cup of stuffing in a mound near the stem end of the leaf. Fold the side of the leaf in around the stuffing and roll it up. Place the stuffed cabbage leaf in a baking tray seam down and continue with the remaining leaves.

Cover the stuffed cabbage leaves with the pureed sauce. Place in the oven and bake for 20 to 30 minutes, until the sauce is bubbling.

To serve, garnish each portion with a dribble of extra virgin olive oil and a sprinkle of parsley.

Serves 4

Note: We never use store-bought pesto as homemade is so easy. See recipe on page 106.

Grilled Eel

Eel is an outstanding fish to grill: It is rich and savory, and the meat is firm enough to take the heat. We love to serve this dish with a green salad, after Capellini with Whiting (see page 113) or Eggs and Tomatoes (see page 100).

Juice of 1 lemon

3 tablespoons extra virgin olive oil

2 garlic cloves, sliced

1 teaspoon chopped rosemary

Salt and freshly ground black pepper or hot pepper flakes

1½ pounds eel, skinned and cut into 2-inch sections

In a nonreactive bowl, combine the lemon juice, oil, garlic, rosemary, and salt and pepper to taste. Add the eel and marinate for 1 hour.

In the meantime, heat the grill.

Remove the eel from the marinade but do not discard the marinade. Grill the eel, turning occasionally, for 3 to 5 minutes per side, until the flesh is white and cooked through. Return the cooked eel to the marinade and allow the eel to marinate for 30 minutes before serving.

Serves 4

Lobsters with Brandy

This is Edward's variation of a dish Pierre Franey used to make at Craig Claiborne's house on Long Island.

5 pounds lobster

4 tablespoons olive oil

1 red bell pepper, seeded and finely chopped

4 shallots, finely chopped

2 tablespoons chopped garlic

Salt and hot pepper flakes

1 cup dry white wine

2 tablespoons finely chopped flat-leaf parsley

4 large fresh tomatoes, peeled, seeded, and chopped

2 tablespoons chopped tarragon

3 tablespoons brandy

12 littleneck clams

Hack the lobster into pieces about 4 inches long. Split the head lengthwise and crack the claws.

Heat the oil over medium-high heat in a skillet or pan large enough to hold all the lobster pieces without overlapping. Add the bell pepper, shallots, garlic, and salt and hot pepper flakes to taste. Cook for about 5 minutes, until the shallots are translucent. Add the wine, parsley, and lobster. Cook, stirring often, until the shells are red all over, about 20 minutes. Remove the lobster pieces and set them aside. Add the tomatoes, tarragon, and brandy to the skillet, and cook the sauce for 10 minutes, until the tomatoes break up.

Smash up the heads of the lobsters and return them, along with any accumulated juices and the remaining pieces of lobster, to the sauce. Cover and cook for another 15 minutes, until the flavors are well blended. Add the clams and cook until they open, a few minutes.

Note: Do not substitute canned tomatoes for fresh in this recipe as the canned will make the dish too tomatoey.

Serves 4

Broiled Mackerel with Peppers

The Italians call mackerel a green fish, because it is oily. You can buy mackerel throughout the year, but Edward used to eat it in the summer, when he was an art student in Provincetown in 1949–50. His fishermen friends would often give him as much mackerel as he could carry home. This is a version of a dish he would commonly make.

1½ pounds whole mackerel, cleaned (1 large or 2 medium fish)

Salt and freshly ground black pepper

2 tablespoons olive oil

1 large red or green bell pepper, seeded and sliced about ½ inch wide and 2 inches long

1 small onion, thinly sliced

2 garlic cloves, thinly sliced

2 scallions, thinly sliced

2 tablespoons finely chopped mint

3 tablespoons balsamic vinegar

2 tablespoons extra virgin olive oil

Lemon wedges, for garnish

Heat the broiler.

Place the mackerel on a broiling tray and broil until the flesh separates easily from the bone, about 20 minutes for a large fish. Allow the mackerel to come down to room temperature. Fillet the mackerel, add salt and pepper to taste, and set aside.

Heat the olive oil in a medium skillet over medium heat. Add the bell pepper and cook until it is almost tender, about 8 minutes. Add the onion, garlic, scallions, and mint. Cover and simmer for 5 minutes. Add the vinegar, cover, and simmer about 3 minutes more. Add salt and pepper to taste.

Place the pepper mixture on top of the mackerel. Dribble the extra virgin olive oil over the peppers. Serve at room temperature garnished with lemon wedges.

Serves 4

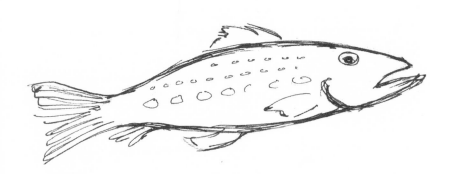

Red Snapper with Zucchini Flowers

You can substitute another white-fleshed fish—such as black bass—or sliced pieces of a bigger fish—like striped bass or cod—for the snapper.

4 tablespoons extra virgin olive oil

1 medium onion, coarsely chopped

8 to 10 large zucchini flowers, chopped

1 tablespoon finely chopped flat-leaf parsley

Salt and freshly ground black pepper

½ cup dry white wine

2 red snapper fillets (about 1½ pounds)

Heat the oven to 450°F.

Heat 3 tablespoons of the oil in a medium skillet over medium heat and add the onion. When the onion becomes translucent, about 5 minutes, add the zucchini flowers, parsley, and salt and pepper to taste. Cover and simmer for 10 minutes, until the zucchini flowers are soft. Add the wine and simmer for another 5 minutes, until the wine is absorbed. Puree the sauce in a food processor, check for salt and pepper, and keep warm.

In the meantime, place the fish in a small baking dish. Add the remaining 1 tablespoon of oil, and salt and pepper to taste. Cover the dish with a cover or aluminum foil and bake in the oven for about 10 minutes, until the flesh separates easily when prodded with a fork.

Divide the fillets into 4 portions and serve with the zucchini flower sauce.

Serves 4

129

Fillet of Sole with Cantaloupe

Edward came upon this ladylike, dainty combination of flavors when he and Elinor were doing separate tasks in the kitchen: Edward was seasoning fish fillets, and Elinor was peeling a cantaloupe.

4 medium fillets of gray sole (about 1½ pounds)

4 tablespoons extra virgin olive oil

Juice of 1 lemon

4 garlic cloves, sliced

2 teaspoons finely chopped tarragon

Salt and freshly ground black pepper

8 pieces peeled cantaloupe, each about 1 inch thick and 2 × 2 inches wide

Heat the broiler.

Place the fillets in a baking tray or shallow dish. Spread 1 tablespoon of the oil on each fillet. Sprinkle each fillet with lemon juice, garlic, tarragon, and salt and pepper to taste. Place the cantaloupe sections around the fillets. Broil close to the heat for about 10 to 12 minutes, until the fish separates easily when prodded with a fork.

Serves 4

Chicken Breasts with Broccoli Pesto

This is a perfect, light summer dish. We like to have a salad afterward, and a piece of fruit. Do not overpuree the broccoli pesto, as a little texture is nice. Sometimes we add another garlic clove to the pesto.

Juice of 3 lemons (about ½ cup)

½ cup extra virgin olive oil

6 garlic cloves, sliced

2 tablespoons chopped rosemary, or 1 teaspoon dried

Salt and freshly ground black pepper

2 whole, skinless and boneless chicken breasts, cut in half crosswise

For the pesto

2 cups broccoli florets

6 tablespoons extra virgin olive oil

3 garlic cloves, sliced

Salt

¼ cup chicken stock or water

Marinate the chicken: In a nonreactive bowl big enough to hold the chicken breasts, combine the lemon juice, oil, garlic, rosemary, and salt and pepper to taste. Add the chicken breasts and marinate them in the refrigerator for several hours.

Heat the grill.

For the pesto: Bring a large pot of salted water to a boil over high heat. Add the broccoli and cook until the water comes up to a boil again. Scoop out about 1 cup of the cooking water, then drain the broccoli. Heat 2 tablespoons of the oil in a small skillet over medium heat. Add 1 tablespoon of the garlic and cook the garlic until it begins to take on color, about 3 minutes. Add the broccoli and about ¼ cup of the cooking liquid. Cook the florets until they are fork-tender, about 10 minutes. Transfer the broccoli and garlic to the food processor. Add the remaining 4 tablespoons of oil, the remaining garlic, and salt to taste and puree to a rough paste. Add the chicken stock a few tablespoons at a time and pulse until the pesto is loose and saucy. Adjust the seasoning.

Grill the chicken breasts over hot coals or gas for about 3 minutes on each side. Do not overcook the chicken. (If cooking on top of the stove, cook in a lightly oiled grilling pan over high heat for 20 minutes, then turn over and cook for an additional 10 minutes.) Remove the breasts and allow them to rest for a few minutes. Slice the breasts on an angle against the grain of the flesh, about ½ inch thick. Garnish with broccoli pesto.

Serves 4

Chicken with Ascoli Olives

This is a simple version of a classic dish from Ascoli Piceno, an ancient city in Le Marche. The olives of Ascoli are unique: Cured in lime (the mineral, not the fruit), they are very large, sweet, and crisp. The Romans coveted these olives and ate them before and after banquets. You can find Ascoli olives in some Italian markets, as well as online at www.chefshop.com. But you can use a large green olive cured in vinegar as well.

4 tablespoons olive oil

1 chicken (4 pounds), cut into 16 pieces

6 garlic cloves, with skins on

1 tablespoon chopped rosemary

Salt and freshly ground black pepper

2 cups dry white wine

20 large green olives, pitted and sliced in half

Heat the oil in a Dutch oven or large heavy-bottomed pot over medium heat. Add the chicken, the garlic, rosemary, and salt and pepper to taste, and cook for 5 minutes, uncovered. Reduce the heat to medium-low and cook the chicken, uncovered, until it begins to brown, about 20 minutes. Add 1 cup of the wine and the olives. Continue to cook, uncovered, stirring often, for about 30 minutes. Add the remaining 1 cup of wine and cook for an additional 30 minutes.

Serves 4

Boiled Chicken with Tomato Pesto

We also like to boil vegetables in the strained broth to serve with the chicken, like small red-skinned potatoes and 2-inch pieces of carrot.

1 whole fresh chicken (about 4 pounds), washed

Salt

2 onions, peeled

2 bay leaves

2 whole cloves

2 large carrots, peeled

2 celery ribs, cut into 3-inch lengths

2 leeks, washed and split (optional)

2 parsnips, peeled (optional)

For the tomato pesto

1½ large ripe tomatoes, chopped

2 scallions, chopped

4 tablespoons pignoli nuts

3 tablespoons extra virgin olive oil

1 tablespoon chopped cilantro

1 garlic clove, chopped

Salt

Put the chicken in a soup pot and cover it with cold water. Remove the chicken and set aside. Add salt to the water, cover, and bring to a boil over high heat.

While you are waiting for the water to boil, prepare the chicken. Remove the wishbone by cutting around the bone with a sharp knife, then yanking it out by its apex with your fingers. Truss the chicken.

Place the trussed chicken into the boiling water, cover, and cook for 1 minute. Then turn off the heat. Do not remove the cover from the pot. Let the chicken rest in the water for 1 hour.

In the meantime, cut a small slice into each onion and insert a bay leaf, pinning it down with a clove.

After an hour, remove the chicken and set aside. Do not discard the water.

Place the carrots, celery, onions, leeks (if using), and parsnips (if using) into the water. Cut up the chicken. Remove the legs, thighs, and breast meat, cover and set aside. Throw the bones into the soup pot with the vegetables. Turn the heat up to high and bring to a boil. Turn down the heat to medium and cook the vegetables at a low boil for 2 hours.

Strain and reserve the stock for boiling fresh vegetables, or some other use. Discard the vegetables.

For the tomato pesto: In a food processor, puree the tomatoes, scallions, pignoli nuts, oil, cilantro, garlic, and salt to taste.

Serve the chicken pieces on a flat platter. Ladle the pesto around them.

Serves 4

Chicken with Shellfish

This recipe calls for chicken legs and thighs, which we like because those parts are so moist; however, you can make this recipe with any chicken part.

4 tablespoons olive oil

6 garlic cloves, with skins on

1 tablespoon chopped rosemary

Salt and freshly ground black pepper or hot pepper flakes

4 chicken legs and thighs, separated

½ cup dry white wine or white wine vinegar

2 medium tomatoes, chopped

1 green bell pepper, seeded and chopped

1 tablespoon finely chopped flat-leaf parsley

1 tablespoon chopped oregano

24 mussels (preferably wild Maine mussels), scrubbed and debearded

¾ pound medium shrimp, peeled and deveined

8 sea scallops (dry pack)

Heat 3 tablespoons of the oil in a large skillet over medium heat. Add the garlic, rosemary, and salt and pepper to taste. Add the chicken and cook until it is lightly browned all over, about 30 minutes. Add the wine, cover, and cook until the wine reduces, mixing often, about 5 minutes.

In a separate pot, combine the tomatoes, bell pepper, parsley, and oregano. Cover and simmer for 10 minutes, until the tomatoes break up, then add to the chicken. Cook for 5 minutes. Add the mussels to the chicken and cook until the mussels open, about 4 minutes.

In the meantime, in a small skillet, heat the remaining 1 tablespoon of oil over high heat. Add the shrimp and scallops and cook until the shrimp turn pink, about 4 minutes. Do not overcook. Add the shrimp, scallops, and their juices to the chicken and mussels and serve.

Note: When choosing mussels, look for wild mussels that are heavy in your palm. A small, light mussel will produce a tiny amount of meat, which will tend to dry out quickly. When choosing scallops, always ask for dry pack or untreated scallops.

Serves 4

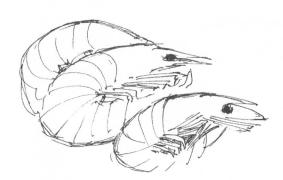

Chicken Sausages with Pole Beans

You can substitute pork sausages for the chicken sausages in this dish. Likewise, you can substitute any large green bean for the pole beans.

1 pound fresh pole beans, trimmed and cut into 1½-inch lengths

2 medium potatoes, peeled and sliced (we prefer Yukon Gold)

6 tablespoons extra virgin olive oil

1 medium onion, thinly sliced

Salt and freshly ground black pepper or hot pepper flakes

2 pounds chicken sausage

2 garlic cloves, coarsely chopped

1 tablespoon finely chopped flat-leaf parsley, for garnish

Bring a large pot of salted water to a boil over high heat. Add the beans and the potatoes and cook for 3 to 5 minutes (if you use a thinner green bean, cook for no more than 3 minutes). Scoop out 1 cup of the cooking water, then drain the vegetables and rinse them in cold water.

Heat 3 tablespoons of the oil in a large skillet over medium heat. Add the onion and cook until it becomes translucent, about 5 minutes. Add the beans and potatoes, the reserved cooking water, and salt and pepper to taste. Cover and cook until the beans and potatoes are tender, about 10 to 15 minutes.

In the meantime, heat the remaining 3 tablespoons of oil in a small skillet over medium heat. Add the sausages and cook, uncovered, for about 5 minutes on each side, until they begin to brown. Add the garlic and continue cooking until the garlic begins to brown—about 2 or 3 minutes.

Add the sausages and garlic to the beans. Cover and simmer for 3 to 4 minutes, until the flavors meld. Add more water if the dish looks dry. Adjust the seasoning and garnish with parsley.

Serves 4

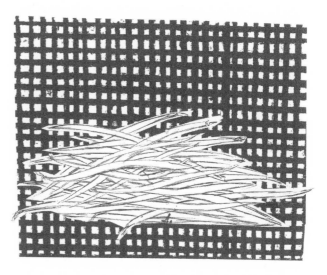

Marinated Grilled Rabbit

Sal Biancardi, whose family owns Biancardi Meats on Arthur Avenue, gave this interesting reversed marinade recipe to Edward. We like to serve this dish at room temperature with a salad.

1 rabbit (about 3 pounds), cut into three sections: hind legs, forelegs, and saddle

½ cup extra virgin olive oil

Juice of 3 large lemons

6 garlic cloves, sliced

Salt and freshly ground black pepper

Submerge the rabbit pieces in a pot of cold water and soak for at least 2 hours. Remove the rabbit and pat dry. Prepare a grill.

Place the meat on the hot grill and grill for about 20 minutes, turning the pieces often. Remove the saddle and forelegs and set aside. Continue to cook the hind legs for an additional 5 minutes. Remove the hind legs and set aside.

Meanwhile, make the marinade. In a large nonreactive bowl, combine the oil, lemon juice, garlic, and salt and pepper to taste.

Cut the rabbit legs in 2 sections per leg. Separate the forelegs from the rib cage, and cut the saddle into 3 sections. Place the meat in the marinade and let it marinate for at least 2 hours, or preferably overnight, turning the rabbit sections occasionally. Serve at room temperature.

Serves 4

Zia Ada's Rabbit with Cognac

Zia Ada makes this dish as part of a classic Offidana dinner. First, homemade salami, then her handmade Gnocchi with Chicken Giblet Sauce (see page 116). She will often serve two meats, which is considered proper for company in the Italian country kitchen: this recipe, and maybe Chicken with Ascoli Olives (see page 132), followed by a salad.

1 rabbit (3 pounds), rinsed

1 gallon water

1 cup salt, plus additional for seasoning

Freshly ground black pepper

1 cup dry white wine

1 cup coarsely chopped fennel greens

½ cup olive oil

4 garlic cloves, finely chopped

1 tablespoon chopped rosemary

20 black olives cured in olive oil

¼ cup cognac

Place the rabbit in a large pot and add the water and 1 cup of salt. Refrigerate for 24 hours. Drain and cut the rabbit into serving pieces, as you would chicken.

Season the rabbit with salt and pepper and place the pieces in one layer in a skillet. Cook the rabbit in the dry skillet over low heat, turning occasionally, until the external moisture on the pieces evaporates. Increase the heat gradually to medium as the liquid is drawn out. Do not brown the rabbit.

Add the wine, fennel, oil, garlic, rosemary, and salt and pepper to taste. Cover, and simmer over medium heat for 35 minutes. Add the olives and continue cooking for another 15 to 20 minutes. Add the cognac, turn up the heat, and cook until the cognac reduces.

Serves 4

THE GARDEN

Since the early 1960s, Edward has maintained a huge garden on a hill above the house in Katonah, and we enjoy a near-vegetarian diet during the summer months. We cook the vegetables simply—one hardly needs a recipe for thick slices of warm boiled potato sprinkled with sliced scallions, boiled beets tossed with fresh chopped parsley, or sliced beefsteak tomatoes sprinkled with a fluff of basil chiffonade—and we always lace them with very fine extra virgin olive oil. I modeled my garden in Colorado on Dad's. We both grow many varieties of tomatoes, for eating fresh and for canning. There is no single canned product we make that is more rewarding—or useful. It doesn't take a lot of tools—just jars with screw-on lids and new caps, and a big pot; nor does it require a big, spacious kitchen. I often can a mere 4 pints of tomatoes at a time—I've even done it on a hot plate. And it is easy, really easy: We simply stuff halved tomatoes (with the skins and seeds removed, or not) into sterilized Ball or Kerr jars, add salt and a couple of fresh basil leaves, screw on the lids and caps, then process the jars in a water bath for a designated amount of time. Stored in a cool, dry place, these tomatoes last at least a year.

We also grow a range of herbs, peppers, leafy vegetables, beans, potatoes, and eggplant, not to mention a crop of spring vegetables and a crop of late fall vegetables. The workload of caring for gardens this size isn't the problem—it's actually very soothing to be digging around in the earth. No, the problem is vermin. Skunks are my nemesis. I usually throw rocks at them, but once, in a gigantic case of misjudgment, we blew away a skunk with a shotgun. For days afterward, my eyes would water every time I went to the garden for a little parsley. Dad is at war with woodchucks. He's got a little tin target that's riddled with shotgun blasts, but he seems less apt at hitting a moving target (unlike my mother, who can shoot a hawk while it's swooping over her chickens). The woodchucks seem to be placed on this earth to torment Edward. They have an elaborate tunnel system that gives them access to all parts of his garden, and they seem immune to trapping, poisoning, or drowning by hose. Woodchuck is one of my father's trigger words. Don't mention it while he is driving if you love your life.

Surprisingly, the vermin do not go after the zucchini. If they did, it would probably be all right, because we grow way too many. At least, I do. Edward has it figured out: He staggers the planting so he has zucchini flowers all summer long. While we love zucchinis, Giobbis are passionate about zucchini flowers.

Every zucchini plant produces both male and female flowers. You can tell the difference because the female flowers grow from a little seedpod and will become the zucchini, and the males grow straight up on a stem. We don't eat the females, unless we want to cook the baby zucchini as well. Usually, we take only the males—all of them, in fact, except for one, as the plant needs one fresh male flower to keep all those females and their baby zucchinis going. You can't say nature isn't consistent.

In the past, we just fried zucchini flowers and ate them as an appetizer, but over the last few years they have been particularly prolific (lots of rain and sun cycles during the summer months), and we have been eating them in a wide variety of ways: in frittatas and lasagnes, on pasta and risottos, and as a sauce on fish. And we continue to invent new uses for them.

Rediscovering a vegetable happens when you've got to figure out new ways to eat the bounty. And that is what makes the chore of gardening so worthwhile: No matter how consistent nature is, she's always full of surprises.

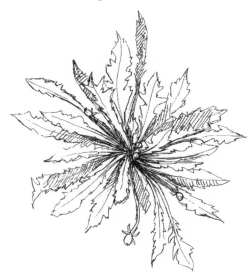

SUMMER VEGETABLES AND SALADS

Broccoli with Olives and Tomatoes

We love to crack eggs on top of this sauce to turn it into an evening dish. Create little indentations with the back of a spoon and crack an egg into each. Cover and cook the eggs until the whites are opaque, about 10 minutes. We serve 2 eggs per person.

3 tablespoons extra virgin olive oil

1 medium onion, thinly sliced

3 garlic cloves, sliced

2 large fresh tomatoes, chopped

1 tablespoon finely chopped flat-leaf parsley

1 pound broccoli, cut into florets and stems peeled

16 black olives cured in oil, pitted

Salt and hot pepper flakes

Heat the oil in a medium skillet over medium heat. Add the onion and garlic and cook until the onion becomes translucent, about 5 minutes. Add the tomatoes and parsley. Cover and simmer for 10 minutes, until the tomatoes break up.

Meanwhile, bring a large pot of salted water to a boil over high heat. Add the broccoli and cook, uncovered, for about 3 minutes. Drain, rinse in cold water, and add to the tomato sauce with the olives and salt and hot pepper flakes to taste. Lower the heat and cook, uncovered, until the broccoli is fork-tender, about 7 minutes. If the sauce gets a little dry, add some water.

Serves 4

Cabbage with Tomatoes and Potatoes

We make this dish with the new cabbage we harvest from the garden in summer.

Half a head green cabbage, chopped (about 3 cups)

1 large potato, peeled and cut into quarters (we prefer Yukon Gold)

Salt

4 tablespoons olive oil

1 large onion, thinly sliced

4 garlic cloves, sliced

2 large fresh tomatoes, chopped

2 tablespoons basil chiffonade

2 tablespoons finely chopped flat-leaf parsley

Hot pepper flakes (optional)

Extra virgin olive oil, for garnish

In a large pot, cover the cabbage and potato with water. Add salt to taste. Bring to a boil over high heat and boil for about 5 minutes. Scoop out 1 cup of the cooking water, then drain.

Heat the oil in a shallow saucepan over medium heat and add the onion and garlic. Cover and cook until the onion becomes translucent, about 5 minutes. Add the tomatoes, basil, parsley, and hot pepper flakes to taste (if using). Cover and simmer for about 10 minutes, until the tomatoes break up.

Add the cabbage and potato, cover, and simmer for about 15 minutes, until all of the vegetables are cooked through and the flavors have melded. Add salt and hot pepper flakes (if using) to taste. If the vegetables seem a little dry, add some of the reserved cooking water.

Garnish each portion with a dribble of extra virgin olive oil.

Serves 4

Baked Corn

Corn cooked in its husk is the only way Edward's family ever prepared corn—never boiled—and we recently enjoyed corn prepared the same way in the zocolos of Central Mexico. It is excellent beside grilled vegetables, Grilled Eel (see page 127), and Marinated Grilled Rabbit (see page 136).

4 ears fresh corn with husks

Extra virgin olive oil

Salt and freshly ground
black pepper

Heat the oven to 400°F.

Wrap each ear of corn in aluminum foil. Bake the corn about 15 minutes. Remove the foil and shuck the corn. Serve it dribbled with extra virgin olive oil and seasoned with salt and pepper.

Serves 4

Polpette di Melanzane

We like to serve these broiled eggplant balls with broiled or baked fish. The balls can also be prepared as patties and a piece of fish served on top. You can double the recipe and add chopped shrimp to the eggplant to make a delicious first course or light entrée. You can also serve this with a raw tomato sauce (see Pasta Primavera on page 108).

3 tablespoons extra virgin olive oil

1 pound fresh eggplant, peeled and cut into ½-inch cubes

1 medium onion, finely chopped

3 tablespoons pignoli nuts

½ cup breadcrumbs

2 tablespoons grated Parmesan cheese

1 small egg

1 tablespoon finely chopped flat-leaf parsley

Salt and freshly ground
black pepper

Olive oil for broiling

Heat the broiler.

Heat the extra virgin olive oil in a medium nonstick skillet over medium heat. Add the eggplant and onion and cook until the onion becomes translucent, about 5 minutes. Add the pignoli nuts and cook, stirring often, until the eggplant is tender, about 20 minutes.

Scrape the eggplant mixture into a food processor and add the breadcrumbs, cheese, egg, parsley, and salt and pepper to taste. Pulse to blend. Do not overprocess: The mixture should be relatively coarse. Form the mixture into 12 balls, each about 1¼ inches in diameter.

Oil a baking tray and place the eggplant balls on it. Sprinkle the balls lightly with olive oil and brown under the broiler for about 5 minutes, until the balls are brown all over.

Serves 4

Eggplant with Ricotta Salata

Ricotta salata is ricotta that has been aged. It is a dry cheese—we grate it on the big holes of a box grater—and very tasty as a garnish. It has much less fat than Parmesan, because it is made primarily from the whey of the milk, so we use it in this variation of eggplant Parmesan. Feta cheese can be used as a substitute.

3 medium eggplant (about 3 pounds)

3 tablespoons olive oil

3 tablespoons extra virgin olive oil

1 medium onion, chopped

1 celery rib, finely chopped

2 garlic cloves, finely chopped

2 large tomatoes, chopped

1 tablespoon basil chiffonade

1 teaspoon chopped oregano

¾ cup grated ricotta salata

Heat the broiler.

Cut the eggplant into slices ½ inch thick. If the eggplant is old, place the slices on a tray lined with paper towels, salt the slices, and let them rest for 30 minutes. Then pat the slices dry before proceeding.

Pour the olive oil onto a baking tray, preferably nonstick, and lay down the eggplant slices. Flip them over in the oil so the slices become lightly coated, then lay them flat. Do not overlap. Broil the eggplant under a low broiler (if you cannot adjust the heat, lower your oven rack). Cook until the eggplant is brown, about 15 minutes. Turn over and broil the other side until browned, about 5 minutes more. Remove and set aside.

Heat the oven to 400°F.

Heat the extra virgin olive oil in a large skillet over medium heat. Add the onion, celery, and garlic and cook until the onion becomes translucent, about 5 minutes. Add the tomatoes, basil, and oregano. Cover and simmer for 10 minutes, until the tomatoes break up.

Place a layer of the eggplant in a medium baking dish. Pour some of the sauce on top of the layer, and add a sprinkling of ricotta salata. Repeat the process until all of the ingredients have been used.

Cover with aluminum foil and bake for about 30 minutes.

Serves 4

Grilled Potatoes

We like to prepare these potatoes when we are grilling meat or fish. To make them in the oven, prepare the potatoes as described below. Pour 2 tablespoons of olive oil into a baking pan. Add the potatoes (do not overlap), salt to taste, and some chopped rosemary, if you like. Place the potatoes in a 450°F oven and roast them for about 10 minutes, turning over with a spatula periodically, until they are brown all over.

2 large potatoes, preferably Yukon Gold

2 to 4 tablespoons olive oil

Salt

Prepare the grill.

Place the potatoes in a medium pot and cover with water. Bring to a boil over high heat. Cook the potatoes for 10 minutes, until they are al dente. Drain and peel the potatoes, then cut into slices ½ inch thick.

Coat the potato slices with the oil and place them carefully on the grill. Cook until brown all over, about 5 minutes per side. Add salt to taste.

Serves 4

Baked Zucchini with Balsamic Vinegar

We use balsamic vinegar in a variety of recipes like this one, which allow its strong, sweet taste to really come forward. For these dishes to work, it is necessary that you use superior balsamic vinegar. Making balsamic vinegar is very labor-intensive, and it requires a long aging process. There is no way you are going to find a good balsamic vinegar that is also cheap. Grocery store balsamic is flavored with chemicals—and you shouldn't bother with it. Rather, make an investment in an excellent vinegar like S. F. Gorrieri Aceto Balsamico or Lorenza di Medici Aceto Balsamico di Modena (see Sources on page 305).

4 tablespoons olive oil

3 large zucchini, about 12 inches long, sliced ½ inch thick and 4 inches long

Salt

⅓ cup balsamic vinegar

Heat the oven to 500°F.

Rub the oil onto two baking trays, preferably nonstick. Place the zucchini slices on the trays. Do not overlap. Turn the zucchini over so the oil lightly coats both sides. Add salt to taste. Bake, uncovered, in the oven for 15 minutes, until the slices begin to brown. Turn the slices over and bake for an additional 5 minutes, until brown.

Place the slices in a nonreactive bowl one layer at a time, drizzling the vinegar between the layers.

Serve warm or at room temperature.

Serves 4

Zucchini Flowers Stuffed with Potato

We love the delicate taste of zucchini flowers, and find subtle tastes like potato make excellent stuffing. You can flavor the potato any way you like. We like parsley and cheese, but other herbs would work just as well.

16 large zucchini flowers

1½ cups all-purpose flour

2 cups dry white wine

2 teaspoons baking powder

Salt

1 medium potato (we prefer Yukon Gold)

1 tablespoon grated Parmesan cheese

1 tablespoon finely chopped flat-leaf parsley

Freshly ground black pepper

Vegetable oil for frying

1 teaspoon rosemary leaves

Check the insides of the zucchini flowers for insects and shake them out. Brush any dirt off the flowers, but do not wash them or your flowers won't be crisp when you fry them.

In a bowl, combine the flour, wine, baking powder, and a pinch of salt and refrigerate for 1 hour (a little more or less is okay).

Place the potato in a medium pot and cover with water. Boil the potato until it is fork-tender, about 20 minutes. Then drain, peel the potato, and mash with a fork—do not blend in a food processor or blender. Add the cheese, parsley, and salt and pepper to taste.

Either use a soft plastic pastry bag or make one by rolling two layers of wax paper into a cone. Cut a small hole in the tip. Spoon a couple of tablespoons of the potato mixture into the wide end of the cone and press the mixture down toward the tip by twisting the top. With one hand, gently open the petals of a zucchini flower. With the other hand, pipe the potato in. You will need about 1 tablespoon of the mixture per flower. Repeat this process with the remaining flowers.

Place ¾ inch of vegetable oil in a large nonstick skillet with the rosemary. Heat the oil over high heat. The oil must be very hot. You can test it by throwing a dash of flour into the oil. If the flour pops, the oil is ready for frying. Dunk the flowers in the batter and place them gently in the hot oil. Don't put too many flowers in at once or it will bring down the temperature of the oil, and they mustn't touch sides or they will stick together. Do not flip the flowers over until you can see that the lower edges have turned golden brown, about 2 minutes. If you are using an iron skillet and the flowers stick, let them cook 30 seconds more. Turn the flowers over with tongs and fry for an additional minute, then remove them and drain them on paper towels. Do not add more battered flowers until you are sure the oil has come up in temperature again. Season with salt to taste.

Serves 4

Green Bean and Purslane Salad

Purslane can be found in some green markets, but before purchasing it, take a look in your garden. Purslane is a weed with thick, round leaves and grows in a crawling pattern. It is very tasty and naturally reduces cholesterol.

¾ pound green beans, trimmed and broken in half

½ cup purslane, with tough stems discarded

2 medium tomatoes, preferably semi-ripe, cut into wedges

1 small sweet onion, thinly sliced

3 tablespoons extra virgin olive oil

Juice of ½ lemon

Salt and freshly ground black pepper

Bring a large pot of salted water to a boil over high heat. Add the beans and cook until they are tender, about 5 to 7 minutes. Drain and rinse in cold water to stop the cooking.

In a salad bowl, combine the beans with the purslane, tomatoes, onion, oil, lemon juice, and salt and pepper to taste, and toss well.

Serves 4

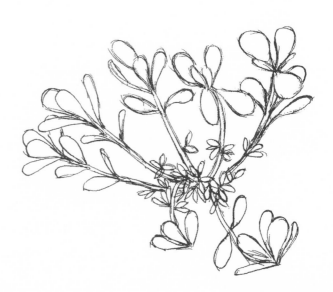

FRUIT FOR DESSERT

Italians eat semisweet buns in the morning with their espresso, and ice cream in the afternoon, but they eat fruit after a meal. It is only on high holidays that you see cakes and other sweets. Often, at the end of a meal, my mother would place a bowl of water filled with fresh peaches on the table, and pass around paring knives. We would peel our peaches, and cut pieces of the sweet flesh into our wine glasses, where the fruit would steep in the red or white wine while we continued to chat. After a few minutes, we'd fish bites of peach out of the glass with a fork. The taste is unparalleled for freshness and sweetness. It is also very elegant in the casual, family style that defines the Italian table.

My parents eat an apple after lunch every day, along with a couple of nuts, or a bit of cheese. That's the humble end of the spectrum. Decades ago, when our family lived for a year in Rome, I was invited to spend the weekend at a school friend's family villa. It turned out the family was somehow related to the Medicis, and the villa was really a castle, with elegant diplomat-type guests and maids in uniforms and a dinner table set for fourteen, with gilt china and polished silver and lacy napery. After a meal consisting of multiple courses, the staff brought out dessert: fruit. But this was fancy fruit; fruit in a five-tiered silver tray, perfectly shined and arranged. Abundant heaps of grapes spilled over the edges of the platters. Glistening plums, apples, and pears were piled in neat pyramids. Fuzzy apricots and figs rolled about. We were offered a beautiful pearl-handled fruit service, but I didn't worry with that. I dug in with my hands. There was so much variety, and the ripeness was so perfect, I ate more fruit in one sitting than I had ever eaten in my life.

I think the best way to eat fruit is *in* the tree from which it grows. Kids know this, and so do very old Italians. My great grandfather liked to eat figs in the tree. When we were kids, again, living in Rome, we used to climb a cherry tree outside my father's studio and gorge on the sweet fruit like birds, spitting pits down on the adults as they talked and drank wine. The area where I own property in Colorado is famous for its fruit: Paonia and Hotchkiss produce beautiful cherries, apricots, peaches, plums, pears, and apples, and my kids are the first to recognize the only proper way to eat an apricot is from a high branch.

During the summer, almost all of our desserts are made from fruits and, in most cases, cooked minimally, in order to retain that fresh, right-off-the-tree flavor and texture. And most of the recipes included in this section are interchangeable; the recipe for broiled apricots is excellent with peaches, and likewise, apricots can be substituted in the recipe for ricotta-stuffed peaches. Cherry sorbet can be made with finely chopped plums. Any pureed fruit will make a fool when combined with whipped cream, and any juice will make a granita, including vegetable juices, as in the case of beet granita. These desserts reflect the Italian position toward dessert in general; fresh seasonal fruits are best. These recipes do as little as possible to interfere with that basic premise.

S U M M E R
D E S S E R T S

Broiled Apricots with Lavender Syrup

You should serve this dish with a dessert knife, as the apricot skins, while delicious to eat, can be difficult to cut with the edge of a spoon. Although lavender is often used in perfumes, it is excellent in an infusion like this syrup.

½ cup water

¼ cup superfine sugar

¼ cup honey

1 tablespoon fresh lavender flowers (or 1 teaspoon dried)

8 apricots, halved and pitted

8 fresh lavender flowers, for garnish

Vanilla ice cream (optional)

Heat the broiler.

Make the syrup: In a small pot over medium heat, combine the water, sugar, honey, and lavender (but not the garnish) and bring to a simmer. Cook until the syrup reduces by half, about 5 minutes.

Place the apricots in a small baking pan. If the apricots are wobbly, cut a small flat spot on the bottom so they sit straight. Dribble the syrup over the apricots. Broil the apricots for about 5 minutes, until they begin to brown.

Serve the apricots plain, garnished with the lavender flowers, or with vanilla ice cream.

Serves 4

Apricot Fool with Peaches

You can eat just a fool for a dessert, but it is very rich. We prefer it as an accompaniment for fresh peaches. It is also good on top of fresh, sliced plums.

6 apricots, halved and pitted

½ cup superfine sugar

1 tablespoon fresh lemon juice

1 cup heavy cream

1 tablespoon Amaretto liquor (optional)

4 ripe peaches, peeled, pitted, and sliced

Place the apricot halves in a food processor and blend to a puree. Transfer to a heavy-bottomed pot and bring to a low boil over medium-low heat. Add ¼ cup of the sugar and the lemon juice, and stir until the sugar dissolves, about 10 minutes. Set aside.

Whip the heavy cream until it forms soft peaks. Gradually whip in the remaining ¼ cup of sugar. Whip in the Amaretto, if using.

Fold the apricot puree into the whipped cream. This is the fool.

Dollop the fool on top of the fresh sliced peaches.

Serves 4

Cherries in Wine

We make this recipe with sour cherries as well. Just add a little more sugar, to your taste.

2 cups red wine

½ cup orange juice

½ cup superfine sugar

8 whole cloves, or ¼ teaspoon powdered cloves

2 cups Bing cherries, pitted

1 teaspoon almond extract

Whipped cream, for garnish (optional)

In a small pot, combine the wine, orange juice, sugar, and cloves. Bring to a boil over medium heat. Add the cherries and boil for about 3 minutes. Remove the cherries and reduce the syrup by half, about 10 minutes. Add the almond extract. Return the cherries to the syrup and allow to cool. Remove the cloves.

Serve in glasses, garnished with whipped cream, if you like.

Serves 4

Peaches Stuffed with Ricotta

This is a very simple dish, and can be adapted nicely. For example, try adding a little lemon zest, orange zest, or a few white raisins to the ricotta mixture. You can substitute apricots for the peaches as well.

2 large peaches, halved and pitted

½ cup ricotta cheese

1 large egg yolk, beaten slightly

1 tablespoon superfine sugar

1 tablespoon peach schnapps

2 Amaretto cookies, ground (about 2 tablespoons)

Heat the oven to 400°F.

Scoop a cavity about the size of a tablespoon out of the peach flesh around the pit area. Place the peaches in a small baking pan or skillet so they fit snugly. If the peaches seem wobbly, slice a small flat area on the bottom so they sit straight.

In a small bowl, combine the ricotta, egg yolk, sugar, and schnapps. Plop about 1 tablespoon of the ricotta mixture into each peach. Do not overload the peach. Sprinkle the Amaretto cookie crumbs over the peaches and bake for 20 minutes, until they become golden.

Serves 4

Lucy's Cookies

Lucille Shannon worked for the Giobbi family in the 1960s. Originally from Arkansas, she was a marvelous southern cook, particularly of desserts. These cookies, when cut thin enough, are delicate and crunchy. We serve them with granitas and sorbet.

14 tablespoons (1¾ sticks) unsalted butter, softened

1 cup sugar

1 egg

1½ cups all-purpose flour, sifted

1½ teaspoons vanilla extract

Using a wooden spoon, combine the butter and sugar in a large bowl. Add the egg and combine. Add the flour and combine. Add the vanilla extract and combine.

The dough is very soft and sticky. Drop the dough into a long log shape onto a large piece of wax paper. Roll the paper over the dough and shape the dough—through the wax paper—into a rough log. Twist the ends of the paper and refrigerate for 6 hours or overnight.

Heat the oven to 350°F.

Cut the cookies as thin as possible and place on a baking tray. The dough will get sticky with handling, but don't add more flour or the cookies will be too heavy. Keep the log in the refrigerator while the batches are baking. Bake the cookies for about 15 minutes, until brown.

As soon as the cookies are cool enough, transfer them to wax paper or a wooden surface so they can breathe; otherwise, they will be soggy.

Makes about 48 cookies

Cherry Crisp

This is an adaptation of a recipe given to us by Marisa Getz, a wonderful Arizona-based pastry chef with roots in Colorado's cherry country. We've made this dish with Bing cherries and Montmorency (sour cherries). We prefer to serve crisps in individual ramekins.

2 cups pitted cherries (slice Bings in half)

4 tablespoons superfine sugar

2 teaspoons all-purpose flour

¼ teaspoon grated orange zest

¼ teaspoon vanilla extract

For the topping

¼ cup all-purpose flour

¼ cup brown sugar

2 tablespoons granulated sugar

4 tablespoons unsalted butter

4 scant tablespoons sliced almonds

Heat the oven to 375°F.

In a small bowl, combine the cherries, sugar, flour, orange zest, and vanilla extract. Divide among four ramekins.

For the topping: In a small bowl, combine the flour, brown sugar, and granulated sugar. Cut in the butter. Scatter the topping on top of the cherries. Sprinkle each ramekin with 1 tablespoon of almonds.

Bake for about 30 minutes, until the topping is just brown and the cherry juice is bubbling through.

Serves 4

Cherry Almond Sorbet

Cherries and almonds are classic go-togethers. This simple little sorbet is delicious because the flavors are so uncomplicated.

1 cup red wine

½ cup superfine sugar

4 cups pitted Bing cherries

1 tablespoon fresh lemon juice

1 teaspoon almond extract

In a saucepan, combine the wine and sugar and bring to a boil over medium heat. Add the cherries and cook until the cherries become soft, about 20 minutes. Remove the saucepan from the heat; add the lemon juice and almond extract. Allow to cool, then puree in a blender or food processor.

Process the cherry puree in your ice cream maker according to its instructions.

Serves 4

Espresso Granita

This is an Italian classic that is incredibly easy to make. It's one of our favorites.

2 cups espresso coffee

½ cup superfine sugar

½ cup heavy cream

1 teaspoon anisette

In a small bowl, combine the espresso and the sugar and stir until the sugar dissolves. Pour the sweetened espresso into a metal pan (we use an aluminum loaf pan) and place the pan in the freezer. Freeze the granita for 15 to 30 minutes, then mash up the ice crystals every 15 to 30 minutes or so by running the tines of a fork through the ice until the crystals are crushed. Do this for about 3 hours, depending on how cold your freezer is, and how small your pan is (wide, shallow pans of granita will freeze more quickly than deep, narrow ones). Every time you do this, the crystals will get smaller. The granita will look like shaved black ice.

Whip the heavy cream until it is thick. Add the anisette and stir it in well.

Serve the granita with the flavored whipped cream on top.

Serves 4

Beet Granita

Every time we boil beets we suffer over having to throw out the beautifully red water that has picked up the flavor of the beets. We've tried drinking it warm (too health-foodie) and making cocktails with it (altogether too weird), but using it to make a granita was divine. Sometimes we make this with less sugar to serve between rich courses.

2 cups beet water (leftover from boiling 6 beets in 6 cups of water)

¾ cup superfine sugar, or to taste

2 tablespoons fresh lemon juice, or to taste

Whipped cream, for garnish (optional)

In a small bowl, combine the beet water, sugar, and lemon juice and stir to dissolve the sugar. Pour into a pan that conducts cold well. (We like to use an aluminum loaf pan.) Place in the freezer, and every 15 to 30 minutes, run the tines of a fork through the ice to break up the crystals. Over the course of 3 hours, the crystals will get small and crumbly.

For a very refined granita, pour into a food processor and pulse to grind the crystals. Then return the granita to the pan and continue to allow it to freeze, running the tines of a fork through it every 15 minutes or so for another 30 minutes.

Serve plain, or in a glass with whipped cream.

Serves 4

FALL

MUSHROOMS

When you really want something to happen, and then it does, it almost seems as if you have a sort of magic at your command. I remember one spring day when I was school age. My father was very upset about something, and I longed to make him feel better. So I went in search of a morel mushroom, which I believed would cheer him up. I walked right to an old rotting apple tree, and at its base was a large morel, brown and brainy, fleshy and slick as a playboy. I longed, and something I longed for happened.

But unfortunately, morels *(Morchella esculenta)* are elusive, and I never found them under the rotting apple tree again. Eventually, the tree was cut down and its stump removed, and my mother planted zinnias in its place. As I grew older and sharpened my personal likes and dislikes, my connection to mushrooms grew apace. On my nineteenth birthday, a friend of my father's, the former *Gourmet* restaurant critic Jay Jacobs, a petite shiitake of a man, took me to lunch at Felidia in New York, where we ate the caps of porcini mushrooms grilled and dressed with olive oil. (Okay, it was a novelty in 1979.) I thought it was the most sumptuous thing I'd ever eaten: rich, light, perfumey. It sealed my passion for fungi. But while I ate many kilos of mushrooms here and abroad, I did not find another truly great specimen for the next twenty years. The truth is, my longings turned elsewhere, and I began to doubt the wisdom of gathering wild mushrooms at all.

I knew from childhood what the genus *Amanita* was: The Death Cap, *Amanita phalloides,* the Destroying Angels, *Amanita bisporigera* and *Amanita virosa,* the pristine white mushroom that felled Caesars and Popes and Babar's king. When eaten, the *Amanita* induces severe vomiting, abdominal pain, and diarrhea, then jaundice, kidney failure, liver deterioration, and convulsions within six to twenty-four hours. Finally, in a matter of days, death. But not all poisonous mushrooms are *that* poisonous: Most will just make you sick. The old wives' tale that warns against eating little brown mushrooms is probably a good one to remember, as lots of little brown varieties will give you a stomachache. Some mushrooms are so slightly poisonous, they don't even affect everyone. We used to buy Christmas trees from Nick, an old Italian who ate a kind of mushroom that my dad thought was poisonous. Nick said they were delicious. "But it's strange," he'd say. "After eating them, I always fall asleep."

In time, I was not sure I could even identify a morel anymore. And then I went on a white truffle hunt with my father's cousin Mario Campinote (he is married to Maria Giobbi from Offida) in Tuscany. Mario is one of those Italians who make love to their language while speaking it. He closes his eyes, a rapturous look on his face, as he rolls his "Rs" and presses his index finger to his thumb as if squeezing the finest articulation from the "t" in *tartufo*.

My parents and I joined him one mid-October morning near the Etruscan town of Certaldo to hunt for truffles. Mario and two crusty buddies, Alfredo and Foscaro, retired grandpas with sunburned necks and calloused hands, led the way down a muddy path that wound through a vineyard and into the dark, tangled brush of a narrow, mist-filled valley. The dogs, called *Lagotta*, are truffle hunters, and quite valuable, although they don't look precious at all. Mario says his are a mixture of Labrador retriever and poodle.

Mario prefers to hunt truffles with dogs because the Tuscan fungi favor overgrown areas, and pigs are just too big to get under the scrub. Secondly, it's very hard to separate a pig from a truffle, while dogs will gladly trade the treasure for a bit of kibble. Nor can pigs cover as much land as dogs. And finally, Mario says that Italians prefer dogs because "you look ridiculous hunting with a pig." All truffles must be hunted with some kind of animal, which can smell the fungus when, upon maturity and a foot deep in the soil, it releases its aroma.

Foscaro pointed under this tree and that with his digging pick (called a *zappino*), using low clucks and clicks to encourage his dog Zara to sniff the earth. When she caught a scent at the base of a willow tree, she started digging furiously. Foscaro grabbed her by the collar, yanked her out of the way, and fell to his knees, scooping a handful of the moist earth up and inhaling deeply. "*Tartufo!*" he said, and began to carefully pick away the dirt, like an archeologist uncovering an artifact, until he had exposed the yellowish, potato-looking fungus. It was like a gas bomb had just gone off: The immediate area was saturated with a sexy, sulfuric fragrance. Foscaro popped the truffle, worth about $25 wholesale, into his pocket, and lit up a cigarette. The rest of us sucked in the last erotic whiffs before they dissipated into the woods.

There are thousands of *Tartufai,* dialect for truffle hunters, throughout Italy. They have been around at least since Roman times, and are protected by an ancient law that allows them to trespass on private land. The *Tartufai* are considered a little disreputable. After all, they tool around in the woods all day and conduct much of their business in cash, but I'm guessing the main reason why they are resented is because they control the volume of a very valuable commodity. When it comes to the fall white truffle, it is the perfume that you're paying for. The *Tuber Magnutum Pico,* also known as the Alba, and the "Diamond of the Table," is probably the most expensive food you can buy—so valuable that supposedly Harry's Bar in Florence locks their truffles in a safe at night.

Picos are high-priced because they are the best and rarest of all truffles. The flavor of a *Pico* is so puissant that it is almost always served raw, either ground, sliced, or grated onto simple dishes like polenta, egg pasta, or eggs. *Picos* are the most perishable truffle—which adds to their cost—and all efforts to cultivate them have failed. Truffles grow on the roots of trees like willow, poplar, hazelnut, and oak, usually at the drip line of the outermost branches. They spring from a mycelium, which, if disturbed, can fail to produce future harvests, so most truffle hunters are very careful about removing the fungus without annoying the mycelium. We encountered a few exposed holes, which Mario covered up with disgust. "People who don't cover their holes are fools," he said.

A truffle hunter's knowledge of where the mycelium lies is key to his success. Indeed, the *Tartufai* are so jealous of their hunting grounds that they pass on the locations only orally, from father to son. Mario and the other hunters parked their doggy-smelling Fiats a real hump away from the valley where the truffles grow, so that other nosy *Tartufai* wouldn't discover their spots. Even trained dogs are not sold locally, for fear they will alert their new owners to their former owner's truffle fields. *Picos* are found in the Piedmont region. Other pockets are found throughout northern Italy and as far south as Rome, as well as a few minor locations in Croatia and Switzerland. "But truffles from anywhere but Italy?" asked Mario rhetorically. The sides of his mouth turned down and he closed his eyes and shrugged. "Why bother?"

Mario and his buddies sell their truffles to a local truffle wholesaler. Some wholesalers, particularly those representing restaurants, hit the homes of known *Tartufai* and make a deal at the kitchen table. And during the truffle festivals, it's not uncommon to see a local hunter on a street corner furtively selling suspect tubers from inside his coat pocket. The white truffle festivals kick in about midway through the fall months. Anybody can visit these events, which vary from rinky-dink fairs to all-out wholesale and retail truffle markets, culminating in October with the ultimate truffle shindig in the Piedmontese city of Alba. A few years back, a drunken construction worker we met in a café drove us (at life-threatening speed) to a little truffle festival in a tiny meadow near Sienna. There was a rickety Ferris wheel, a dance floor and band, and a half-dozen picnic tables set up near an outdoor kitchen. Local ladies, in sacky dresses and gold hoop earrings, boiled up bowls of tagliatelle, tossed the al dente pasta in sweet butter and black pepper, and shaved big curls of white truffles on top. That's the kind of meal you remember for a lifetime.

When we returned to Mario's house after the hunt, our cousin Maria had prepared a feast. First, saltine crackers spread with a puree of white truffles, butter, and black pepper; then a variety of Tuscan crostini (chicken liver; porcini mushroom; garlic, with a little crushed tomato). The pasta course was an opulent handmade tagliatelle dressed with truffles, egg yolks, and mascarpone cheese, followed by a dish Maria always makes when we visit and that I have had no success recreating: boar stew, thick and maroon-colored and so rich and oily it is served only in small portions. Oh, my God, the taste! This concoction of wild boar, unsweetened chocolate, cinnamon, pignoli nuts, and cured black olives is both sweet and sour, strong and mild, aromatic, addictive, indulgent. One can imagine Lorenzo de Medici asking for seconds of this surprising dish, and indeed, Maria said it is based on one that originated in the Renaissance kitchens of the Tuscan nobility. There were more dishes, of course, all delicious, all forgotten. Between white truffles and purple boar stew, our tastebuds were overloaded, intoxicated, incapacitated.

That night, back in Florence, we went to dinner at Camillo's, where we ate a simple risotto with white truffles shaved on top. Afterward, Dad stopped a couple of unsuspecting American tourists and opened his jacket, where he had a truffle stashed in the inside pocket, and encouraged the hesitant Milwaukeeans to "Go ahead. Take a sniff." My mother, lady that she is, tried to pretend she didn't think he was hilarious.

After the truffle hunt, I was ready to become reacquainted with my inner mycologist. I bought books like *Mushrooms of Colorado* and the *Encyclopedia of Food,* which told me mushrooms, the fruiting body of a fungus, are about 90 percent water (like us); that they are organized by genus and species; by families, orders, classes, and subdivisions, and that they are all in the Kingdom of Fungi. I learned fungi don't make their own food but must get it from an outside host, and that they produce spores, not seeds. It's kind of creepy how much like an animal mushrooms really are. But reading is not the same thing as doing, and I knew the only way I was going to learn was if I had a teacher. Mushrooming for the table is, ultimately, an oral tradition.

We have a place in Colorado because my husband is one of those hiking people. His first Christmas gift to me was a sleeping bag. But I couldn't understand the attraction of clambering over scree only to reach the top. I recognize that other people find this immensely rewarding, but the Giobbis always connected to nature via food. I never really felt much of a need to find my place in the circle of life any other way. Then I met blue-eyed Peggy Tomaski, masseuse and mycologist, who shared her hunting grounds with me. Not all mushroom hunters are so generous. I've sunk so low as to get my friend Yvon Gross, a terrific French chef in Hotchkiss, drunk and then tried to trick him into telling me where he finds chanterelles. But Yvon can hold both his liquor and his tongue.

But thanks to Peggy and an equally beloved huntress, Linda Rubick, and using my own common sense and luck, I now find chanterelles, delicious milky caps, king boletus (porcini), hawk's wings, and many others. In Long Island, I have gathered bluing boletus, paying a quarter for each mushroom my entrepreneurial kids can find, and endured a hundred sand flea bites in the bargain. In Montana, I searched for morels in the forest fire burn site of the Flathead National Park, where we followed the hoof prints of elk in the ashy muck, each one home to a morel, and camped with the commercial pickers—Laotians, Cambodians, Mexicans—who follow the wild mushroom blooms across the northwestern states.

The magic one conjures in finding mushrooms can be contagious. The Giobbis often meet for Sunday lunch in the fall, when Dad's garden is at its richest. We eat more meat and poultry than in summer: pasta with chicken livers followed by quail with figs, and mushrooms, lots of mushroom dishes like spaghettini with botarga (the smoked roe of the red mullet) and wild mushrooms, followed by a tangy skirt steak with wild mushrooms cooked down to the point of caramelized nuttiness. After one such Sunday lunch in Katonah—I think we had pasta with a rich guinea hen sauce and tender duck baked in salt, followed by ginger pears—I announced I was going into the Purple Forest, a large pine forest about half a mile from the house, to search for mushrooms. The rest of the family—full, a little sleepy on homemade wine, and comfy in front of the fireplace with the papers—wished me luck and turned back to the crossword puzzle.

I walked under the lavender branches of the fir trees, pine needles yielding under my feet, listening to the sounds of nature that I can hear only when I am not thinking about my petty complaints, when I can stop being self-conscious long enough to remember I am a part of all things living right now. And then I heard rustling in the woods behind me, and my husband emerged, carrying a knife and basket. We began gathering yellow coral mushrooms, speaking only occasionally to direct each other to another patch. Our tranquillity was soon interrupted, however, by what seemed to be a virtual unloading of a bus of Giobbis. Hooting and hollering through the woods came everyone else, Lisa and Paul and Snow, Carson and Mo, Cham and Laine—lugging the baby and steering the manic toddling of Val—Mom and Dad, all of them carrying baskets and knives and calling for the littlest children not to touch a mushroom until a grown-up had looked at it. One kind of revelry replaces another, I thought, as I watched my kin fan out.

The fact that mushrooming can be a life and death endeavor—one always hears about famed mushroomers whose pride did them in—marks fungi as the most profound of plants. Indeed, it is through mushrooming that I have learned an important lesson of old age—that living in the moment is the greatest living of all. For years, Dad tried unsuccessfully to identify a mushroom that grew near his root cellar in Katonah. I remember the kitchen reeking of compost as he conducted spore tests on the dinner table. Often, at meals with chefs, he would ask them about this mysterious mushroom, and they would grunt in French and shrug. It was as if Dad could conjure the mushroom, but not make it real. Finally, after we Giobbi kids had grown up and were conducting lives of our own, he decided to taste it. He chopped the mushrooms and sautéed them with garlic and olive oil, and garnished them with parsley from his garden. He tasted them in the morning, so he could get to the doctor during the day if necessary. It turned out they were the honey mushroom, *Armillaria ostoyae*—not an incredibly choice specimen, but one precious to him. It was the mushroom Dad ate as a child; the mushroom he smelled one day in Austria when he was pinned facedown in the earth by Nazi machine-gun fire; the mushroom that his father had picked 60 years before, and cooked with rabbit and rosemary and wine.

When I first heard this story, I thought my dad was nuts to risk his health. But now I know: One has reached a state of grace when life boils down to the taste of a wild mushroom.

ESSENTIALS OF MEAL PLANNING

We are grateful for the bounty of fall because our appetites are increasing. Cooler weather demands higher-calorie foods, and at the same time, the vegetable garden is at its most glorious in September and October. We eat ripe tomatoes for the first part of fall, and as the season progresses, we prepare more recipes calling for green tomatoes and feast on the other foods that hold out for the season, like eggplant, parsnips, butternut squash, cardoons, beets, and herbs. In the fall, the radicchio produces its second growth, and we eat the sweet red buds in salads.

We indulge in game birds—ducks and quails—once hunting seasons open, and check all our spots for wild mushrooms: the tree by the wine cellar for oyster mushrooms, Jay's front yard for honey mushrooms, the Purple Forest for bright orange coral mushrooms.

We also take advantage of the tuna catch. After feasting their way up the coast, the albacore, yellowtail, and big eye have swollen to enormous sizes, and we gorge on them in delicate sausages, or grilled steaks served with black pepper and a squeeze of lemon.

One of our most treasured fall foods is the cranberry bean, which comes in around Thanksgiving. We use it in everything—soups, stews, vegetable dishes. We even simmer them in chicken broth and garnish the dish with caviar, a dish that has surprised some of our friends for its blatant mix of high and low ingredients. But people always get bogged down with the meaning of gourmet. Is cauliflower with cranberry beans gourmet? Of course it is. What determines fine dining, in the Italian mind, is not the preciousness of the ingredient, or the birthing pains of a recipe. For Italians, the definition is clear: A simple preparation of extremely fresh ingredients is the secret to truly elegant eating.

ABOUT PASTA

In the 1960s, Dad started to write and speak about pasta, and his early intervention in breaking down the spaghetti and meatballs model contributed to America's sophistication about Italian food in general and pasta specifically. And there were gates to storm: When I was a kid, my usual birthday dinner request was spaghetti with green sauce—basil pesto. This disgusted my fourth-grade schoolmates so thoroughly that we had to drive one dry-heaving child home. No one except Italian home cooks knew about pesto back then. Dad also put the word out about De Cecco pasta. He hated the American alternatives and, through his relationship with Craig Claiborne of the *New York Times,* helped promote the product throughout the United States. Today, I can find De Cecco pasta at my grocery store in Hotchkiss, Colorado. Since the advent of De Cecco, a number of excellent pastas have arrived on the scene. Two of our favorites are Sapori Di Casa (a handmade pasta) and Rustichella D'Abruzzo, wonderful pastas with great texture and delicate taste. They are expensive, but we eat small amounts (although we do eat it frequently). Too often, pasta is eaten as filler food, and it shouldn't be—unless you are a college student living on a couple of dollars a day. This is one of many persistent misconceptions about Italian food, despite America's growing awareness of what real Italian food tastes like.

At a French Culinary Institute class, a little leftover class time was spent on the preparation of "chicken cacciatore." Meaning hunter-style, cacciatore usually includes forest mushrooms. The chicken is browned in a small amount of oil. Aromatics like onions and garlic are added, then wine and herbs. The chicken is cooked until the alcohol cooks out. Then vegetables are added and the chicken is stewed in them: tomatoes, wild mushrooms, whatever. Our chef prepared a classic French chicken casseur (shallots, tarragon, mushrooms) but added marinara sauce after the chicken had browned—typical of Ital-American cuisine. And when a student asked what was traditionally served with the dish, the chef said "pasta, of course."

Italians don't eat pasta *with*. They eat pasta *before*. Small servings are eaten before a second course—which can be anything from an elaborate meat and vegetable plate to a simple salad. Traditionally, pasta does not sit beside an entrée like a potato. In fact, you don't even see rice served next to an entrée that often (osso buco with risotto Milanese is one exception). More likely, the carbohydrate aspect of a meal happens at the beginning of the meal, and in the same serving size as Ital-American cooks will place beside an entrée.

The word *pasta* means paste, referring to the dough made by combining durum wheat flour with a liquid. The term is used to describe a wide variety of noodles made from this kind of dough. There are dozens of shapes, sizes, and thicknesses, as well as stuffed pastas and flavored pastas. In Italian cookery, certain types of pasta are specific to certain types of sauces and methods of cooking. Thin pastas, like spaghettini and capellini, are served with fish and broth sauces. They tend to cook a little quicker than other pasta cuts and are preferred when pasta is finished in the sauce. Egg pasta, like tagliatelle and pappardelle, are pastas fortified with eggs; they are ideal with meat and cream sauces. Cut or shaped pastas, like penne and rigatoni, are excellent with slightly chunky meat and vegetable sauces; the bits of sauce will adhere to the ridges and spaces of cut pasta. We don't recommend those strange "homemade" pastas that you find in the refrigerator section of the supermarket. They are gummy and nasty and don't boil up nicely. We buy stuffed pasta prepared by local pasta shops in New York, who roll out their own dough to prepare ravioli and tortellini (although we do make it ourselves, on holidays and snowy afternoons). And we make gnocchi from potatoes or squash with a small amount of flour and eggs.

We find eating a small portion of beautifully prepared pasta to be a great way into a meal, and that it often satisfies our appetite just enough to ensure we don't overeat. To that end, all the pasta recipes in this book are for small servings to be served as a first course. Please, if you double the recipe, double the people too.

F A L L
F I R S T   C O U R S E S

Beet, Potato, and Tuna Salad

We also serve this dish as an entrée, following a soup.

4 medium potatoes (we prefer Yukon Gold), scrubbed

4 medium beets, scrubbed

1 medium onion, thinly sliced

2 cans (6 ounces) Italian tuna fish packed in oil, drained

4 tablespoons extra virgin olive oil

4 tablespoons chopped flat-leaf parsley

2 tablespoons white wine vinegar

2 teaspoons mustard (we like Coleman's)

Salt and black pepper

Place the potatoes in a medium pot and cover with cold water. Bring to a boil over high heat. Place the beets in another medium pot and cover with cold water. Bring to a boil over high heat. (We use separate pots so the red beets will not discolor the potatoes.) Cook both until tender, about 20 minutes. Drain the beets and potatoes and set aside until they are cool enough to handle. Peel and slice the beets and potatoes. In a serving bowl, combine the beets and potatoes with the onion, tuna fish, oil, parsley, vinegar, and mustard, season with salt and pepper, and serve at room temperature.

Save the water from boiling the beets Beet Granita (see page 155).

Serves 4

Tuna with Beans

This is a very popular dish in Italy, and in American restaurants as well. We like to serve this dish with a piece of Bruschetta (see page 17).

¼ cup extra virgin olive oil, plus more for garnish

1 medium onion, coarsely chopped

2 garlic cloves, sliced

1 tablespoon tomato paste

1 cup water

1 bay leaf

Salt and freshly ground black pepper

1 can (15 ounces) cannellini beans (we prefer Goya brand), drained

1 can (6 ounces) Italian tuna fish packed in oil, drained

Heat the ¼ cup oil in a small saucepan over medium heat, add the onion and garlic, and cook until the onion becomes translucent, about 5 minutes. Add the tomato paste and cook, stirring often, over low heat for 3 minutes. Add the water, bay leaf, and salt and pepper to taste, cover, and simmer for 10 minutes. Add the drained beans, cover, and simmer for 15 minutes. Add the tuna fish, turn off the heat, and allow the dish to come down to room temperature. Remove the bay leaf.

Dribble some extra virgin olive oil on each serving.

Serves 4

Grilled Eel and Eggplant Salad

We make this dish from August through October, when the eggplants are in. This salad is excellent prepared a day in advance, giving it plenty of time for the flavors to meld. Store in the refrigerator, and allow to come to room temperature before serving.

1 large eel, about 1½ inches in diameter at thickest part, skinned, cut into 2-inch sections

Salt

1 medium eggplant, cut into ¼-inch thick slices

6 tablespoons extra virgin olive oil

6 garlic cloves, sliced

Juice of 1 lemon or 3 tablespoons balsamic vinegar

1 tablespoon finely chopped flat-leaf parsley

Freshly ground black pepper or hot pepper flakes

Heat the grill.

Grill the eel until it begins to brown, about 5 minutes.

If the eggplant is a little old, sprinkle salt over the eggplant slices and allow to rest for 15 minutes. Wipe dry. Brush 2 tablespoons of the oil over the eggplant slices. Place the slices on the grill and grill until they are lightly browned, about 5 minutes on each side. Cut the grilled eggplant into pieces.

In a mixing bowl, combine the eel, eggplant, the remaining 4 tablespoons of oil, the garlic, lemon juice, parsley, and salt and pepper to taste. Allow the salad to rest for at least 15 minutes before serving.

Serves 4

Snails alla Marchigiana

This is a recipe Edward's mother used to make. When he was a boy, only Moroccan snails were available. Now you can buy Italian land snails all year round (though we prefer to eat them in the cool months). Italian snails are brown with white stripes, and they should be alive. After they've been cooked, we discard the intestinal tract of large snails, but we don't bother with smaller specimens. We find them on Arthur Avenue; ask your fishmonger to order them.

1 pound Italian snails (about 30 snails)

4 tablespoons olive oil

6 garlic cloves, chopped

Hot pepper flakes

2 tablespoons tomato paste

½ cup dry white wine

1 teaspoon dried marjoram

1 teaspoon crushed dried rosemary

2 bay leaves

½ cup water

Salt

1 tablespoon finely chopped flat-leaf parsley

Italian bread, for serving

Wash the snails in warm salted water and rinse them 6 to 10 times, until the water is clean and there is no slime. The snails will come out of their shells in the warm water.

Bring a small pot of water to a boil. Add about 10 snails, one at a time, into the water. They should be partly out of their shells by the time they are put in the boiling water. They will die as soon as they hit the water and will remain partially out of their shells. Scoop out with a slotted spoon and continue with the remaining snails. Set aside.

Heat the oil in a medium skillet over medium heat. Add the garlic and hot pepper flakes to taste. Cook until the garlic begins to take on color, about 2 minutes. Add the snails, cover, and cook about 10 minutes. Add the tomato paste and stir well. Cook for several minutes, reduce the heat to low, and then add the wine, marjoram, rosemary, and bay leaves. Cover and simmer for 15 minutes. Add the water and salt to taste. Cover and simmer for 15 minutes more, mixing often. Add the parsley and cook for several minutes more.

Remove the bay leaves. Serve with toothpicks to remove the snails from the shells, and Italian bread to dip into the sauce.

Serves 4

Cranberry Bean Soup with Corn

This is a version of the bean soup Edward's grandfather used to make. If you use canned beans, we recommend Goya cannellini. Simmer the sauce for 45 minutes before adding canned beans.

1 tablespoon olive oil

¼ cup chopped pancetta or Canadian bacon

1 medium onion, finely chopped

2 garlic cloves, finely chopped

2 large tomatoes, chopped

2 celery ribs, finely chopped

1 tablespoon chopped flat-leaf parsley

1 bay leaf

Salt and freshly ground black pepper or hot pepper flakes

1 cup fresh cranberry beans (about 1 pound in the shell)

4 cups water

2 ears fresh corn, husked and cut into 2-inch lengths

½ cup grated Parmesan cheese, for garnish

Heat the oil in a large soup pot over medium heat. Add the pancetta and cook until the fat is partially rendered, about 5 minutes. Add the onion and garlic and continue cooking until the onion becomes translucent, about 5 minutes. Add the tomatoes, celery, parsley, bay leaf, and salt and pepper to taste and bring to a boil. Add the fresh beans and the water, cover, turn down the heat to medium-low, and simmer for about 1½ hours. Add the corn and cook for an additional 15 minutes. Remove the bay leaf. Garnish with the grated cheese.

Serves 4

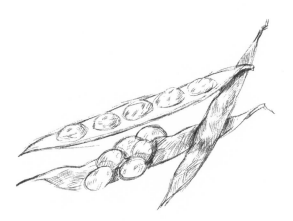

Stracciatelle Soup with Cardoons

Cardoons are tough, so they are usually boiled for 30 minutes before a final cooking. In the case of this recipe, boil the cardoons for only 15 minutes. Stracciatelle, the egg mixture, is usually served in chicken soup with spinach. This recipe is a specialty of Le Marche.

1 pound cardoons, chopped

Juice of half a lemon

2 cups water

1 tablespoon all-purpose flour

8 cups chicken stock

6 eggs

2 tablespoons grated lemon zest

6 tablespoons grated Parmesan cheese

Salt

Place the cardoons in a small bowl and cover with cold water. Soak, with the lemon juice, for 30 to 45 minutes. Drain the cardoons and place in a small pot with 2 cups water and the flour. Gently boil the cardoons for about 15 minutes over medium-low heat. Drain.

Heat the stock in a soup pot over high heat. Boil the cardoons in the stock for 15 minutes. Lower the heat to bring the stock to a simmer.

In a bowl, combine the eggs, lemon zest, cheese, and salt to taste and mix well. Add the egg mixture to the simmering stock. Turn up the heat and bring the stock to a boil again. As soon as it is boiling, take the stock off the heat altogether. Allow the stracciatelle to sit for several minutes before serving.

Serves 6

Leek and Chestnut Soup

Every fall, one of the men from the younger generation—son or son-in-law—goes out to Katonah to help Edward make wine. After a morning crushing the grapes, amidst those smells, and others, of dying leaves and wet dogs and chimney smoke, they sit down to a hot bowl of this creamy, sweet leek and chestnut soup and a glass of last year's red wine.

1 cup fresh chestnuts

4 tablespoons olive oil

2 large leeks, whites only, rinsed and sliced

1 cup beer

4 cups chicken or beef stock

2 medium potatoes, peeled and cut into chunks (we prefer Yukon Gold)

½ cup heavy cream

Salt

Toasted croutons, for garnish (see page 32)

Score the chestnuts, put them in a small pot, and cover with water. Boil for 3 minutes. Drain the chestnuts, then peel and skin them, and chop.

Heat the oil in a large heavy-bottomed soup pot over medium heat. Add the leeks and chestnuts, and cook until the leeks are soft, about 5 minutes. Add the beer and continue to cook for 5 minutes. Add the stock and potatoes and cook until the chestnuts are very soft, about 30 minutes.

Push the soup through a food mill or sieve (you can use a processor, but the potatoes will become a little sticky). Return the soup to the pot, swirl in the cream, and add salt to taste.

Serve this soup warm garnished with toasted croutons.

Serves 4

Butternut Squash and Rice Soup

An excellent soup to serve before Meatballs, Marchigiana-Style (see page 203).

2 tablespoons extra virgin olive oil

1 medium leek, white only, rinsed and chopped

1 small onion, finely chopped

4 cups chicken stock

4 tablespoons rice (we like Uncle Ben's or basmati)

1 pound butternut squash, peeled, seeded, and cut into small dice

1 tablespoon finely chopped flat-leaf parsley

Salt and freshly ground black pepper

4 tablespoons grated Pecorino or Parmesan cheese, for garnish

Heat the oil in a medium soup pot over medium heat. Add the leek and onion. Cover and cook until the onion becomes translucent, about 5 minutes. Add the stock and simmer for 15 minutes. Add the rice and cook for 5 minutes, then add the squash. Cook for 10 minutes, until the rice is cooked and the squash is tender. Add the parsley and salt and pepper to taste. Garnish each portion with grated cheese.

Serves 4

Tripe Soup with Beans

This soup is hearty, yet delicate and sweet. Tripe is sweet because of its high gelatin content, and not greasy at all. Beans are a natural complement, and this combination is often used in Northern Italy. It is low in saturated fats and is excellent for joint health.

½ pound tripe

6 cups chicken stock

1 carrot, coarsely chopped

1 celery rib, coarsely chopped

2 bay leaves

1 tomato, chopped

1 leek, white only, rinsed and chopped

1 tablespoon basil chiffonade

Salt and freshly ground black pepper

½ pound Savoy cabbage, cut into large chunks

2 small potatoes, peeled and cut into large chunks (we prefer Yukon Gold)

1 cup fresh cranberry beans (about 1 pound in the shell)

3 tablespoons grated Parmesan cheese, for garnish

Prepare the tripe: Bring a large pot of salted water to a boil over high heat. Add the tripe and cook for 5 minutes. Drain and rinse in cold water. Turn the tripe comb-side down and trim off the fat with a sharp knife. Cut the tripe into strips ½ inch wide and 2 inches long.

In a large soup pot, combine the tripe, stock, carrot, celery, and bay leaves. Place over medium heat and boil gently for 1 hour. Add the tomato, leek, basil, and salt and pepper to taste, and cook for 30 minutes more. Add the cabbage and potatoes and cook for 15 minutes. Add the beans and cook for about 45 minutes, or until tender. Remove the bay leaves.

Serve each portion sprinkled with grated cheese.

Serves 6

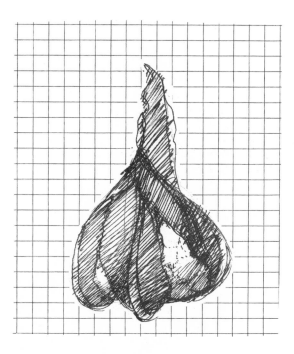

175

Penne with Cabbage

There is no simpler dish than this surprisingly flavorful recipe. We make it with Savoy cabbage in the fall, but it is wonderful with fresh summer cabbage during the hot months.

4 tablespoons extra virgin olive oil, plus additional for garnish

1 large onion, thinly sliced

1½ pounds Savoy cabbage, shredded

Salt

¾ pound cut pasta, such as penne

6 tablespoons grated Parmesan cheese

Freshly ground black pepper

Heat the 4 tablespoons of oil in a large skillet over medium heat. Add the onion, cover, and cook until it becomes translucent, about 5 minutes. Add the cabbage and salt to taste. Reduce the heat to medium-low, cover, and continue cooking for about 15 minutes, until the cabbage is tender.

In the meantime, bring a large pot of salted water to a boil over high heat. Add the pasta and cook until it is al dente. Scoop out about 1 cup of the cooking liquid, then drain the pasta.

Toss the cabbage and pasta together in a serving bowl. Add some reserved water if it seems dry, ¼ cup at a time. Toss with the grated cheese and serve each portion with a drizzle of extra virgin olive oil and a few cranks of freshly ground black pepper.

Serves 4

Farfalle with Green Tomatoes

This is a specialty of Abruzzo, and the recipe comes from a relative of Edward's. We make this dish in early summer as well, when the tomatoes are just coming in.

3 tablespoons olive oil

2 tablespoons diced pancetta or Canadian bacon

1 onion, finely chopped

2 garlic cloves, finely chopped

1 tablespoon basil chiffonade

3 large green tomatoes, sliced

2 tablespoons pignoli nuts, toasted

1½ cups chicken stock

Salt and freshly ground black pepper

¾ pound cut pasta, such as farfalle

2 tablespoons grated Pecorino cheese

4 tablespoons toasted bread-crumbs, for garnish

Extra virgin olive oil, for garnish

Heat the olive oil in a medium skillet over medium heat. Add the pancetta and cook until it begins to release its fat, about 3 minutes. Add the onion and cook, uncovered, until translucent, about 5 minutes. Add the garlic and cook several minutes more, until the garlic begins to take on color. Add the basil, tomatoes, pignoli nuts, stock, and salt and pepper to taste. Cover and simmer for 20 to 25 minutes, until the tomatoes become soft.

In the meantime, bring a large pot of salted water to a boil over high heat. Add the pasta and cook until it is al dente. Drain.

Toss the pasta, sauce, and cheese together in a bowl. Garnish with the breadcrumbs and the extra virgin olive oil.

Serves 4

Spaghettini with Botarga and Wild Mushrooms

In Le Marche there are pasta dishes called Mare e Monte, *or "sea and mountains." This is our version. Botarga, the smoked roe of the red mullet, can be found in many specialty stores and online at www.freshcaviar.com. Grate it on the large holes of a box grater. You can use any wild mushroom you please, but we prefer porcini.*

3 tablespoons unsalted butter

3 tablespoons minced shallots

½ pound fresh porcini mushrooms, thinly sliced

5 tablespoons finely chopped flat-leaf parsley

Salt

½ cup olive oil

4 garlic cloves, minced

Hot pepper flakes

¾ pound spaghettini

1 scant cup grated botarga (about 1 lobe of a large roe)

Heat the butter in a small skillet over medium heat. Add the shallots and cook until translucent, about 5 minutes. Add the mushrooms and cook for about 5 minutes, until the liquid cooks out. Add 3 tablespoons of the parsley and salt to taste. Set aside.

Heat the oil in a small pot over medium heat until it is very hot. Add the garlic and hot pepper flakes to taste. Cook until the garlic is soft, not brown, about 1 minute. The garlic should sizzle gently. Remove from the heat and set aside.

Bring a large pot of salted water to a boil over high heat. Add the spaghettini and cook, stirring often to avoid sticking, until the pasta is al dente. (It takes spaghettini a little less time to cook than a thicker cut pasta.) Drain and place the spaghettini in a serving bowl.

Toss the pasta with the oil and garlic. Toss in the mushroom mixture, then scatter in the botarga with one hand as you toss the pasta with the other. Adjust the seasoning and toss well. Garnish with the remaining 2 tablespoons of parsley and serve immediately.

Note: Sometimes the botarga clumps, so be sure to scatter it throughout the pasta by hand.

Serves 4

Spaghetti with Tuna and Anchovies

We tested this recipe with a very fine canned tomato called Vaegri—indeed, the best we ever tasted beside our own homemade. We buy it at Tino's Deli in the Bronx (see Sources on page 305). We prefer fresh or salted anchovies over tinned, filleted and washed. It's easier to fillet the anchovies before soaking.

4 tablespoons extra virgin olive oil

1 small onion, finely chopped

4 garlic cloves, finely chopped

4 salted anchovies, filleted, soaked for a few minutes, and chopped, or 8 oil-packed anchovies, rinsed and chopped

1 can (6 ounces) Italian tuna fish packed in oil, drained

1 tablespoon finely chopped flat-leaf parsley

Hot pepper flakes

1½ cups chopped fresh ripe tomatoes or whole canned Italian tomatoes

Salt

¾ pound spaghetti

Heat the oil in a large saucepan over medium heat. Add the onion, garlic, and anchovies. Cover and simmer until the garlic begins to take on color, about 3 minutes. Add the tuna fish, parsley, and hot pepper flakes to taste. Cook for several minutes, breaking up the tuna with a wooden spoon. Add the tomatoes, cover, and simmer for 20 to 30 minutes, until the sauce is the consistency of a marinara (all the tomato should be cooked down). If the sauce is dry, add a little water to loosen it up. Add salt to taste.

Bring a large pot of salted water to a boil over high heat and add the spaghetti. Cook until it is al dente. Drain and add to the sauce. Toss well and serve.

Serves 4

179

Fettucine with Guinea Hen Sauce

When we first tasted this dish in Certaldo, a beautiful town in Tuscany, we thought it was a red-meat sauce, yet it wasn't greasy. It turns out guinea hens make for a very rich sauce with little fat.

For the stock

1 guinea hen (3½ pounds)

2 medium carrots, cut in thirds

1 parsnip, cut in half

1 celery rib, cut in thirds

1 medium onion, peeled

1 small leek, cleaned and cut into thirds

5 garlic cloves

2 bay leaves

2 tablespoons chopped flat-leaf parsley

Salt and freshly ground black pepper

For the stock: Bone the guinea hen. Refrigerate the meat, fat, and skin, which you will use later, for the sauce. Place the bones and the carrots, parsnip, celery, onion, leek, garlic, bay leaves, and parsley in a large soup pot and cover with water. Season with salt and pepper to taste. Boil the stock gently over medium heat for about 2 hours. Strain the stock. Discard the bones and vegetables. Reserve 2 cups of stock for the sauce and refrigerate the rest.

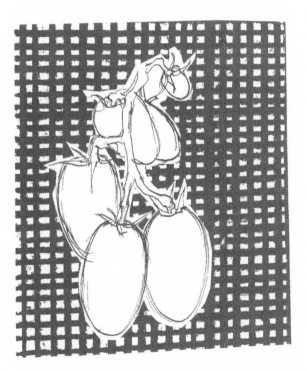

For the sauce

½ cup chopped pancetta or Canadian bacon

1 small onion, peeled and stuck with 5 cloves

3 garlic cloves, chopped

Salt and freshly ground black pepper

1 cup dry white wine

2 ounces dried porcini mushrooms, soaked in warm water for 10 minutes (retain the water)

1 tablespoon dried basil

2 cups whole canned Italian tomatoes, chopped

1 medium carrot, cut in half

3 tablespoons olive oil

½ pound wild mushrooms, chopped

1½ pounds fettucine

¾ cup grated Parmesan or Pecorino cheese, for garnish

For the sauce: Place the pancetta in a large skillet with the reserved skin and fat from the guinea hen and the onion stuck with cloves and cook over medium heat until the skin has completely rendered its fat, about 10 minutes. Pick out the skin and discard.

Cut the guinea hen meat into strips and chop and add it to the skillet. Add the garlic and salt and pepper to taste. Cook over medium heat, stirring often, for about 10 minutes, until the meat is browned. Add the wine, dried porcini mushrooms with their water, and the basil. Cover, reduce the heat to medium-low, and simmer until the wine is absorbed and no longer smells winey, about 5 minutes. Add the tomatoes, carrot, and the reserved 2 cups of guinea hen stock. Cover and simmer for 2 hours. Remove the carrot and onion. Place the sauce in a food processor and pulse to blend until the sauce is the consistency of double-ground meat, and then return it to the pot.

Heat the oil in a small saucepan over medium heat. Add the wild mushrooms and cook for about 5 minutes, until the mushrooms give up their liquid. Add salt and pepper to taste. Add the wild mushrooms to the sauce and continue cooking over low heat for 1 hour. The sauce cooks for a total of 3 hours.

Bring a large pot of salted water to a boil over high heat and add the pasta. Cook until it is al dente. Drain and pour into a serving bowl. Add the sauce, mix well, and garnish with the grated cheese.

Note: If you want to serve this dish to fewer than 8 people, make only 1 pound of pasta, and save about one-quarter of the sauce for another day.

You can also make this dish with a 3½ pound duck, in which case, render the skin and then pour off the fat after it's rendered.

To find guinea hens, ask your butcher or go to www.dartagnan.com.

Serves 8

Tagliolini with Saffron

Edward first tasted this dish in a very good restaurant called Trattoria Antico Fattore, in Florence. It is very exotic and super easy. The quality of the pasta will make a difference in this dish.

2 cups chicken stock

½ teaspoon saffron

¾ pound imported cut pasta, such as tagliolini, farfalle, or penne

1 teaspoon unsalted butter

1 teaspoon all-purpose flour

Freshly ground black pepper

4 tablespoons grated Parmesan cheese

1 teaspoon grated lemon zest, for garnish

4 teaspoons finely chopped flat-leaf parsley, for garnish

Bring the stock to a boil in a medium skillet over high heat. Add the saffron. Cover and boil for about 5 minutes, until the saffron dissolves. Set the broth aside.

Bring a large pot of salted water to a boil over high heat. Add the pasta and cook until it is almost al dente. Drain and set aside.

Mash the butter and flour together between your fingers until they are a smooth paste. Return the saffron broth to the stove and bring to a low boil over medium-low heat. Add the butter/flour mixture in a couple of small pinches, whisking all the time, and cook until the sauce is about the thickness of light cream, about 5 minutes. The broth must boil about 3 minutes in order to cook out the raw taste of the flour. If the sauce gets too thick, add some more warm chicken stock. Add pepper to taste.

Add the drained pasta to the broth and cook, mixing often, until the pasta is al dente, about 3 minutes. Add the grated cheese and mix well. Garnish each plate with a pinch of lemon zest and parsley. Serve immediately.

Serves 4

Fettucine with Chicken Livers

We save the livers whenever we buy whole chickens and use them in this sauce. We find the livers from free-range chickens to be superior to industrial chicken livers. When buying livers, be sure the source is a good one, like Whole Foods.

2 tablespoons unsalted butter

2 tablespoons extra virgin olive oil

1 large onion, finely chopped

2 garlic cloves, finely chopped

½ pound chicken livers

Salt and freshly ground black pepper

1 cup dry Marsala wine

1 tablespoon chopped marjoram or 1 teaspoon dried

1 tablespoon chopped rosemary or 1 teaspoon crushed dried

¾ pound fettucine or tagliolini

4 tablespoons grated Parmesan or Pecorino cheese, for garnish

2 tablespoons finely chopped flat-leaf parsley, for garnish

In a medium skillet, heat the butter and oil over medium heat. Add the onion and garlic and cook until the onion becomes translucent, about 5 minutes. Add the livers, and season with salt and pepper. Turn the heat up to high and cook for several minutes, stirring constantly. Add the wine, marjoram, and rosemary and continue cooking for several minutes more, until the livers plump up and turn slightly brown. Remove the livers and cut them into tiny pieces.

Bring a large pot of salted water to a boil over high heat and add the pasta. Cook until al dente. Drain and toss in a serving bowl with the sauce and the livers. Garnish with the grated cheese and parsley.

Note: Livers should be pink inside. If overcooked, they become dry and mealy.

Serves 4

Spaghettini in Duck Broth

We make this broth with the carcass from Duck Baked in Salt (see page 202). It is an excellent substitute for chicken broth in all of our recipes. We often serve a simple bowl of this broth, garnished with a squirt of lemon, before a main course.

1 duck carcass, plus the neck, and the oranges from inside the cavity

2 large carrots, cut in half

1 leek, with greens, rinsed

2 large celery ribs, cut into 3-inch lengths

1 parsnip, scraped and washed

1 large onion, peeled

3 bay leaves

8 black peppercorns

4 quarts water

Salt

3/4 pound spaghettini

Juice of half a lemon

Grated Parmesan cheese, for garnish

In a large soup pot, place the carcass, carrots, leek, celery, parsnip, onion, bay leaves, peppercorns, and water. Partially cover and bring to a boil over high heat. Lower the heat to medium-low and simmer for 3 hours, until the stock is aromatic. Strain the stock and discard the solids. Defat the stock. Return the stock to a clean pot and cook over medium heat to reduce by half. Season with salt to taste.

Add the spaghettini and the lemon juice to the broth and cook until the spaghettini is al dente. Allow the spaghettini to absorb most of the broth. If needed, add some water.

Garnish with grated cheese.

Serves 4

Spaghetti with Pork and Onions

This is an incredibly savory pasta course, excellent before poultry, game, or other meat dishes. We also serve the sauce over soft polenta.

5 tablespoons olive oil

1 tablespoon unsalted butter

2 pounds onions, thinly sliced

2 cups beef or chicken stock

1 tablespoon chopped marjoram or 1 teaspoon dried

Salt and freshly ground black pepper

1 pound lean ground pork

½ cup dry white wine

¾ pound spaghetti

¼ cup chopped flat-leaf parsley

Grated Parmesan cheese, for garnish

Heat 3 tablespoons of the oil and the butter in a Dutch oven or heavy-bottomed pot with a fitted top over medium heat, then add the onions and cook, covered, for 30 minutes, stirring occasionally, until the onions are very soft. Add the stock, cover, and continue cooking for about 75 minutes, until the onions and stock become stewy. Add the marjoram and salt and pepper to taste.

Heat the remaining 2 tablespoons of oil in a medium skillet over medium heat. Add the pork, season with salt and pepper, and cook, stirring often, until the pork is brown, about 10 minutes. Discard the fat and add the wine. Cook until the wine is absorbed and no longer smells winey, about 5 minutes. Set aside.

Bring a large pot of salted water to a boil over high heat. Add the pasta and cook until it is al dente. Drain and add the pasta to the onion mixture. Mix for 1 minute over medium heat. Add the parsley and continue to mix for a minute more.

Serve garnished with the pork and grated cheese.

Serves 4

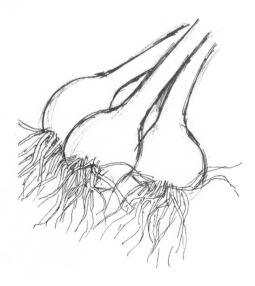

185

Timbalo Gigi

Edward made this dish for the baptism of Gigi, Cham and Laine's daughter. Butternut squash is the unique ingredient here. It makes for a very sweet, luscious lasagne.

1 pound eggplant, cut into ½-inch slices

Olive oil

1 medium butternut squash (about 2 pounds)

3 eggs

8 tablespoons grated Parmesan cheese

Salt and freshly ground black pepper

1 pound ricotta

2 tablespoons finely chopped flat-leaf parsley

Dash of grated nutmeg

4 sheets no-boil lasagna, preferably Delverde, or 12 strips imported (see note, page 37)

4 cups warm marinara sauce (see page 258)

Heat the oven to 500°F.

Place the eggplant slices on a lightly oiled baking tray. Flip the slices over in the oil to lightly coat. Do not overlap. Bake until the bottoms of the slices are brown, about 15 minutes, then flip over and brown the other side, about 5 minutes. Set aside.

Cut the squash in half and remove the seeds. Place the squash on a baking tray and bake until soft, about 30 to 45 minutes. Remove and as soon as it is cool enough to handle, scoop the meat out of the peel with a spoon and place in a bowl.

Turn the oven down to 400°F.

Combine the cooked squash with 1 egg, 2 tablespoons of the Parmesan, and salt and pepper to taste.

In another bowl, combine the ricotta with the 2 remaining eggs, 4 tablespoons of the Parmesan, the parsley, nutmeg, and salt and pepper to taste.

If you are using a lasagna variety other than no-boil, bring a large pot of salted water to a boil over high heat and cook the lasagna until it is al dente. Drain off half the water and set the pot under cold running water to cool the lasagna enough to handle. Lay the lasagna on paper towels. Do not overlap or they will stick together.

Spoon about ½ cup of warm marinara sauce into the bottom of the pan that came with the no-boil lasagna or a 9-inch square baking dish. Place a layer of pasta on top, then a layer of ricotta, then a layer of the eggplant. Add another ½ cup of sauce, and another layer of pasta. Add a layer of squash and a layer of pasta, and so on. Top the lasagne off with a layer of marinara and the remaining 2 tablespoons of grated Parmesan.

Cover the lasagne with aluminum foil and bake for 30 to 40 minutes, until it is piping hot and bubbling throughout. Allow the lasagne to rest for 10 minutes before serving.

Serves 8

Risotto with Quail

We were very excited to discover that D'Artagnan sells an excellent boned and butterflied quail. (See Sources on page 305 for information.) The quail, which are fresh, farm-raised birds, weigh about ¼ pound each. They are wired open, making them very easy to cook on top of the stove. One quail per person is adequate for a first course. Serve 2 birds per person as a second course dish.

For the quail

2 tablespoons olive oil

4 tablespoons chopped pancetta or prosciutto

Salt and freshly ground black pepper

4 quail, boned and butterflied

1 tablespoon chopped rosemary or 1 teaspoon crushed dried

¼ pound wild mushrooms, sliced

1 medium onion, finely chopped

2 garlic cloves, finely chopped

2 tablespoons finely chopped flat-leaf parsley

1 tablespoon chopped mint or 1 teaspoon dried

1 cup dry white wine

For the risotto

3 tablespoons extra virgin olive oil

1 small onion, finely chopped

1 cup Valone Nano rice or Arborio rice

½ cup dry white wine

4 to 5 cups warm chicken stock

Salt and freshly ground black pepper

4 tablespoons grated Parmesan or Pecorino cheese, for garnish

For the quail: Heat the oil over medium heat in a skillet large enough to hold all 4 quail. Add the pancetta and cook until the fat is rendered, about 5 minutes. Do not burn.

Salt and pepper the quail to taste. Sprinkle with the rosemary and place in the skillet. Turn the heat up to medium-high. Cook the quail, uncovered, for about 5 minutes on each side, until they are lightly browned. Remove the quail and keep warm. Add the mushrooms, onion, garlic, parsley, and mint to the skillet. Turn the heat down to medium, cover, and cook until the onion becomes translucent and the mushrooms release their liquid, about 5 minutes. Add ½ cup of the wine and bring it to a boil. Add the quail and the remaining ½ cup of wine, cover, and cook over high heat for about 5 minutes, until the mushrooms are cooked and the birds have heated through. Keep warm.

For the risotto: Heat the oil in a heavy-bottomed 2-quart saucepan over medium heat. Add the onion and cook until it becomes translucent, about 5 minutes. Add the rice and cook for a few minutes, stirring to coat the rice with the oil. Add the wine and cook until the wine is absorbed, about 3 minutes. Add about 1 cup of the warm stock to the rice and stir well. The rice will absorb the stock in about 5 minutes or less. Add another cup of stock, and so on, stirring frequently, until the rice is tender and creamy. The rice will cook for a total of about 20 minutes. Add salt and pepper to taste.

Ladle the risotto onto serving plates. Add 1 tablespoon of cheese on top of each portion, then place the quail and some sauce on top.

Serves 4

Zia Ada's Scripelle Timbalo

Scripelle are Italian crepes. They are used in place of pasta, and as a result, this delicious dish is surprisingly light— a real treat for lasagne lovers. The meat sauce can be made ahead of time. We like to serve this recipe before Quail with Fig Sauce (see page 201), or Stuffed Veal Bundles with Red Pepper Sauce (see page 206).

For the sauce

4 tablespoons olive oil

1 medium onion, finely chopped

3 garlic cloves, finely chopped

½ pound lean ground pork

½ pound lean ground beef

2 cups whole canned Italian tomatoes, strained

1 teaspoon dried marjoram

3 whole cloves, crushed (see Note)

Salt and freshly ground black pepper

1 cup frozen peas

For the scripelle

8 eggs, lightly beaten

½ cup grated Parmesan cheese

4 tablespoons milk

4 tablespoons all-purpose flour

½ teaspoon grated nutmeg

Salt

2 tablespoons unsalted butter

For the sauce: Heat the oil in a medium saucepan. Add the onion and garlic. Cook until the onion becomes translucent, about 5 minutes. Add the pork and beef and cook for about 10 minutes, stirring often to break up the meat, until browned. Add the tomatoes, marjoram, cloves, and salt and pepper to taste. Reduce the heat to medium-low, cover, and simmer for about 1 ¾ to 2 hours, until the meat breaks down.

Bring a small pot of salted water to a boil over high heat and add the peas. Cook until they are tender, about 5 minutes. Drain and add to the sauce. Set the sauce aside.

For the scripelle: In a medium bowl, whisk together the eggs, cheese, milk, flour, nutmeg, and salt to taste. Have ready a baking tray lined with wax paper.

Heat a small nonstick crepe pan over medium heat. Rub the pan with some of the butter and pour in about 2 tablespoons of the scripelle batter. Swirl the batter around the bottom of the pan. Cook for about 30 seconds, and then slide the pancake onto the wax paper. Repeat until you have used all the batter, rubbing the pan with butter as needed. This will make about 20 scripelle.

For the besciamella

4 tablespoons unsalted butter

4 tablespoons all-purpose flour

2 cups milk

Salt and freshly ground
black pepper

Dash of grated nutmeg

For assembly

1 cup grated Parmesan cheese

For the besciamella: Heat the butter in a small pot over medium-low heat. Slowly add the flour and whisk until blended. Add the milk and whisk rapidly. Continue cooking for about 3 to 5 minutes more, until thickened. Season with salt, pepper, and nutmeg.

For assembly: Heat the oven to 400°F. Heat the meat sauce.

Pour about ¼ cup of meat sauce in the bottom of a 12 × 8 × 3-inch baking dish. Lay down 2 scripelle side by side. Ladle about ¼ cup of meat sauce over the scripelle. Spoon about 4 tablespoons of besciamella on top, and then sprinkle with grated cheese. Continue until you have used all the ingredients, finishing the timbalo with meat sauce and grated cheese.

Place in the oven and bake for 25 minutes, until the flavors are melded and the timbalo is hot all the way through. Remove from the oven and allow the timbalo to rest for about 5 minutes before cutting.

Note: When we crush whole cloves, we just put them between sheets of plastic and pound away with a mallet.

Serves 6

CULINARY HUNTING

My mother comes from a family of bird hunters. Since the mid-1970s, various relatives have owned a duck-hunting club called Claypool's Wild Acres, in Arkansas. The club is situated along the Mississippi flyway, which is a kind of highway for migrating waterfowl, and there are a lot of ducks. Since the banning of DDT, and with the efforts of conservation-minded folks—mainly hunters—who have worked to preserve duck breeding grounds farther north, the population has been growing. I wanted to go duck hunting with my southern kin because I am very interested in eating duck, particularly wild duck, which has a wonderful, livery taste that is rich and mysterious. But while I went down south to get ducks to eat, I actually came back with much more.

The clubhouse is a frumpy, old farmhouse with a semi-attached boot shed, plunked in the middle of a big gravel driveway. The property is primarily flooded woods and reservoir, surrounded by flat, rich rice and soybean country. At dawn, when we arrive, we can hear ducks quacking in the distance, and see thousands of them flying overhead in long fluttery ribbons. After negotiating with various family members as to where everyone is going to hunt, struggling into our waders, and churning through the swamp in a muddy little all-terrain vehicle, we arrive at Well Island, a grove of pin oaks in a flooded wood. There are decoys floating in the clearing, and blinds hidden around the perimeter. We settle into our spots; the Labradors hush, shivering with anticipation on their floating stands, and we load our guns and pull on our masks, and wait for the water to still. And then everything stills. We wait, breathing the vast oxygen-rich air, eyes on the sky, fingers growing numb as they grasp the gun's shaft. So concentrated is the quiet that the slow zigzag of a leaf falling from the canopy captures the attention of all the hunters. Uncle Norfleet lights up a Carlton, and I can see the glowing tip of his cigarette and the long black barrel of his gun peeping out from the blind.

As the sky turns orange and pink, we shoot mallards and tiny, zippy teal for their sweet, tender meat. With every bird that falls like a feathery stone, the dogs leap off their stands and lope through the water to retrieve the duck in soft jaws, their tails wagging fiercely. The ducks are so stuffed with rice from their nightly feed that their craws make a crunching sound like a bean bag chair when we hang them in the crook of a nearby willow bush. When we get home, we will grill the breast meat and serve it with a velvety brown sauce, or bake the birds whole in salt and dress them with a sweet sauce made from Marsala wine and raisins.

It is always exciting to bag a duck, but something else happens while we are waiting in the blinds, in the damp closeness of the pin oaks. We hunker down in a cathedral of tree trunks, slick and inky against the predawn sky. One has to be very silent, so silent that every drip of moisture in the thick, cold air becomes perceptible, every snapping twig, every soft rustle in the forest. It is a state of intense stillness, agitation without stir, sublime intuition. Only in the waiting do I perceive the invisible connections between wild things and myself.

Through patience comes respect for the life that is lost so that we may dine. Hunting not only connects me to nature, but it also connects me to my food. Some people object to duck hunting, but from my perspective it's not controversial at all. Dad raised rabbits and chickens and pigeons, all for the table, and I was used to seeing these animals killed quickly and mercifully, and cleaned efficiently. We were more European in our sensibilities—connected with, not divorced from, the origins of our food. I look at meat in the supermarket, precut and wrapped in plastic, and I see a product dissociated from the life (and death) involved in its making. Our responsibility toward that animal is taken from us, like we are children who can't handle the realness of where our food comes from. When we have no connection with something, what does it matter if we throw it away?

We hunt for only two hours—a club rule that limits disruption of the flock—and then settle down to breakfast prepared by local Weiner, Arkansas, ladies in the clubhouse. The table, by a picture window that looks out on pieces of farm equipment and a duck resting pond, is set with thick ceramic plates, pitchers of orange juice and milk, and bowls of jelly, jam, and marmalade. The ladies march out of the kitchen with platters of scrambled eggs and another of fried eggs, a basket of steaming homemade biscuits, a mound of curly bacon, and a bowl of white gravy with the handle of a ladle sticking out of it. Everyone is pretty quiet for the first few minutes of furious piling on plates, and then the hunters do something you just don't see that much anymore—not without dogma and righteousness and politics.

They give thanks, for having had a safe hunt, for the bounty of nature, for the gift of food.

FALL
SECOND COURSES

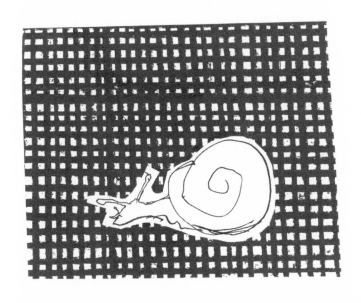

Savoy Cabbage alla Valdostana

In Italy, Savoy cabbage is served in the fall and winter, as the taste is best after the plant has been exposed to a frost. Savoy cabbage has a crinkly leaf and a more flattened sphere than green cabbage. This is a robust, cold-weather dish, wonderful after a bowl of cranberry bean soup.

1 pound sweet Italian pork sausages

5 tablespoons extra virgin olive oil

1 medium onion, thinly sliced

4 garlic cloves, sliced

1 pound Savoy cabbage, leaves separated and blanched in salted water for 1 minute

3 medium potatoes (we prefer Yukon Gold), peeled and cut into ¼-inch slices

Salt and freshly ground black pepper

1 slice boiled ham, about ¼ inch thick, cut into pieces ½ inch wide and 2 inches long

Hot pepper flakes

1 cup chicken stock

2 tablespoons extra virgin olive oil or Parmesan cheese shavings, for garnish

Heat a medium skillet over medium heat. Prick the sausages and place them in the skillet. Brown all over, for about 5 minutes. Add 3 tablespoons of the oil, the onion, and garlic. Cook until the onion becomes translucent, about 5 minutes. Remove the sausages and cut them into slices. Return the sausages to the skillet with the onions.

Place the remaining 2 tablespoons of oil in a shallow, wide braising pan. Add 1 layer of cabbage leaves, then one layer of sliced potatoes, salt and pepper to taste, then another layer of cabbage leaves, followed by the ham and then the sausages and onion and hot pepper flakes to taste, and finally, another layer of cabbage leaves. Pour in the stock and simmer over low heat, with the liquid boiling gently, for 45 minutes.

Garnish each portion with a drizzle of extra virgin olive oil or cheese shavings.

Serves 4

Stuffed Cabbage, Baked with Beans

We have served this as a first course for 8, and as a second course for 4. It is also very nice on a buffet table.

1 cup fresh cranberry beans
(about 1 pound in the shell)

2 cups chicken stock

1 small carrot, scraped

Half a medium onion, peeled

4-inch piece of celery rib

For the stuffing

1 pound lean ground pork

4 tablespoons grated Parmesan
cheese

2 tablespoons basil chiffonade or
1 teaspoon dried

3 tablespoons breadcrumbs

6 dried figs, chopped

2 tablespoons pignoli nuts

Salt and freshly ground
black pepper

8 large Savoy cabbage leaves,
blanched in salted water for 1
minute and then rinsed in cold
water

Heat the oven to 400°F.

Place the beans in a medium soup pot and cover with the stock. Add the carrot, onion, and celery and bring to a low boil over medium heat. Cook until the beans are tender, about 45 minutes. Drain the beans; reserve the stock but discard the carrot, onion, and celery. Set aside.

For the stuffing: In a medium bowl, mix together the pork, cheese, basil, breadcrumbs, figs, and pignoli nuts. Season with salt and pepper.

Spread out the cabbage leaves on your work surface and place an equal amount of stuffing in the middle of each leaf. Fold the side of the leaves in over the stuffing and then roll the leaves up. Place the rolls in a baking dish, seam side down.

Pour the beans and stock over the cabbage rolls. Cover and bake for 30 minutes.

Note: You can substitute 1 can (15 ounces) of drained cannellini beans for the fresh cranberry beans. Cook them in the stock, with the aromatics, for 30 minutes.

Serves 4 to 8

Eggplant Rolls

This recipe is adapted from one we've enjoyed at Tino's Deli on Arthur Avenue in New York.

Vegetable oil for frying

3 eggs

1 tablespoon water

1 pound eggplant, sliced lengthwise into ¼-inch thick slices (about 8 slices)

All-purpose flour for dredging

2 cups breadcrumbs

½ cup ricotta

1 tablespoon finely chopped flat-leaf parsley

2 tablespoons grated Parmesan cheese

Salt and freshly ground black pepper

½ cup marinara sauce (see page 258)

Heat about ½ inch of oil in a nonstick skillet over medium heat. Lightly beat 2 eggs with the water. Dust the eggplant slices in flour, then dip both sides in the egg and water mixture. Dust the slices in breadcrumbs. Place the eggplant slices in the hot oil and fry until each side is golden brown—less than a minute. Drain on paper towels.

Heat the oven to 400°F.

In a large bowl, combine the ricotta, parsley, Parmesan, the remaining egg, and salt and pepper to taste and mix well. Place about 1 tablespoon of the ricotta filling on the lower third of an eggplant slice and fold the eggplant over. Close with a toothpick, if necessary. Place the rolls in a baking dish so they fit snugly. Spoon 1 tablespoon of marinara sauce over each roll. Cover with aluminum foil. Place in the oven and bake for about 20 minutes. There is not a lot of sauce, so if the marinara in the bottom of the dish begins to burn, add a little water.

Note: If eggplant is garden fresh, you do not need to salt it. But if it's been hanging around in your fridge or the supermarket, salt the slices and allow them to rest for 15 minutes before wiping them dry with a paper towel.

Serves 4

Swiss Chard with Squid

This dish is a variation on a Tuscan specialty, squid with spinach. When cleaning Swiss chard, remove the string that forms along the stalk—it's similar to celery and rhubarb. When buying squid, select bone squid over summer squid. Summer squid are small with a light purplish tint, and the flesh is thin. Bone squid come in all sizes, and the flesh is white and thick, with a more delicate taste.

1 pound Swiss chard, string removed from stalk, chopped coarsely (about 6 cups)

2 medium potatoes, peeled and cut into quarters (we prefer Yukon Gold)

4 tablespoons olive oil

1 medium onion, coarsely chopped

4 garlic cloves, sliced

1½ pounds bone squid, cleaned, skinned, and sliced (include the tentacles if available)

1 tablespoon chopped flat-leaf parsley

Salt and hot pepper flakes

½ cup dry white wine

Bruschetta (page 17), for serving

Bring a large pot of salted water to a boil over high heat. Add the Swiss chard and potatoes. Cook for about 3 minutes. Scoop out 1 cup of the cooking water, then drain, rinse the chard and potatoes in cold water, and drain again.

Heat the oil in a medium braising pan over medium heat. Add the onion and garlic and cook until the onion becomes translucent, about 5 minutes. Add the squid, parsley, and salt and hot pepper flakes to taste. Cover and cook over high heat for about 3 minutes. Add the wine, reduce the heat to medium-low, and cook, covered, for about 5 minutes, until the wine no longer smells winey. Add the boiled Swiss chard and potatoes and the reserved water. Adjust the seasoning, cover, and cook over medium heat for about 45 minutes, until the squid is tender. Add more water if the vegetables look dry.

Serve immediately with bruschetta.

Serves 4

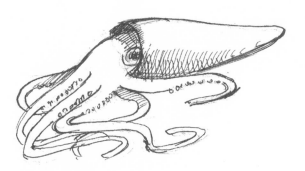

Tuna Sausages with Red Peppers

We can tuna in the fall, when the albacore, yellowtail, and big eye are running off the northeastern coast. We often make these sausages with the bits and ends of meat that don't make it into our jars. Sausage making is extremely easy and very satisfying. You can buy casings from most butchers.

2 pounds fresh tuna, skinned, boned, and coarsely ground (1 pound tuna belly and 1 pound tuna steak)

4 tablespoons grated ricotta salata

¼ cup red wine

4 garlic cloves, chopped

2 tablespoons chopped pignoli nuts

2 tablespoons finely chopped flat-leaf parsley

1 tablespoon grated orange zest

1 tablespoon chopped mint or 1 teaspoon dried

1 teaspoon hot pepper flakes or freshly ground black pepper

Salt

30 inches sausage casings, soaked in cold water for 1 hour

2 tablespoons extra virgin olive oil

2 tablespoons balsamic vinegar

2 large red bell peppers, roasted, peeled, and seeded, cut into strips

Lemon wedges, for garnish

In a large bowl, mix together the tuna, cheese, wine, garlic, pignoli nuts, parsley, orange zest, mint, and hot pepper flakes with salt to taste.

Slip an inch or so of the casings over your faucet and run cold water through the casing, allowing the water to run out at the other end.

Slip one end of the casings over the mouth of a sausage funnel (a funnel with a spout about ¾ inch in diameter). Slide the entire casing up the spout, as if putting on a stocking, leaving only a bit of casing hanging off the end. Tie this bit off with culinary string. Hold the funnel and casing with one hand and stuff the tuna mixture into the funnel with the other. Allow the casing to gradually slip away from the spout as it fills with the tuna mixture. Tie the sausages off every 5 inches or so, or twist the sausage completely around to make links. If you see any air bubbles in the sausage, prick them to let the air escape. This will make eight 5-inch sausages.

To cook the sausages, sauté them in a skillet in the oil for several minutes on each side, until golden brown. Add the vinegar, and toss one minute.

Serve the tuna sausages on a bed of red peppers, with lemon wedges for garnish.

Serves 4

Chicken with Lobster

We love to eat chicken with shellfish, as the combined tastes are very savory. We made this dish for dinner one Halloween night on Long Island, to entertain the adults while the children trick-or-treated. Edward cooked in costume: two small devil's horns glued to his head and a long chef's apron.

6 tablespoons olive oil

1 chicken (3½ to 4 pounds), cut into 8 serving pieces

Salt and freshly ground black pepper or hot pepper flakes

4 whole garlic cloves, with skins on

1 tablespoon chopped rosemary or 1 teaspoon crushed dried

2 bay leaves

1 lobster (1½ to 2 pounds), tail cut into 2-inch sections, claws cracked

½ cup dry white wine

2 large red bell peppers, seeded and sliced

3 garlic cloves, sliced

3 semi-ripe tomatoes, sliced

¼ cup white wine vinegar

2 tablespoons basil chiffonade

2 tablespoons chopped flat-leaf parsley, for garnish

Heat a medium skillet over medium heat. Add 3 tablespoons of the oil. Season the chicken parts with salt and pepper. Add the chicken to the oil, skin side down, along with the whole garlic cloves, the rosemary, and bay leaves. Cook, uncovered, turning periodically, until the skin is brown, about 25 minutes. Pour off the fat and add the lobster pieces. Cook for 5 minutes, then add the wine, cover, and simmer until the wine is absorbed and no longer smells winey, about 5 minutes. Pour the chicken and lobster and its juices on a platter and keep warm. Remove the bay leaves. Keep the garlic in the skillet.

In the same skillet, heat the remaining 3 tablespoons of oil over medium heat. Add the bell peppers and sliced garlic, and cook, uncovered and stirring often, until the peppers are tender, about 10 minutes. Add the tomatoes, vinegar, basil, and salt and pepper to taste. Cover and simmer for about 5 minutes, then add the chicken and lobster and its juices. Cover and simmer for 10 minutes.

Serve garnished with parsley.

Serves 4 to 6

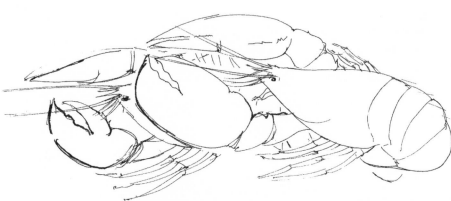

Chicken with Fennel and Mint

Edward is a fierce defender of his chickens. Many years ago a neighbor owned a dog named Dusty that Edward suspected was killing his birds. We were walking around near the barn on a fine fall afternoon when we spotted a loose chicken pecking in the grass, its back leg stretched out behind it. Our eyes followed the long string that was tied to the struggling chicken's leg, a string that traveled up in the air and to the roof of the barn, where Edward had stationed Cham with the shotgun. He didn't see the dog that afternoon, and eventually the neighbors moved away, but to this day "Dusty" is one of Edward's trigger words.

2 medium fennel bulbs, cored and quartered

4 chicken legs and thighs, separated

3 tablespoons extra virgin olive oil

4 garlic cloves, with skins on

1 tablespoon chopped rosemary

3 bay leaves

Salt and freshly ground black pepper

¾ cup dry white wine

1 large onion, sliced

2 large potatoes, peeled and sliced (we prefer Yukon Gold)

1 cup chicken stock

1 tablespoon chopped mint or 1 teaspoon dried

Heat the oven to 450°F.

Bring a medium pot of salted water to a boil over high heat. Add the fennel and blanch for 3 minutes. Drain and set aside.

Place the chicken, skin side down, on a baking tray. Do not overlap. Add the oil, garlic, rosemary, bay leaves, and salt and pepper to taste. Place the chicken, uncovered, in the oven and bake for about 30 minutes, turning occasionally, until the chicken browns. Drain off the fat. Add the wine, cover with foil, and continue to bake until the wine no longer smells winey, about 5 minutes. Add the onion, fennel, potatoes, stock, and mint. Cover and return the tray to the oven and bake until the potatoes and fennel are tender, about 20 minutes. Remove the bay leaves.

Note: If you can find fresh mint this late in the season, use it. In fact, anytime you can find fresh herbs, use them over dry. Just use three times the amount of fresh as you would dried.

Serves 4

Guinea Hen with Chestnuts

Elinor keeps a small flock of free-range guinea hens in Katonah. They are excellent parents, taking on the care of baby chicks abandoned by the heartless chickens in her flock. One year, we ordered 20-day-old guinea hen chicks, but when they arrived, they didn't look like guinea hens at all. We put them in the coop and after 6 weeks, when they still didn't look like guinea hens, we decided to eat them. Edward killed a couple and they were good . . . whatever they were. But after that first meal, whenever Edward returned to the coop, the adult guineas would go crazy, squawking at him and running about. When he went to slaughter a couple more, the grown hens made such a terrible commotion that Edward realized they didn't want him to kill the young birds, and so he opened the coop and let them join the rest of the flock. The adults herded the chicks and took them out, and they've taken care of them ever since. As a result, the hens used in this recipe were bought at the meat market.

2 tablespoons olive oil

3 tablespoons chopped pancetta or Canadian bacon

3 tablespoons chopped prosciutto

1 guinea hen (2½ to 3 pounds), cut into serving pieces

6 garlic cloves, with skins on

Salt and freshly ground black pepper

1 tablespoon crushed dried rosemary

1 small onion, finely chopped

¾ cup dry Marsala wine

1 teaspoon dried marjoram

10 chestnuts, split and boiled for 5 minutes, with shells and skins removed

2 tablespoons tomato paste

Heat the oil in a large skillet over medium heat. Add the pancetta and prosciutto. Cover and cook for about 3 minutes, then add the guinea hen pieces, skin side down. Add the garlic and salt and pepper to taste and cook, uncovered, for 5 minutes. Turn the pieces over, add the rosemary and onion, and cook until the hen is lightly browned, about 25 minutes. Add the wine and marjoram. Cover and bring to a boil. Add the chestnuts and tomato paste, stirring to incorporate the paste into the wine. Reduce the heat to medium-low, cover, and cook for 20 minutes more. Add some warm water or warm chicken stock if the pan looks dry.

Note: To find guinea hens, ask your butcher or go to www.dartagnan.com.

Serves 4

Quail with Fig Sauce

Edward adapted this dish from a Tuscan specialty, boar with fig sauce. It is wonderful served with soft polenta.

4 tablespoons olive oil

1 garlic clove, finely chopped

1 tablespoon chopped rosemary or
1 teaspoon crushed dried

1 tablespoon chopped sage or 1
teaspoon crushed dried

8 quail, butterflied

6 dried figs, coarsely chopped

1 cup dry Marsala wine

3 tablespoons chopped pancetta

3 tablespoons minced shallots

1 cup chicken stock

8 fresh figs, halved, for garnish

In a large bowl, combine 3 tablespoons of the oil, the garlic, half the rosemary, and half the sage. Add the quail, mix well, and set aside for 30 minutes. Place the dried figs and wine in a small bowl and set aside until the figs begin to soften, about 30 minutes.

Heat the remaining 1 tablespoon of oil and the pancetta in a large skillet over medium heat. Cook until the fat is rendered, about 10 minutes. Remove the pancetta with a slotted spoon and set aside. Add half the quail with marinade to the skillet and brown for about 6 minutes on each side. Remove and keep warm. Repeat with the remaining quail and marinade.

Add the shallots to the skillet and cook until soft, about 3 to 5 minutes. Increase the heat to medium-high and add the dried figs and wine. Cook until the pan is almost dry, 5 to 10 minutes. Add the stock, bring to a simmer, and cook until the figs are very soft, about 10 to 15 minutes. Return the pancetta to the sauce with the remaining rosemary and sage. Warm the quail in the sauce, in batches, about 5 minutes per batch. Transfer the quail and sauce to a platter and serve, garnished with the fresh figs.

Serves 4

Duck Baked in Salt

This is an ideal recipe for duck, because the salt absorbs the fat without making the meat salty. Boiling the duck first opens the pores of the skin and allows the fat to escape more efficiently. The carcass makes an excellent stock to eat as a broth or to cook with spaghettini (see page 184), so be sure to save it, as well as the oranges.

For the duck

1 duck (7 pounds), giblets reserved for the sauce

2 oranges, pricked with a fork

3 tablespoons chopped rosemary or 1 tablespoon crushed dried

5 garlic cloves, slivered

Freshly ground black pepper

2 pounds coarse (kosher) salt

For the sauce

Reserved duck giblets

2 tablespoons olive oil

Half a medium onion, finely chopped

2 garlic cloves, minced

Salt and freshly ground black pepper

2 cups chicken stock

½ cup sweet Marsala wine, or other sweet wine

2 tablespoons golden raisins

4 dried figs

2 bay leaves

For the duck: Put the duck in a large pot and cover it with water. Remove the duck and bring the water to a boil over high heat. Lower the duck into the boiling water and boil it for 2 minutes. Drain, wipe the duck dry (this is to reduce some of the fat), and prick the skin all over with a fork.

Stuff the oranges, 1 tablespoon of the rosemary, and 1 tablespoon of the garlic slivers into the cavity of the duck. Truss the duck and slip the remaining garlic slivers under the skin of the breast. Rub the remaining 2 tablespoons of rosemary and black pepper to taste all over the duck.

Heat the oven to 425°F.

Pour ½ inch of salt into the bottom of an ovenware pan large enough to hold the duck. Place the duck on the salt and pour the remaining salt over the duck so that it is completely covered. Place the duck in the oven and bake for 3 hours.

For the sauce: While the duck bakes, cut the giblets into small dice, keeping the liver separate.

Heat the oil in a medium saucepan over medium heat. Add the onion and garlic and cook until the onion becomes translucent, about 5 minutes. Add the gizzard and the heart, sauté for 10 minutes, then add the liver and salt and pepper to taste; cook until the liver changes color, about 3 to 4 minutes. Add the stock, wine, raisins, figs, and bay leaves and simmer, covered, for 1 hour. Remove the bay leaves.

Remove the duck from the oven and gently remove the duck from under the salt. The duck will be very tender and want to fall apart. Carefully brush the salt off the meat and serve the meat with the sauce.

Serves 6

Meatballs, Marchigiana-Style

This dish is excellent served with rice or potatoes, following a soup like Butternut Squash and Rice Soup (see page 174) or Leek and Chestnut Soup (see page 173). If we serve a pasta course first, we will not make a starch to attend the meatballs.

For the meatballs

½ pound lean ground pork

½ pound ground beef

½ cup chopped walnuts

1 cup fresh breadcrumbs

½ cup grated Parmesan cheese

2 teaspoons salt

Freshly ground black pepper

2 tablespoons finely chopped flat-leaf parsley

1 egg, lightly beaten

4 tablespoons olive oil

For the sauce

2 tablespoons olive oil

1 medium onion, coarsely chopped

1 medium leek, white only, rinsed and chopped

4 garlic cloves, sliced

½ pound white mushrooms, sliced

½ cup dry white wine

1 cup chicken stock

6 dried apricots, cut into ¼-inch strips

1 package (10 ounces) frozen peas

2 teaspoons dried mint

Salt

For the meatballs: Heat the oven to 450°F.

In a bowl, mix the pork, beef, walnuts, breadcrumbs, cheese, salt, pepper to taste, parsley, and egg. Form 20 balls, each about the size of a golf ball. Place the meatballs on a baking tray and add the oil. Roll the balls around until they are covered in oil. Bake, uncovered, until they are golden, about 10 minutes. Discard the fat and oil and set the meatballs aside.

For the sauce: Heat the oil in a shallow saucepan over medium heat. Add the onion, leek, and garlic. Cook until the onion becomes translucent, about 5 minutes. Add the mushrooms and cook for 5 minutes, then add the meatballs and wine. Cover and reduce the heat to medium-low. Cook until the wine is absorbed and no longer smells winey, about 5 minutes. Add the stock and apricots. Turn the heat back up to medium and bring to a boil. Add the peas and mint. Add salt to taste, cover, and simmer for about 20 minutes.

Serves 4

Skirt Steak with Eel

We have never been fans of "surf and turf"—steak with shrimp or lobster. But we do think skirt steak and eel work together very well. We like to serve this dish with boiled potatoes dressed with good olive oil, or sliced avocado, which is soothing next to the grilled taste, followed by a green salad.

1 large eel (about 1½ inches in diameter at thickest part), skinned,
cut into 2-inch sections

1 skirt steak (about 1 pound), cut
into 3 sections

Juice of 2 lemons

4 tablespoons extra virgin olive oil

4 garlic cloves, sliced

Salt and freshly ground
black pepper

Heat the grill.

Grill the eel pieces, turning often until they begin to brown, about 5 minutes. Place the steak on the grill and cook for about 2 minutes on each side for medium rare.

Place the eel pieces in a bowl with the lemon juice, oil, garlic, and salt and pepper to taste. Allow to marinate for 10 to 15 minutes. Cut the steak into slices about ½ inch thick. Add the steak to the eel and mix well.

Serves 4

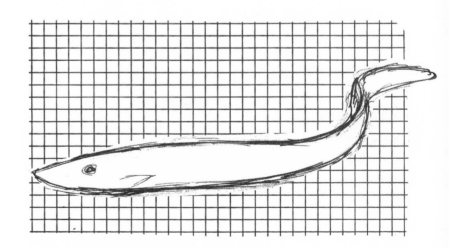

Skirt Steak with Lobster Mushrooms

Edward uses cock's comb mushrooms in this recipe, as they grow on a tree near his kitchen, but we've never seen them in the market. Lobster mushrooms (Hypomyces lactifluorum) *from the Pacific Northwest, which are similar, are abundant in our markets. They are red and fleshy, with a crunchy texture (and they don't taste like lobster). But any of the fall wild mushrooms will do in this dish. You can also use any type of grilled and thinly sliced steak.*

1 skirt steak (about 1 pound), cut into 3 sections

Salt and freshly ground black pepper

1 pound lobster mushrooms or other wild mushroom

4 tablespoons olive oil

6 garlic cloves, sliced

4 tablespoons balsamic vinegar

2 tablespoons chopped flat-leaf parsley, for garnish

Heat the grill or the broiler.

Season the steak with salt and pepper. Grill or broil it for about 2 minutes on each side for medium rare. Remove the steak, let it rest for about 5 minutes, then slice it thinly on the bias. Set aside.

Cut the mushrooms into lengthwise slices about ¼ inch thick. Heat the oil in a nonstick skillet over medium heat. Add the mushrooms and reduce the heat to low. Cook the mushrooms very slowly for about 20 minutes. Add the garlic and salt and pepper to taste, and continue cooking until the edges of the mushrooms begin to caramelize, about 15 minutes more. Add the vinegar and turn the heat up to medium. Toss for several minutes, then add the sliced skirt steak. Toss for a minute or two until the flavors meld and serve immediately, garnished with the parsley.

Note: Because the vinegar taste is very prominent in this dish, please use a high-quality balsamic.

Serves 4

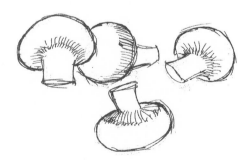

Stuffed Veal Bundles with Red Pepper Sauce

Edward first came up with the recipe for red pepper sauce, which he originally served on pasta, back in the 1970s. Since then, we've seen variations on this recipe in many cookbooks, and for good reason. It is quite delicious. Some folks use roasted red peppers, but we don't recommend it. It is the caramelizing of the vegetables that lends the sauce its sweetness.

For the sauce

4 tablespoons olive oil

2 large red bell peppers, seeded and sliced

1 medium onion, thinly sliced

3 garlic cloves, finely chopped

Salt and freshly ground black pepper

1 cup chicken stock

For the veal bundles

1/2 pound mozzarella, thinly sliced, then chopped

1/4 pound boiled ham, coarsely chopped

4 tablespoons finely chopped flat-leaf parsley

1/4 teaspoon grated nutmeg

Salt and freshly ground black pepper

8 veal cutlets (about 2 pounds), pounded thin

1 tablespoon unsalted butter

1 tablespoon olive oil

3/4 cup dry Marsala wine

2 tablespoons crushed dried rosemary

For the sauce: Heat the oil in a large skillet over medium heat. Add the bell peppers and cook, uncovered, for about 15 minutes, until the peppers begin to brown. Add the onion, garlic, and salt and pepper to taste, cover, and continue cooking until the onion begins to caramelize, about 15 minutes.

Puree the vegetables in a food processor. Add the stock, 1/4 cup at a time, until the sauce is about the consistency of light cream.

For the veal bundles: In a mixing bowl, combine the mozzarella, ham, parsley, nutmeg, and salt and pepper to taste. Place about 2 tablespoons of the mozzarella mixture in the middle of each slice of veal. Start to roll the veal around the filling, then fold in the side, and finish rolling. Tie the bundles with a piece of culinary string or close with a toothpick.

In a medium skillet, heat the butter and oil over medium heat. Add the veal bundles, toothpick side down. Turn the heat up to high and brown the bundles, about 2 minutes on each side. Remove the bundles and set aside. Pour the wine into the skillet, and when the wine comes to a boil, return the veal bundles to the skillet. Cook for about 30 seconds, then turn them over and cook for an additional 30 seconds to glaze with the wine. Add the rosemary and salt and pepper to taste. Add the red pepper sauce, cover, and simmer for about 5 to 8 minutes. Serve 2 veal bundles per person, with a couple of spoonfuls of sauce on top.

Serves 4

Veal Tails with Butternut Squash

We love to serve this simple, tasty dish on top of polenta. We find veal tails in our supermarkets. Ask your butcher for them. Oxtails can be substituted for the veal tails.

2½ pounds veal tails

Salt and freshly ground
black pepper

4 tablespoons olive oil

1 medium onion, chopped

6 whole garlic cloves, peeled

½ cup dry white wine

1 tablespoon chopped rosemary

2 large tomatoes, chopped

1 tablespoon chopped basil or
flat-leaf parsley

2 bay leaves

1½ cups chicken stock

1 cup fresh lima beans

1 pound butternut squash, peeled
and cut into bite-size pieces

Season the veal tails with salt and pepper. Heat the oil in a large skillet over medium heat. Add the veal tails and cook until lightly browned, about 3 minutes on each side. Add the onion and garlic. Cook until the onion becomes translucent, about 5 minutes. Add the wine and rosemary. Cover and cook until the wine is absorbed and no longer smells winey, about 5 minutes. Add the tomatoes, basil, and bay leaves. Cover and boil gently for 30 minutes. Add the stock and cook, covered, for an additional 30 minutes. Add the lima beans and squash and cook, covered, for an additional 20 minutes, until the squash is almost fork-tender. Remove the cover and continue cooking to reduce the sauce by about 25 percent, around 20 minutes. Remove the bay leaves.

Serves 4

Stuffed Pigskins with Pignoli Nuts

Pigskins are very delicate and tasty, and just about pure protein. This recipe is common in southern Italy—Edward first tasted it there in 1954. Pigskins tend to stick to the pan, so be sure you use a nonstick pan or a very well-seasoned iron skillet. As pigskins are not commonly available on supermarket shelves, ask your butcher for them. We like to serve these with Fall Vegetable Medley (see page 218).

4 pieces of pigskin, about 4 × 8 inches each

4 tablespoons pignoli nuts

4 tablespoons golden raisins

2 tablespoons finely chopped flat-leaf parsley

Salt and freshly ground black pepper

8 tablespoons olive oil

2 medium onions, chopped

8 garlic cloves, sliced

2 tablespoons tomato paste

2 teaspoons dried oregano

2 cups chicken stock

Spread the pigskins out on your workspace. In the center of each skin, add 1 tablespoon of pignoli nuts, 1 tablespoon of raisins, ½ tablespoon of parsley, and salt and pepper to taste. Roll the skin around the stuffing and tie with culinary string.

Heat the oil in a medium nonstick skillet over medium heat. Add the onions, garlic, and pigskin rolls. Cook for several minutes, then turn over the rolls and cook for several minutes more, until the onions become translucent. Add the tomato paste and stir. Add the oregano and stock. Cover and simmer for about 1 hour and 15 minutes, until the skins are fork-tender.

Serves 4

VEGETABLES FOR DINNER

My mother, Elinor, comes from an old Memphis family, distinguished by its community leaders, its businessmen, and its high-style southern dysfunction. From bank presidents to hysteric invalids, they run the gamut of proper and properly crazy—but I suppose that can be said of all families. Certainly, we experienced the most common type of collapse when my grandmother, Elinor Sr., died (after a long bout of a strange dementia where her conscious self left her body for periods of time): the battle of the loot. But we were able to resolve most bad feelings by coming together around the table. It was a solution determined by my mom, who may not be an Italian, but she eats like one.

Problems started at the funeral. My Uncle Norfleet, a sometimes impatient man, thought the funeral procession, with its ponderous hearse and procession of cars and noisy police escort, was going TOO DAMN SLOW, and so he kidnapped my mother and took off in his aging hatchback to beat the procession to the cemetery.

Twenty of us waited around Grandma's casket on the top of a windy hill for fifty minutes before Uncle Norfleet came roaring up, spewing exhaust fumes and complaints about suspicious street changes. I think, if I may indulge in a little roadside psychology here, that Uncle Norfleet just didn't want to bury his mom, and so he took a very long route to the cemetery.

Grandma had a lot of antiques, flatware, dishes, doodads, and whatnots. There was some nice stuff—and lots and lots of junk that needed to be sorted and disposed of. Mom asked me to come to Memphis to help her, as I am one of those people who can divest easily. She also knew, due to some pre-house-emptying phone calls, that the designation of household fill might be a little antagonistic. And so she made a rather brilliant move. Mom hired two ladies to cook classic southern soul food, lunch and dinner, for whomever was around. This brought the sometimes cantankerous players to the table at mealtimes, where they were soothed with collard greens and sweet potatoes, corn pones and grits.

As in Italian cookery, there is a grand tradition of all-vegetarian dining in the south (okay, many of the vegetables are cooked in pork fat), and I have always preferred to dine on vegetables when in Memphis. One of my favorite joints is The Little Tea Shop near the river, where Brooks Brothers–clad bankers (usually white men) are bossed around by chubby, feisty waitresses (usually black ladies), and served hot, stewed country vegetables, minty iced tea, and sass. My grandmother's cook, Luella Johnson, was a fantastic chef, bringing out the delicate flavors of local vegetables with only pork fat, salt, and pepper. Her cooking is impossible to reproduce, because she compensated for a million variations in the product—its freshness, age when picked, and storage conditions—with slight alterations in her cooking time and heat. She had a limited repertoire, but she was master of it.

Back to Grandma's house: I came to clear, and I was ruthless. I handled coat closets and attic boxes full of moldy photographs and kitchen drawers full of bent spoons and frayed dishrags, while Mom and her brother took turns selecting pieces of furniture. But it was uncomfortable for them, and the circumstances were emotionally charged. Weird sibling baggage started to play out between them—differing opinions as to what Grandma's intent would have been vis-à-vis that art work, this rug, that bowl spoke a subterranean language of disappointment and regret. And complicating matters somewhat was ninety-two-year-old Aunt Lizzie, my grandmother's younger sister. Ever the lady in her linen skirt suits, Aunt Lizzie sat in the middle of all the chaos and roiling emotions and insisted that "Somebody, somebody must take this duck head–handled umbrella. Now I want to know, who is going to take this umbrella?"

Thank God for lunch. The table was set with all of Grandma's old-fashioned dinnerware, water glasses, and individual butter pats. There were numerous people gathered: core family, cousins whom we tried to hoist items on, well-wishers who hoped we would hoist items on them. All in the vicinity at mealtime joined us. We ate baby butter beans and black-eyed peas and sweet turnip greens with homemade corn sticks. And by the time a plate of homemade cookies had made its way to the table, Uncle Norfleet was suggesting to Mom that he didn't really want the rug and Mom was suggesting to Norfleet that the fish platter would look nicer in his house. Aunt Lizzie left after lunch with the duck head umbrella.

Peace reigned for a while, and inevitably passions would flare up again. But no situation seemed insurmountable, as dinner wasn't so long away.

FALL VEGETABLES AND SALADS

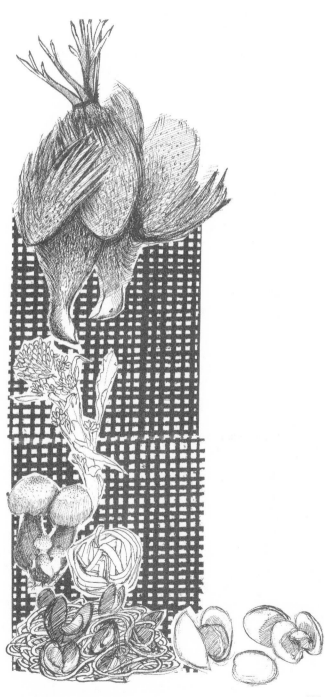

Baked Beets and Potatoes

This is a perfect fall side dish, which we eat with roasted birds. We always boil beets and potatoes separately, otherwise the beets will stain the potatoes red. Save the beet water to make Beet Granita (see page 155). We prefer slicing potatoes and beets to cubing them because the large faces can pick up more of the seasoning.

2 medium potatoes (we prefer Yukon Gold)

2 medium beets (save the greens to add to Fall Vegetable Medley, see page 218)

1 medium onion, thinly sliced

4 tablespoons olive oil

Salt and freshly ground black pepper

Heat the oven to 450°F.

Fill two pots with cold water. Add the potatoes to one pot and the beets to the other. Bring to a boil over high heat and cook for 10 minutes. Drain, peel, and cut the potatoes and beets in ½-inch thick slices.

Place the potatoes, beets, and onion in a baking dish. Sprinkle the oil over them and add salt and pepper to taste. Bake, uncovered, in the hot oven, turning occasionally, until the potatoes are browned, about 15 minutes.

Serves 4

Cham's Baked Brussels Sprouts

Cham made these for Thanksgiving one year, and they are delicious. Paul, Lisa's husband, also makes them, as a garnish for beef stews and chicken soups. These are very good if they are a little burnt.

½ pound Brussels sprouts, stem ends trimmed and light, outer leaves removed

4 tablespoons extra virgin olive oil

4 garlic cloves, finely chopped

Salt and freshly ground black pepper

Heat the oven to 400°F.

Cut the sprouts in half lengthwise and place on a baking tray, cut side up. Do not overlap. Drizzle with 3 tablespoons of the oil. Sprinkle with 1½ tablespoons of the garlic and season with salt and pepper.

Bake, uncovered, until the edges of the sprouts brown, about 20 minutes. Remove from the tray and toss in a serving bowl with the remaining garlic and 1 tablespoon of oil. Adjust the seasoning.

Serves 4

Cauliflower with Beans

We often serve a side dish like this one next to a roasted chicken, or as part of a vegetable second course. However, to turn this dish into a light supper, add a can of drained Italian tuna fish and serve at room temperature.

1 cup fresh cranberry beans
(about 1 pound in the shell)

Salt

2 bay leaves

2 pounds cauliflower, broken into
florets

1 large semi-ripe tomato, diced

1 cup arugula, torn into bite-size
pieces

4 tablespoons extra virgin olive oil

1 tablespoon finely chopped
flat-leaf parsley

Freshly ground black pepper

Place the beans in a medium saucepan and cover them with about 1 inch of water. Add a pinch of salt and the bay leaves. Cover and simmer over medium heat for about 45 minutes, until the beans are tender.

Bring a large pot of salted water to a boil over high heat. Add the cauliflower and cook until it is fork-tender, about 5 minutes. Do not overcook.

Drain the cauliflower and the beans and remove the bay leaves. Combine the cauliflower and beans in a serving bowl with the tomato, arugula, oil, parsley, and pepper to taste.

Note: You can also use dried cranberry beans. Either soak them overnight or cover them with water and bring to a hard boil for a couple of minutes. Then drain, and proceed with the recipe. The dried beans will take longer to become tender.

Serves 4

Cauliflower with Roasted Peppers

This dish can be made as soon as the peppers come in, in the early fall, and is good through the winter. We love it with chicken.

2 pounds cauliflower, broken into
florets

2 large red bell peppers, charred,
peeled, seeded, and cut into strips
about ¾ inch wide

1 tablespoon finely chopped
flat-leaf parsley

1 tablespoon fresh lemon juice

3 tablespoons extra virgin olive oil

Bring a large pot of salted water to a boil over high heat. Add the cauliflower and boil for about 4 to 5 minutes, until the cauliflower is al dente. Drain.

In a large bowl, combine the cauliflower, the pepper strips, and the parsley, lemon juice, and oil. Toss gently and serve at room temperature.

Serves 4

Sweet and Sour Cipollini

Cipollini are small, flat, and sweet onions—a real winter treat. They can, however, be difficult to peel, so soak the onions first, as you would pearl onions. These onions are excellent with boiled and grilled meats. They also are a great addition to an antipasto plate, or as part of a vegetable second course.

3 tablespoons extra virgin olive oil

18 whole cipollini onions, peeled

2 garlic cloves, sliced

1 tablespoon sugar

3 tablespoons white wine vinegar

1 small ripe tomato, peeled, seeded, and pureed

Salt and hot pepper flakes

1 large red bell pepper, charred, peeled, seeded, and sliced

1 tablespoon finely chopped flat-leaf parsley, for garnish

Heat the oil over medium heat in a skillet large enough to hold the onions without overlapping. Add the onions and garlic. Cover and cook the onions for about 5 minutes, until they begin to brown on the bottom. Turn the onions over and cook them for an additional 5 minutes.

Dissolve the sugar in the vinegar, and then add the vinegar mixture to the onions, along with the tomato puree and the salt and hot pepper flakes to taste. Cover and simmer for 15 minutes.

Toss the cipollini with the roasted pepper and serve garnished with the parsley.

Serves 4

Kale and Cabbage

You can substitute other leafy greens like Swiss chard or collard greens in this dish. Swiss chard will cook more quickly than the tougher greens.

1 pound kale, tough stems removed, chopped

1 pound Savoy cabbage, chopped

2 medium potatoes, peeled and cut into quarters (we prefer Yukon Gold)

3 tablespoons olive oil

4 garlic cloves, sliced

Salt and hot pepper flakes

Bring a large pot of salted water to a boil over high heat. Add the kale and boil, uncovered, for about 10 minutes, then add the cabbage and potatoes and continue boiling for 5 minutes. Reserve 3 cups of the cooking water, then drain.

Heat the oil in a large skillet over medium heat. Add the garlic and cook until it begins to color, about 2 minutes. Add the drained vegetables, salt and hot pepper flakes to taste, and about 1 cup of the reserved water. Reduce the heat to medium-low. Boil gently, partially covered, for about 30 minutes, until the potatoes are tender. If the vegetables get too dry, add a little more of the reserved water to moisten. Smash the potatoes with a fork and blend with the vegetables. Adjust the seasoning.

Serves 4

Puree of Parsnips and Potatoes

We like to serve this side dish with roasted birds and meats.

2 parsnips, scraped and cut in half

1 carrot, scraped and cut in half

1 potato, peeled and cut in half
(we prefer Yukon Gold)

Salt and freshly ground
black pepper

4 tablespoons extra virgin olive oil

Half a medium onion, chopped

1 tablespoon chopped flat-leaf
parsley, for garnish

In a large pot, combine the parsnips, carrot, and potato and cover with water. Add salt and bring to a boil over medium-high heat. Cook the vegetables until tender, about 20 minutes. Drain the vegetables and mash them by hand or with a potato ricer. Add salt and pepper to taste.

Heat 2 tablespoons of the oil in a small skillet over medium heat. Add the onion and cook, covered, until it becomes translucent, about 5 minutes. Add the onion to the parsnip mixture and stir it in well. Garnish with the remaining 2 tablespoons of oil and the parsley.

Serves 4

Red Peppers with Onions and Potatoes

This is an excellent side dish for poultry. You can also double this recipe and poach an egg on top of the cooked vegetables (see instructions on page 17). We often eat eggs with vegetables for supper.

2 medium potatoes (we prefer
Yukon Gold)

4 tablespoons olive oil

1 large red bell pepper, seeded
and sliced

1 medium onion, sliced

1 tablespoon chopped flat-leaf
parsley

Salt and freshly ground
black pepper

Place the potatoes in a medium pot and cover with water. Bring to a boil over medium-high heat and boil for 5 minutes. Drain. When the potatoes are cool enough to handle, peel them and cut into slices about ½ inch thick. Set aside.

Heat 3 tablespoons of the oil in a large skillet over medium heat. Add the bell pepper and cook, uncovered, for about 12 minutes, until the pepper becomes soft. Add the onion, parsley, and salt and pepper to taste, cover, and continue to cook over medium heat until the onion becomes translucent, about 5 minutes. Remove the onion and pepper with a slotted spoon and add the remaining 1 tablespoon of oil. Add the potato slices one at a time—do not overlap—and cook them over medium-low heat for about 10 minutes, until the bottoms are golden brown. Turn the potatoes over, add salt, and continue cooking until that side is brown as well, about 5 minutes. Add the pepper and onion back to the skillet, cover, and cook for several minutes more, to warm them through and meld the flavors.

Serves 4

Roasted Peppers with Purslane and Wild Rucola

We love this with grilled meats or fish. Wild purslane and rucola come up in our garden in the fall. You can substitute sliced endive and domestic arugula.

2 large red bell peppers

1 cup purslane

1 cup wild rucola leaves

4 tablespoons balsamic vinegar

3 tablespoons extra virgin olive oil

2 garlic cloves, sliced

Salt and freshly ground black pepper

Roast the bell peppers over an open flame or under your broiler until they are blistered all over. Remove the charred skin and split the peppers open. Remove the seedpods and discard. Slice the peppers into ¾-inch slices and gently mix in a serving bowl with the purslane, rucola, vinegar, oil, and garlic. Season with salt and pepper to taste.

Serves 4

Boiled Pears and Potatoes

This is a very unusual dish, excellent with birds or pork. The cooking time will depend on the ripeness of the pears. Be careful not to overcook, or the pears will fall apart.

4 small potatoes, sliced (we prefer Yukon Gold)

1 bay leaf

2 firm pears, peeled, cored, and sliced

1 tablespoon olive oil

1 tablespoon unsalted butter

3 tablespoons chopped pancetta or Canadian bacon

1 medium onion, thinly sliced

Salt

Bring a small pot of salted water to a boil and add the potatoes and the bay leaf. Cook until the potatoes are tender, about 20 minutes. Drain. Remove the bay leaf.

Bring a small pot of salted water to a boil. Add the pears and cook until tender, about 2 minutes. Drain.

In a medium skillet, heat the oil and butter over medium heat and add the pancetta. Cook until the pancetta renders its fat, about 5 minutes. Add the onion. Cook until it becomes translucent, about 5 minutes. Add the potatoes, pears, and salt to taste to the skillet, and gently mix.

Serves 4

Rape with Fresh Tomatoes

Brocoletti di rape, or rabe, as it is called in dialect, is related to both the cabbage and turnip families. It is a slightly bitter, leafy green vegetable with florets something like broccoli. When selecting rape (pronounced RA-pay), look for bunches heavy with florets. This is a lovely vegetable dish, but it is also good served on pasta. Just cut the rape into bite-size pieces. Boil a cut pasta like penne until it is al dente and serve the vegetables on top, garnished with a little extra virgin olive oil.

2 bunches rape, stems removed

3 tablespoons extra virgin olive oil

4 garlic cloves, sliced

Hot pepper flakes (optional)

1 fresh tomato, chopped

Salt

Bring a large pot of salted water to a boil over high heat. Add the rape and cook 2 minutes. Drain and rinse in cold water.

Heat the oil in a large skillet over medium heat. Add the garlic and hot pepper flakes to taste (if using) and cook until the garlic softens, about 3 minutes. Add the tomato, cover, and simmer for about 10 minutes, until the tomato breaks up. Add the rape and salt to taste. Simmer, uncovered, for 10 minutes, until the rape is tender.

Serves 4

Butternut Squash alla Parmesan

This is a very warm and filling side dish that also works well as a main course, and it's perfect for a buffet table.

Vegetable oil for frying

2 pounds butternut squash, cut in half, seeds removed, peeled, and cut crosswise into $1/4$-inch thick slices

Salt and freshly ground black pepper

All-purpose flour for dredging

2 eggs, lightly beaten, or 4 egg whites

2 cups marinara sauce (see page 258)

$1/2$ pound fresh mozzarella, sliced thin (optional)

$3/4$ cup grated Parmesan cheese

Heat the oven to 450°F.

Heat $1/2$ inch of oil in a large nonstick skillet over medium heat. Season the squash with salt and pepper. Dust the squash slices in the flour, then dip them in the eggs. Slip the squash slices into the oil a few at a time and fry until golden brown, about 3 minutes on each side. Drain on paper towels. Repeat until you have fried all of the squash slices.

Pour $1/4$ cup of sauce into the bottom of a 9 × 3 × 9-inch baking dish. Add a layer of cooked squash slices, and then another $1/4$ cup of sauce, then a layer of mozzarella and/or grated Parmesan. Continue building up the casserole until you have used all the ingredients.

Bake in the oven for 30 minutes.

Serves 8

Roasted White Turnips

We harvest white turnips during the summer and fall. These are excellent served beside broiled shrimp and scallops, and broiled whole fish.

4 or 5 medium white turnips, peeled and sliced

4 tablespoons olive oil

1 teaspoon chopped rosemary

Salt and freshly ground black pepper

As soon as you cut them, place the sliced turnips in cold water, as they tend to discolor.

Heat the oven to 450°F.

Place the sliced turnips on a baking tray—do not overlap. Add the oil, rosemary, and salt and pepper to taste. Bake until they are golden brown, about 12 minutes. Turn them over and brown the other side, about 8 minutes more.

Serves 4

Fall Vegetable Medley

We harvest lima beans, cabbage, and leeks in the fall, but you can substitute other fall vegetables, like beet greens, Brussels sprouts, kale, and boiled cranberry beans.

4 tablespoons olive oil

1 medium onion, coarsely chopped

4 garlic cloves, crushed

Half a small head of Savoy cabbage, cored and chopped

4 small potatoes, peeled and sliced (we prefer Yukon Gold)

1 medium leek, white only, rinsed and cut into 4 sections

1 cup chicken stock

Salt and freshly ground black pepper

1 cup fresh lima beans

1 tablespoon chopped basil or flat-leaf parsley

Extra virgin olive oil, for garnish

Heat the olive oil in a medium saucepan over medium heat. Add the onion and garlic, cover, and cook until the onion becomes translucent, about 5 minutes. Add the cabbage, potatoes, leek, and stock, and season with salt and pepper. Cover and simmer for 15 minutes. Add the lima beans and basil. Cover and cook until the beans are fork-tender, about 10 minutes.

Garnish each portion with extra virgin olive oil.

Serves 4

ABOUT NUTS

The Giobbi family always eats nuts after a meal. The onset of walnuts in the fruit bowl is as sure a sign of fall as tangerines and red maple tree leaves and honking ribbons of geese flying high in the wet, gray sky. Some of my favorite desserts are a slice of quince paste served with a handful of walnuts, or a scoop of vanilla ice cream flavored with kahlua and sprinkled with chopped walnuts. We love Torta Adelaide, a rich walnut and date cake that we first tasted when our friend Flavia Destefanis brought it one Thanksgiving. Likewise, we eat many almonds, all year round. But in fall we grind them into a flour and make almond poppy seed cake. Even the dogs appreciate nuts.

Mike (1984 to 1998) was able to shell a peanut with his teeth. Speed Racer (1969 to 1982), who was buried standing up because rigor mortis set in before my parents were finished digging the hole, ate nuts, and more. It was 1972, and we were living in Rome for the year. Speed Racer, a Labrador retriever who was about twice the size of a typical Roman dog, had come with us. He was an exceptionally good-natured animal, with a high tolerance for pain, a constant loopy joy, and a love of swimming. We children used to walk him all over our neighborhood of the Piazza Di Spagna, allowing him to swim in the fountains and poop indiscriminately on the swanky Via della Croce. One cold November afternoon, Lisa, Cham, and I were walking Speed Racer through the Borghese Gardens, at the top of the Spanish Steps. We stopped to buy a paper cone of freshly broiled chestnuts from one of the many vendors who dot the park, squatting beside hot braziers, the fingertips of their gloves cut off and their noses red from the raw park air. We were quite independent for school-age kids, and we could speak enough Italian to make our wishes known. We continued along the path, peeling our steaming chestnuts while Speed enjoyed the buffet of Italian park smells, only to discover that most of the nuts were brown and putrid, rotten to the core. We returned to the vendor—three children, ages nine, ten, and twelve—and showed him the rotten nuts, asking for others or a refund. Upon closer inspection, he was not as picturesque and apple-cheeked as he had seemed, but a decrepit bum, with decaying teeth and mean eyes, rags around his shoulders, and shoes separating from their soles. He told us, basically, to get lost. We were surprised and frustrated as we didn't know what recourse we had; we were kids, and we knew he was jerking us around because we were young. We argued a bit more, just to retain some sense of dignity. And as we did, Speed Racer, in a glorious moment of canine intuition, lifted his leg and put out the man's brazier.

The vendor jumped up and started yelling at us and waving his dusty arms, and we kids dropped our rotten chestnuts and took off running through the garden and down the Spanish Steps and back to the doorway of our apartment, where we giddily fitted the key in the lock. Speed Racer was right there beside us, his tail wagging happily, guilty as the old stone streets of Rome.

FALL
DESSERTS

Almond Torte with Poppy Seeds

In the search for desserts that use up extra egg whites, we found a version of this simple torte in The United National International School Cookbook. *This recipe is very grown-up: It is not too sweet and very light. It is best served fresh from the oven.*

6 egg whites

¼ teaspoon cream of tartar

1 cup sugar

1 cup finely ground almonds

½ cup all-purpose flour

8 tablespoons (1 stick) unsalted butter, melted

2 teaspoons almond extract

1½ teaspoons grated lemon zest

1 tablespoon poppy seeds

Confectioners' sugar or whipped cream, for garnish (optional)

Heat the oven to 375°F. Butter a 9-inch round cake pan.

In a large bowl, beat the egg whites and cream of tartar with a whisk until they form soft peaks, then beat in the sugar. Lightly but thoroughly fold in the almonds, flour, butter, almond extract, lemon zest, and poppy seeds. Pour the batter into the pan and bake for about 35 minutes, until a thin knife plunged into the center of the cake comes out clean.

Serve with confectioners' sugar or whipped cream.

Serves 8

Ginger Pears

This is a simple, refined dessert that is both sweet and spicy. It is best served at room temperature.

2 slightly underripe Bosc pears

2 cups water

½ cup superfine sugar

1 tablespoon grated fresh ginger

4 sprigs mint or 4 slivers lemon zest, for garnish

Peel and halve the pears. Core the pears but leave the stems on. Set aside.

In a shallow pot with a fitted cover, combine the water and sugar and heat over medium heat until the sugar dissolves.

Add the pears and ginger. Cover and poach over medium heat for 15 minutes. Turn off the heat and allow the pears to cool in the liquid.

Remove the pears. Cook the liquid over medium-high heat until it is reduced by two-thirds, about 5 minutes.

Serve the pears dribbled with the reduced sauce and garnished with a mint sprig or sliver of lemon zest.

Serves 4

Chestnut Puree with Whipped Cream

We first tasted this simple dessert in Hungary, where it is often served, although we learned that it is also popular in Fruili, in the northeast corner of Italy. You need to serve only a small scoop, as the puree is very rich. Indeed, we've made truffles with it. Refrigerate the puree until quite cold, roll into small balls and freeze them on a baking tray, then dip in melted dark chocolate and return to the fridge until the chocolate is hard. Keep the chestnut truffles refrigerated.

24 chestnuts

½ cup plus 1 tablespoon sugar
(or more to taste)

3 tablespoons dark rum
(or more to taste)

½ teaspoon vanilla extract

½ cup heavy cream

To prepare the chestnuts, score them and place them in a medium pot. Cover with water and bring to a boil over medium-high heat. Allow the chestnuts to boil for about 20 minutes, until they soften. Drain. When the chestnuts are cool enough to handle, shell and skin the chestnuts (the warmer they are, the easier this will be).

Puree the chestnuts in a food processor with ½ cup of the sugar, or more to taste, and 2 tablespoons of the rum, or more to taste, and the vanilla extract. Puree to a smooth consistency.

Press the puree through a food mill to aerate it—the puree should be fluffy after going through the mill. Scoop the puree into dessert glasses.

Beat the cream until it is almost stiff. Add 1 tablespoon of sugar and 1 tablespoon of rum and whip until the cream forms peaks. Plop dollops of the whipped cream on top of the puree and serve.

Serves 4

Fig and Pear Tart

We often experiment with an apple tart recipe we learned at New York's French Culinary Institute—and this is one example. It is most impressive to watch our friend, the chef Arlene Jacobs, spread apples on top of her tarts like a dealer at a black jack table.

For the pastry

1 cup all-purpose flour

1 tablespoon confectioners' sugar

⅛ teaspoon salt

8 tablespoons (1 stick) unsalted butter, cold

1 egg yolk

For the filling

30 small figs, peeled

1 cup water

1 cup granulated sugar

Juice of half a lemon

3 firm pears, peeled, cored, and sliced (we like Bosc)

Heat the oven to 400°F. Butter a 10-inch tart pan.

For the pastry: In a mixing bowl, combine the flour, confectioners' sugar, and salt. Cut in the cold butter until it is crumbly. Add the egg yolk and combine until the dough holds together when gently squeezed. If it does not hold together, add a teaspoon or two of cold water. Do not knead. Pull out a walnut-size pinch of the dough. Press the dough with the heel of your hand against a cool hard surface, like a piece of marble. Smear the dough until the butter in the flour mixture is smooth, then scrape it off the board and set aside. Do this with all of the dough. Form the dough into a disk, wrap with plastic, and refrigerate for 30 minutes or more.

For the filling: In a medium pot, combine the figs, water, granulated sugar, and lemon juice and cook, uncovered, over medium-low heat for 1 hour, until the water evaporates and the figs are very soft. (It will take less time to cook the figs if they are very ripe.) Roll the pastry out and fit it into the tart pan. Return the pastry to the refrigerator for 10 minutes.

Remove the pastry from the refrigerator and pour in the cooked figs. Arrange the pear slices on top in an overlapping pattern. Bake the tart for 10 minutes, and then lower the temperature to 350°F and bake for an additional 50 minutes, until the crust and pear slices are golden brown.

Allow to come to room temperature before serving.

Serves 8

Torta Adelaide

We first tasted this lovely, rich dessert when our friend Flavia Destefanis brought it to Thanksgiving lunch one year. It is very simple to make, and best served with a dollop of whipped cream.

1 cup walnuts

1 cup dates, pitted (about 10 large)

1 cup sugar

6 eggs, separated

1 teaspoon baking powder

Sweetened whipped cream, for serving

Heat the oven to 350°F. Butter and flour a 10-inch springform pan.

Chop the walnuts in a food processor to a flourlike consistency. Chop the dates finely; if you prefer to use a food processor, pulse to chop with ¼ cup of the sugar. Avoid overchopping or the dates will mash together.

In a large bowl, beat the egg whites until almost stiff, then gradually add the sugar, beating all the while. Fold in the egg yolks, combining gently but thoroughly. Fold in the dates and walnuts. Sift the baking powder into the mixture and fold in gently but thoroughly.

Pour the batter into the pan and bake for about 30 minutes, until a toothpick inserted in the center comes out clean. The cake will have risen, but it will fall as it cools. It's okay.

Serve with sweetened whipped cream.

Serves 8

Apple Compote Crumble

This dessert is a favorite of the kids, and easily put together. We often make the apple compote and the crumble ahead of time, and keep them in the fridge in (separate) containers.

4 apples (we like Golden Delicious)

2 tablespoons water

2 tablespoons granulated sugar

½ cup brown sugar

¼ cup all-purpose flour

2 tablespoons unsalted butter

½ teaspoon ground cinnamon

½ cup heavy cream

¼ teaspoon vanilla extract

Heat the oven to 350°F.

Peel and core the apples. Cut them into large cubes and place in a medium pot. Add the water and 1 tablespoon of the granulated sugar. Cook, partially covered, over medium heat, for about 15 minutes, until the apples are tender and their juices evaporate. We prefer the apple compote to be on the chunky side. Take off the heat and cool to room temperature.

In the meantime, prepare the crumble. In a small pie plate, combine the brown sugar, flour, butter, and cinnamon, crumbling the ingredients with your fingers until they are well combined. Place the crumble in the oven and bake for 15 minutes. Remove the crumble and fluff it up with a fork. Return the crumble to the oven for another 5 minutes. Be careful not to burn it.

Remove the crumble and allow it to harden, periodically fluffing the crumbs up with a fork. You may need to squeeze some of the bigger pieces between your fingers to break them up.

Beat the cream until it forms soft peaks. Add the remaining 1 tablespoon of granulated sugar and the vanilla extract.

To assemble, place ½ cup of apple compote in a dessert glass. Sprinkle a tablespoon or more of crumble on top, then a dollop of whipped cream.

Note: For a more adult taste, add a tablespoon of Calvados to the whipped cream.

Serves 4

Concord Grape Granita

Bluish-black concord grapes are quite resistant to cold, which is why they are plentiful in late fall in the Northeast. We usually make jelly with the strong juice, but this recipe is a delicious and graceful alternative. We love it as a simple dessert for company, or part of our Thanksgiving feast. If you do not have a jelly bag, line a sieve with a few layers of cheesecloth and place over a bowl.

1½ pounds concord grapes

1½ cups water

½ cup superfine sugar

Whipped cream (optional)

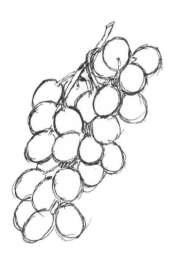

Wash the grapes and remove the stems. Place the grapes in a medium heavy-bottomed pot and add 1 cup of the water. Bring to a boil over medium heat and boil the grapes for about 15 minutes, until they are soft. Pour the grapes and juice into a jelly bag hung over a bowl. Allow the juice to strain through the bag. As it cools, squeeze the bag to extract as much juice as possible. You should have about 1¼ cups of juice.

In a small pot, bring the remaining ½ cup of water and the sugar to a boil over medium heat and boil until the sugar dissolves, a couple of minutes. Combine the juice and sugar syrup in a pan that conducts cold well. (We like to use an aluminum baking pan.) Place in the freezer and every 15 to 30 minutes, run the tines of a fork through the ice to break up the crystals. Over the course of 3 hours, the crystals will get small and crumbly.

For a very refined granita, pour into a food processor and pulse to grind the crystals. Then return the granita to the pan and continue to freeze, running the tines of a fork through it a couple of times over the next 30 minutes.

Serve plain in a glass, or with whipped cream.

Note: How quickly the granita freezes will depend upon your freezer. The granita can be kept in a plastic container in the freezer for up to 1 week. The recipe does work with Welch's grape juice, but it's not as delicious.

Serves 4

WINTER

CENA DELLA VIGILIA

My mother's Christmas cactuses always bloom right on time. They explode from their heavy earthenware pots and drop fat red starbursts over the rim. My brother, sister, and I are assigned the job of moving them, but we have to be careful. Although they look sturdy, the blossoms fall off easily when disrupted. But disrupt we must, as the Christmas tree goes into the bay windows where the cactuses have flourished.

The living room of the house in Katonah is rarely used, except on Christmas Eve, when this part of the house is revealed like an icon on a feast day, and the room becomes a sort of church where the rituals of Christmas are enacted. It was the holiest room in my childhood, except, of course, for my own personal holy places—a rock in the woods, a spring down the road, a nook in the pond where there were always frogs.

The tree is decorated with decades worth of homemade ornaments: little Nina, Pinta, and Santa Maria made from walnut shells; love beads strung on sagging wires once shaped like stars; papier-mâché Santas and angels, all decaying and colorless, or chewed into unidentifiable lumps by the late Thelma, a cat who indulged in the digestive aid of tinsel. Over the years my sister, brother, and I have forgotten who made which of the repugnant flour ornaments, including Dad's series of penises and testicles that he made to our great delight and our mother's feigned disgust. "I think I made that one," says I, pointing to a rather artful ornament. "No," corrects Cham. "I did." Childhood memories are fiercely protected things, and so each of us tells our spouses who really made what.

But the tree is a sideline to the real action of the house: the cooking. It actually starts the day before, when Dad leaves the house at 7:00 a.m. in order to be first in line at Randazzo's fish store on Arthur Avenue in the Bronx. Arthur Avenue is lined with nondescript tenement apartments, two- and three-family houses, and commercial buildings that reflect classic

Italian-American ticky-tack. But the street is alive with activity. Goods from shops spill out their doors, with foodstuffs, crockery, and knickknacks piled high on makeshift bleachers. A deli owner packs his Cadillac with cheese as a young man in butcher's white totes a quarter of a cow's carcass down the avenue on his shoulder. At the café in the vegetable market, grandpas sip espresso and read *Il Giornale,* and grandmas with complicated braids argue over the dates of baptisms and weddings held a generation ago. Arthur Avenue is really a lot like Italy, only without the ancient architecture and the modern motor scooters.

Dad has become friends with many of the shop owners, and when I tag along to carry his bags, he tells them, "*Lei ha nata in Firenze* [she was born in Florence]." "*Brava!*" is the standard response. Dad chats up the geezers who have been cutting meat or handling mushrooms their whole lives and departs every store with a recipe, a cooking tip, or a couple of extra clams.

Every Arthur Avenue veteran's first stop this time of year is the fishmongers, because the traditional Christmas Eve Cena della Vigilia (the "vigil dinner") is an all-fish meal. Outside Randazzo's there is already a line of people who carefully eye the bags of customers exiting the store, worried that the triglia will all be gone before their turn. Dad knows the store like he does the layout of his bedroom, and promptly picks out whitebait and smelts for frying, shrimp, clams, scallops, and a flounder fillet to stuff in green olives for our antipasto plate, crabs for pasta, sole fillets and crabmeat for the entrée. Since 1912, the Randazzo family has been selling a wide variety of pristinely fresh fish—up to a hundred, in fact. The Randazzo men are proud. Proud fishmongers, proud New Yorkers, proud Rangers fans. With their full approval, my father fingers a plump smelt. He lifts the fish and sniffs it. "Very fresh," he tells me. "You can tell because it smells like cucumber."

Our next stop is the vegetable market, a 17,500 square foot indoor marketplace at the epi-center of Arthur Avenue, and home to about twenty booths. Around the perimeter of the space are businesses like Rosa's dry goods and Mike's organ meats. In the center there is a green maze of vegetable vendors selling flower-heavy brocoletti di rape, speckled cranberry beans, and boxes of tangerines that smell so sweet I can't even smell the puffing cigar of the old fellow who sells them. We load up on our vegetables, and before dropping them off in the car, stop by Teitel Brothers. One doesn't really browse here. If you pause ever so briefly over the many buckets of beans and olives, one of the Teitels usually starts yelling, "What are you looking for? You want capers?" Actually, we need hunks of Parmesan cheese and dried figs.

With our change, Dad is handed that most ubiquitous of Italian Christmas foods, a sweetened yeast bread called panettone.

There are a few sumptuous meat stores on Arthur Avenue, but the one that Dad goes to is Biancardi's. Rabbit, goat, baby lamb, capon, duck, pig's feet, rack of lamb, veal, and twelve different kinds of sausage are available every day, as well as pork and lamb liver, hearts, and tripe, and around the holidays, veal sweetbreads. When we enter, all the countermen shout "Edwardo!" Walking along Biancardi's counter with my father is akin to hiring headphones at a museum exhibit: As we stop before each example of animal flesh, he explains just how he'd like to cook that particular beast. But we buy only what we need: ground pork for the lasagne, and a large capon for Christmas Day. Sal Biancardi gives Dad a panettone with his change.

Our final stop is Tino's Deli, packed with Italian goodies: two-inch-square knots of home-smoked mozzarella; imported *finochiata,* a fennel-flavored salami from Tuscany; a rare Marchigiana prosciutto called carpenia; and a heavy, pale wheel of *Pecorino di fossa*—Pecorino cheese that has been aged in ditches. When Dad enters the door, the owner, Giancarlo, maneuvers through the crowd to give him a welcome hug. We buy pasta, Primus Novello olive oil from Sicily, Palmera tuna (for our caponata), and rich Villa Balsemico di Modena vinegar, and sip a shot of sweet espresso. On our way out, Giancarlo hands Dad a panettone.

On Christmas Eve day a large pot of cranberry bean soup boils gently on the stove—lunch for the worker bees. During the course of the morning we have minced clove after clove of garlic; roasted, peeled, and sliced peppers; chopped parsley; grated Parmesan cheese into mounds like small mountains of cream-colored snow; passed cups and cups of home-canned tomatoes through the sieve; rolled out piecrusts; tearfully chopped onions; and all the while the dog—and there is always a big fat Lab around at Christmas—trolls the edges of the counter, dragging his long pink tongue along the floor where the linoleum meets the cabinetry, licking up loose breadcrumbs and bits of cheese.

Pots and knives and skillets are washed over and over, so many times that our hands become as chapped and scaly as the paws of a tortoise. The kitchen is warm and steamy, and smells of wine and parsley. The panettone shift from one tabletop to another, to make room for prepped ingredients, until finally finding a home on top of the washing machine. Cham and his wife, Laine, chase down toddlers. Mom wraps, and scrounges through the re-gifting closet as she remembers people she has forgotten. Or she decorates, opening boxes loaded with thick green candles, red ribbon, and plastic bags of pinecones, some small as an acorn, others large as a softball, that roll off her arrangements and under the couch, to be discovered, incongruously, in mid-summer. Lisa, efficient as always, chops, and then disappears for a smoke on the cold front porch, to ponder, I think, the old decaying weeping willows that hover over the pond. Her husband, Paul, makes eggnog with a very free hand, and we all stay slightly tipsy on it for the remainder of the holiday. Kevin entertains the kids.

It is usually snowy at Christmas, and Kevin helps the kids drag their sleds up the hill above the frozen pond, where the dog waits, tail wagging, brown eyes locked on a child. Mo settles himself on the oval sled, grabs the sides, and orders Kevin to push. With a shove he whips down the hill, skidding the surface of the packed snow, down to the banks of the pond, up over the short rock ledge, and then bang! Onto the ice for another 10 feet of skidding, during which the dog comes running, his toenails scratching the ice, his feet sliding out from under him, loping and slipping toward Mo as he finishes in a slow spin, and then the dog is on him, barking uproariously and humping the back of Mo's blue parka with uninhibited doggy-style joy.

Carson, who is on the threshold of adolescence and considers both her brother and the dog's antics to be the lowest ebb of humanity, sits in an igloo, listening to rap on her iPod.

At lunch we come together for cranberry bean soup flavored with a little bacon fat, bread, and a salad; and maybe a few of the ever-present tangerines of Christmas, and a couple of walnuts. Dad crunches two of them together in his hand, which seems a feat of gargantuan strength to the children. Their eyes open wide in wonder at their grandpa's uncanny strength. He smiles, and tells them his reflexes are so fast he can catch a flying bug in his hand, too. Then he points his finger at the smallest grandchild and tells him to pull and then promptly farts. The older children laugh uproariously. It is a trick that works only once per grandchild.

After lunch we combine breadcrumbs, parsley, cheese, and olive oil to make the stuffing for shellfish, combine the roast peppers and boiled shrimp, the scallops and artichokes, the tuna mixed into the caponata. The crab sauce simmers on the stove, emitting a lovely herby smell. The sole fillets are rolled around their stuffing of ricotta and parsley, and the shrimp shell sauce, pink and sweet, bubbles in a saucepan nearby. The pies are filled with lemon pudding and piled high with snowy meringue. After sink upon sink of dishes have been washed, the kitchen floor swept, the wreaths hung, the table set with the best linen from my mother's southern past, the children unhappily crowbarred into jackets and ties, we wait, in our fancy clothes, for the sound of our guests' tires in the driveway. Then Dad begins frying. Out of the hot oil, into the straw baskets to drain, dashed with salt. We eat sperling, little cuttlefish, baby octopus, slivers of squid, and sometimes a whole, small smelt, which we eat like corn on the cob. We open champagne and toast each other, and the family, and friends.

There are always guests for the Christmas Eve dinner. They come for years at a time, and then drop out of circulation. There was the decade of Bob and his housemate, Gene. Bob was a snippy man, with eyes unwilling to love us, but Gene was a miracle. He was an opera singer and after dinner would sing Christmas carols with a voice so resounding the music would fill all the volumes of the downstairs rooms, and then creep up the stairs and into the bedrooms on the second floor, where we children waited in our beds for the miracle of Santa Claus. Then, for many years, the Roloffs, he in double-breasted suits and ascots, and she in dirndls or miniskirts—you never knew. Or the years Jinkie and her husband, Bob, came over and Bob, who claimed to be psychic, predicted everyone's future (mine involved horses and a cute boy—incorrectly, by the way, as by the time I was into boys, I was out of horses).

Craig Claiborne often spent Christmas Eve with us, loving and distracted as a southern belle. He brought adult presents for us children—once a collection of home decorating items from Gucci, which we tried, vainly, to reconcile with our Barbie dolls and Peanuts comic books. The food writer Jay Jacobs came as well. Small and tidy, Jay enjoyed a martini or two or three before dinner. One year when he came, he was the only guest. Throughout her childhood, my sister had written a Christmas list and at the top of it had asked for a monkey. By the time Lisa was an adult, she didn't want the monkey anymore, but wrote it down on a list for our mother as a kind of keepsake of passions past. That Christmas, Mom and I had gone to the pet store to pick up a peacock for Dad (for many years peacocks roamed the property). The peacock was so large and disagreeable that a monkey, in a nearby cage, seemed quite charming. We decided on the spur of the moment to get Lisa her monkey. During the course of the meal, family members in the know kept leaving the table to feed bananas to the monkey. By dessert, only Jay and Lisa were left at the table, and Jay, having had a few more martinis, snored, while Lisa ate alone in silence.

For most, the verb "to fast" evokes images of abstinence: knees sore from praying, tummies growling with annoyance. But not in Italy. Indeed, La Vigilia, the traditional holy fast of Christmas Eve, is more of a feast. Composed of three, seven, nine, or twelve fish dishes, the vigil Italians keep in anticipation of the birthday of Christ is one long, delicious celebration.

As a child, I used to love to count the Cena della Vigilia fishes, but when I'd ask my father what the seven sacraments were, he'd say, "pasta alla vongole, Brodetto alla San Benedetto . . . ." Different regions of Italy interpret the number and types of fish dishes different ways—sometimes tradition will differ within a specific region from one village to the next. Cena della Vigilia is of Roman Catholic origin. Up until the days of the Second Vatican Council, which began in the early 1960s, the vigil of Christmas was a day of fast and abstinence. Only one meal was allowed for the day, and Catholics abstained from eating meat. It is out of this prohibition that the feast of the fishes arose. The dinner was traditionally served before the family attended midnight mass, and it served multiple purposes: its largesse satisfied hunger, celebrated the imminent birth of Christ, and kept everyone awake until midnight. The number of fishes served, however, is a relatively arbitrary one.

Christianity, like most religions, employs numerology in its ritual. And when it comes to Cena della Vigilia, the application of numerological significance is fairly liberal. Some towns serve 9 fish, representing the 9 months of gestation. Others serve twelve, for the twelve apostles. Or three, for the three kings, or the holy trinity. I've heard the seven fishes representing, besides the seven sacraments, the seven O Antiphons from Vespers, the days of the week, and the 52 weeks in the year (the numbers five and two equaling seven). The Roman Catholic altar is set with three candles on each side, with Christ's image in the center—another seven. There are the seven hills of Rome. And a partridge and a pear tree. Whatever the number of courses, the art of Cena della Vigilia is to use recipes that will not fill the diners before they are served the main course, and to serve them in a modest, steady flow. Dishing up the antipasto on family-style platters inevitably encourages guests to take seconds, and long pauses between courses induce diners to munch on bread. Another consideration in planning Cena della Vigilia is presentation. We learned the hard way not to cook a large whole fish and divide it up. Not only is it difficult to prepare for a large group, but also serving it is a mess when the final course should be the most appetizing. "For years I thought this was a feast of abundance," says Dad. "But it's not." It's a feast of celebration in restraint.

The antipasti dish is a merry, diverting course, varied in taste and texture, and beautiful as well. Indeed, one consideration is the color of the foods: Stuffed black mussels, boiled shrimp with green artichokes, grilled white scallops with roasted red peppers, pink tuna with fresh cranberry beans, all served on one plate. The children depart shortly after this course is served, to lie on their backs under the Christmas tree and gaze up through the branches at the vast possibilities of their futures. We adults continue to eat, knowing that life is short.

For the pasta course we eat a delectable linguine with crab sauce, followed by tender sole with crabmeat, or Brodetto alla San Benedetto, a piquant fish stew which calls for green tomatoes, red peppers, and vinegar, ladled on a piece of garlic-rubbed bruschetta, the only bread we serve. The meal ends with a lemon meringue pie, or poached pears, and then everyone finds an after-dinner drink and heads out for the annual visit to the living room. A fire is stoked, and Mom worries the stereo system (we are one of those low-tech families) until she can get the tape to play.

We settle onto couches. Children lay across dogs, couples rest in each other's arms, and the older folks let their lids fall closed and their breathing become deep. The stereo plays a tape of Dylan Thomas reciting his prose poem, *A Child's Christmas in Wales,* and the Giobbis (those who are awake) mouth all of the words and watch the candles burn, and wonder at the wonderousness of coming together. The smallest children fall asleep, as do the dogs, who conk out as soon as they lay down anyway. When the recording is over, the oldest and the youngest stumble upstairs to bed, while those in middle age have another egg nog and try to put together robots and dollhouses, listening for the pad of a small, suspicious foot at the top of the stair. After the stockings have been stuffed, their jingle bells muffled, and hours of consultations with the directions for assembling a bicycle, we find, upon exhausted completion, that the handlebars are screwed on backward.

We drink espresso and eat Arthur Avenue panettone in the morning, knee-high in holiday debris: the gift-wrapping, ribbons and Styrofoam peanuts; mothers make thank-you lists, and the children search, in vain, for one more overlooked present. Those of us who can head back to the kitchen to help Dad prepare lunch. Christmas Day we eat sweet, slippery lasagne followed by a glistening brown capon stuffed with clementines and dressed with drippings, giblets, and pureed figs; brocoletti di rape; and sweet potatoes baked to a crisp with olive oil and garlic. We toast the day with glasses of deep red, fruity homemade wine and attack with vigor the pies filled with butternut squash. Although various family members (mainly spouses), overcome by the plethora of gifts and the two days of orgiastic eating, announce they intend to go to Bermuda for the holidays next year, no one does. We all come back, year after year, to these same sunny rooms, just like the blossoms on our mother's Christmas cactuses.

ESSENTIALS OF MEAL PLANNING

We eat richer foods in the winter than at any other time of year: thick soups, pasta with meat sauces, and stewy main courses. Winter vegetables tend to be starchy and robust: We eat sweet potatoes and white potatoes (throughout we recommend Yukon Gold, our general use favorite) and turnips regularly. Brussels sprouts, cauliflower, brocoletti di rape, Savoy cabbage, kale—all are excellent cooked in their own blanching juices with garlic and hot pepper, and we prepare any number of vegetable combinations this way. For salads we eat thinly sliced fennel dressed with fine extra virgin olive oil, lemon juice, and salt and pepper. We also cook fennel a number of ways: braised, then sprinkled with cheese and broiled, for example, and cooked with other vegetables.

One of the most exciting seasonal foods in winter is Maine shrimp, or sweet shrimp, as the Japanese call them (you'll see them on sushi menus this time of year). Maine shrimp have never been frozen. They are small, sometimes minuscule, but usually about two to three inches long with the heads on, and run about forty to the pound. They are, without doubt, the sweetest shrimp we've ever tasted, and so tender! Slightly gelatinous, they cook very quickly and are divine any way you choose to prepare them.

During the winter months we always have nuts, dried figs, quince paste, tangerines, and pears in the house. Most of our winter desserts involve these ingredients. Indeed, we particularly love the fruits of winter. As children, we often visited our maternal grandmother at her house in Florida, a tidy little stucco structure surrounded by a large flank of rough grass that dropped to the beach. There were royal palm trees in the view corridor, and the carpeting was white shag: Very West Palm Beach, circa 1977. A favorite outing was to the Ter Marsch fruit stand, where we would buy January and February's exquisite honeybell oranges and eat them in the car, dribbling juice all over the upholstery. We still order honeybells every year.

MAKING SOUP

Ironically, a Giobbi family drinking story is as much about drinking soup as drinking booze. When Edward was a young man studying art in Italy, he and a friend of his challenged his grandfather to a wine-drinking contest. Sure their youth would take the day, the boys were shocked to be out-drunk by a seventy-year-old man. His secret, he told them, was eating bean soup earlier in the day. I've always kept that in mind, and can remember one occasion in New York, when I joined a group of friends to hit the gay piano bars in the Village. I ate a big bowl of homemade bean soup before going out, and was able to drink and sing *Over the Rainbow* on key for most of the night. Not so my rowdy college companions, who not only became totally inebriated, but were soundly bounced from the bar for demanding the pianist abandon Rodgers and Hammerstein and play *Ramblin' Man* instead.

The older my parents get, the more often they eat soup. They eat soup every day, followed by a salad and an apple. It is highly digestible, wonderfully healthy, and I think even psychologically comforting. When I suffered from stomach disorders during the year following the 9/11 disaster, I ate soup until my stomach healed. Lisa's daughter, Snow, who began life as a picky eater, first discovered the joys of flavor when we mashed a few beans in the broth from a bean soup. Now she's an enthusiastic consumer of all things soupy.

While we make soup from all types of beans, one of our favorites is the cranberry bean, which is sold fresh starting around Thanksgiving and through the winter. Cranberry beans, also called shell beans (as are other traditionally dried beans when they are sold fresh), are white with rusty speckles. When cooked, they turn a pale beige. Making soup with fresh beans is particularly delightful, as the texture remains firm and consistent throughout and there are no tough skins.

Soups are made from prime ingredients, like the white part of the leek, chopped vegetables, grains, legumes, and cuts of meat. Everything you put in will end up on your spoon. In contrast, stocks are made from lesser ingredients, like the green parts of the leek, fennel tops, the odds and ends of vegetables in the fridge, Parmesan cheese rinds (which are now showing up in cheese stores), and bones from raw and cooked meat, fish, and birds, pan drippings, all types of herbs, even lemons that have lost either their skin to zesting or some of their juice to juicing. We've made stock with the leftover sauce from osso buco, the leftover crabs from linguine with crab sauce, and the leftover carcasses of whole fish. And of course, birds. The big birds, like the Thanksgiving turkey and the Christmas capon, are fought over at our house, and it is the sly Giobbi sibling who graciously declines slices of leftover meat, taking home only the carcass. Likewise, the remains of a baked ham or a smoked turkey make flavorful stocks. Savory vegetables like onions, leeks, and garlic, herbs, and root vegetables like carrots and turnips get thrown in, and the whole mess is simmered for two hours. After straining, we defat the stock by either using a defatting cup, or using Edward's messy but very effective technique of pouring the stock into a jar set in a bowl, allowing the fat to rise to the top, then pouring in a bit more stock to send the fat over the rim and into the bowl. For clear stocks, we make sure not to boil the pot too vigorously, and we remove the scum that rises to the top continuously. Our Zia Ada in Le Marche keeps her chicken stock clear by putting the chicken in the pot, covering it with water, and boiling for five minutes. Then she discards all the water and returns the chicken to the pot with fresh water and the remaining ingredients. This does the same thing as skimming the scum—the bits of blood and other proteins that cloud the stock are discarded with the first boil.

Stocks can be kept indefinitely in the refrigerator if they are re-boiled every third day. We often use stocks from one batch to start off a new one. Although we mix poultry and meat broths, we do keep fish broths separate. Fish broths love fennel, otherwise known as anise, a licorice-tasting bulb with feathery greens (which we sometimes substitute with a hit of anisette), and bay leaf. With them, we make light, aromatic fish soups like Fish Soup with Anisette, or prepare Risotto with Crabmeat. In a pinch, we simply boil a portion or two of linguine fini in fish stock instead of water, then garnish with herbs. We also cook spaghettini in chicken, game bird, or beef broth, garnished with Parmesan cheese. The dish is simple and tasty enough to please children, and elegant and unusual enough to impress guests. In short: an utterly Italian take on the first course—light, quick, and delectable.

WINTER
FIRST COURSES

Green Olives Stuffed with Fish

This dish is a variation on one concocted by the chefs along the lungomare, *or beachfront, in San Benedetto, which is a variation of the country classic, Olives Ascoli-Style. We eat them as part of our appetizer plate at the Cena della Vigilia. It is best to use green olives that have been cured in lime—they are crisper and greener—however, you can use green olives cured in brine. Just soak them in cold water for several hours before using.*

38 large green olives

2 tablespoons olive oil

1 pound white fish fillet, like sole, flounder, or whiting

⅓ cup sherry

2 tablespoons finely chopped flat-leaf parsley

Hot pepper flakes

2 tablespoons grated Parmesan or Pecorino cheese

2 tablespoons fine breadcrumbs, plus additional for dredging

All-purpose flour for dredging

1 egg, beaten

Vegetable oil for frying

Salt

Lemon wedges, for garnish

Pit the olives by paring away the flesh in a long continuous curl from end to end, the way you would peel an orange. If you cut off a piece by mistake, don't throw it away, you'll still be able to use it.

Heat the olive oil in a small skillet over medium heat. Add the fish, sherry, parsley, and a pinch of hot pepper flakes. Cook, breaking the fish up with a wooden spoon, until it is cooked through and falls apart, about 5 minutes. Do not brown. Let the fish cool down.

In a small bowl, mash the fish and add the grated cheese and 2 tablespoons of the breadcrumbs.

Form 1 teaspoon of the stuffing into an oblong shape. Carefully wind the olive flesh around the stuffing. You can patch on some of the pieces of olive if you cut off any by mistake. A gentle squeeze will meld the olive and stuffing together. Repeat for the remaining olives.

Have ready three plates: one with flour, one with the beaten egg, and one with breadcrumbs. Dredge the stuffed olives in the flour, then dip the olives in the egg, then roll briefly in breadcrumbs.

Heat the vegetable oil in a small skillet. The oil must be very hot. You can test it by throwing a pinch of flour into the oil. If the flour pops, the oil is ready for frying. Fry the olives until they are golden brown, about 1 minute per side. Drain on paper towels, add salt to taste, and serve on a platter with lemon wedges.

Makes 38 olives

Cranberry Beans with Caviar

We find paddlefish caviar, which is not from an endangered fish, to be delicious. This dish is very elegant and indulgent, without all the silliness of crackers and condiments that usually accompany caviar.

2 cups chicken stock

1 cup fresh cranberry beans (about 1 pound in the shell), or ³/₄ cup dried great Northern beans, soaked overnight and drained

Half a celery rib

2 garlic cloves, with skins on

1 bay leaf

Salt and freshly ground black pepper

Extra virgin olive oil

4 tablespoons paddlefish caviar

4 slices bruschetta, for serving (see page 17)

Bring the stock to a boil in a medium soup pot over medium heat. Add the beans, celery, garlic, and bay leaf, cover, and cook at a low boil until the beans are tender, about 45 minutes (about 1½ hours for dried beans).

The beans should be loose and slightly soupy. Pick out the celery, garlic, and bay leaf and discard. Pour the beans into small bowls. Add salt and pepper to taste. Lace the bowls with extra virgin olive oil and serve with a tablespoon of caviar on top of each portion.

Serve with a piece of bruschetta.

Serves 4

Shrimp and Artichoke Salad

We've often served this colorful, sassy dish as a part of the first course of Christmas Eve's Cena della Vigilia. You can replace the artichokes with sliced roasted red peppers.

1 pound medium shrimp

2 jars (6½ ounces each) marinated artichoke bottoms, packed in oil

2 tablespoons finely chopped flat-leaf parsley

2 garlic cloves, finely chopped

4 tablespoons olive oil

4 teaspoons fresh lemon juice

Salt and freshly ground black pepper

Place the shrimp in a medium saucepan and cover with water. Bring the water to a boil, and cook until the shrimp turn pink, about 4 minutes. Drain the shrimp.

When the shrimp are cool enough to handle, peel and devein them. Cut each shrimp crosswise on the bias into thin slices.

Drain the artichoke bottoms and chop them finely. Put the artichokes into a mixing bowl and add the parsley and garlic. Blend well. Add the shrimp, oil, and lemon juice. Add salt and pepper to taste. Toss and serve.

Serves 4

Cranberry Bean and Faro Soup

This is the perfect winter soup. Add a few tablespoons of boiled tubettini or other small cut pasta to the bottom of each bowl before adding the soup to make it even more substantive. The quality of faro varies in cooking time and price. We recommend the Faro Perlato brand.

4 tablespoons olive oil

1 medium onion, coarsely chopped

3 garlic cloves, finely chopped

1 cup whole canned Italian tomatoes, chopped

1½ cups fresh cranberry beans (about 1½ pounds in the shell)

5 cups water

1 medium carrot, chopped

1 cup chopped Savoy cabbage

1 celery rib, chopped

2 tablespoons chopped flat-leaf parsley

1 teaspoon dried basil

Salt and hot pepper flakes

4 tablespoons faro (spelt)

Grated Parmesan cheese, for garnish

Extra virgin olive oil, for garnish

Heat the olive oil in a soup pot over medium heat. Add the onion and garlic and cook until the onion becomes translucent, about 5 minutes. Add the tomatoes, reduce the heat to low, cover, and simmer for about 10 minutes, until the tomatoes break up. Add the beans, water, carrot, cabbage, celery, parsley, basil, and salt and hot pepper flakes to taste. Cover and boil gently for about 1½ hours, until the beans are tender but firm. Add the faro and cook for an additional 45 minutes, or until tender.

Serve the soup garnished with grated cheese or a drizzle of extra virgin olive oil.

Serves 4

Ceci Bean Soup with Shellfish

This is a version of a Marchigiana specialty. Ceci beans are also known as garbanzo beans.

4 tablespoons olive oil

¼ cup chopped pancetta or Canadian bacon

1 leek, white only, rinsed and chopped

1 medium onion, chopped

4 garlic cloves, finely chopped

2 tablespoons chopped flat-leaf parsley

2 cups whole canned Italian tomatoes, chopped

2 celery ribs, chopped

1 pound dried ceci beans, soaked in water overnight and drained

6 cups water

2 teaspoons dried basil

2 bay leaves

Salt and freshly ground black pepper

1 cup small cut pasta such as tubettini

24 medium shrimp, peeled and deveined

32 mussels, scrubbed

Heat the oil in a large soup pot over medium heat. Add the pancetta. When the fat is partially rendered, about 5 minutes, add the leek, onion, garlic, and parsley. Cook until the onion becomes translucent, about 5 minutes. Add the tomatoes and celery, cover, and simmer for about 10 minutes, until the tomatoes break up. Add the beans, water, basil, bay leaves, and salt and pepper to taste. Cook at a low boil over medium heat until the beans are tender, about 2 hours. Remove 2 cups of the beans and puree them in a food processor. Return the pureed beans to the soup. (You can puree more of the beans if you like, but the beans must be quite soft, otherwise the puree will be nubbly.)

Bring a medium pot of salted water to a boil over high heat. Cook the pasta until almost al dente. Do not cook the pasta completely to al dente; it will finish cooking in the soup. Drain and add to the soup. Add the shrimp and mussels to the soup and continue cooking until the mussels open, about 5 minutes. Remove the mussels from the shells (set aside 16 mussels in their shells for garnish). Return the mussels to the soup and discard the shells. Remove the bay leaves from the soup.

Serve each portion garnished with two mussels in the shell.

Serves 8

Fish Soup with Anisette

The licorice taste of anisette is wonderful in this elegant fish soup. It is a perfect first course when followed by Broiled Sardines with Breadcrumbs (see page 270), Codfish with Brocoletti di Rape (see page 268), or Fillet of Sole Stuffed with Crabmeat (see page 273).

¼ cup olive oil

2 leeks, whites only, rinsed and chopped

1 medium onion, chopped

2 garlic cloves, minced

2 cups whole canned Italian tomatoes, chopped

1 teaspoon saffron, soaked in 1 tablespoon warm water

1 cup dry white wine

2 bay leaves

1½ teaspoons chopped thyme or ½ teaspoon dried

Salt and hot pepper flakes

3 cups crab or fish stock, warmed (see pages 260 and 25)

2 medium potatoes, peeled and diced (we prefer Yukon Gold)

2 pounds fish fillets, like sole or red snapper, skinned and cut into 3-inch pieces

2 tablespoons anisette

8 slices bruschetta, for serving (see page 17)

4 tablespoons finely chopped flat-leaf parsley, for garnish

Heat the oil in a large Dutch oven or heavy-bottomed pot over medium heat. Add the leeks, onion, and garlic, and cook until the vegetables become soft, about 5 to 8 minutes. Add the tomatoes and saffron water. Cook until the tomatoes break up, about 10 minutes. Add the wine, bay leaves, thyme, and salt and hot pepper flakes to taste. Cook about 5 minutes, until the wine no longer smells winey. Add the stock, turn the heat up to medium-high, and bring to a boil. Lower the heat to medium and add the potatoes. Cook the soup at a low boil until the potatoes are tender when prodded with a fork, about 20 minutes.

Add the fish and cook for 5 minutes, until the fish is cooked through. Remove the bay leaves. Add the anisette, adjust the seasoning, and serve with two pieces of bruschetta in the soup, or on the rim of the bowl, if you like. Garnish with the parsley.

Note: You can make this dish richer by placing a dollop of garlic-flavored mayonnaise (preferably homemade) on top of each slice of bruschetta.

Serves 4

Capon Broth with Angel Hair Pasta

After the big meals of Christmas Eve and Day, no one is much interested in eating—certainly not anything heavy. That's why we always make this broth on December 26th, with the leftover carcass.

8 cups water

Carcass and skin of a 10-pound capon

2 medium carrots, cut into thirds

2 celery ribs, cut into thirds

2 clementines (from inside the capon)

1 large onion, peeled and stuck with 4 whole cloves

1 leek, whites and greens, washed and cut into thirds

5 sprigs flat-leaf parsley

2 bay leaves

Salt

4 angel hair nests, or 1/2 pound fidelini pasta

Juice of half a lemon

Grated Parmesan cheese, for garnish

In a large soup pot, combine the water, carcass, carrots, celery, clementines, onion, leek, parsley, and bay leaves and bring to a low boil over medium heat. Cook for about 2½ hours, until the broth tastes strong.

Strain the broth and discard the bones and vegetables. Defat the broth and add salt to taste.

Boil the pasta in the broth until al dente, about 5 minutes. Add the lemon juice.

Serve garnished with a sprinkle of grated cheese.

Serves 4

Potato, Rice, and Sausage Soup

We like to serve this soup for lunch, followed by fennel salad and a piece of cheese.

3 tablespoons olive oil

1 large onion, coarsely chopped

2 garlic cloves, chopped

1 cup whole canned Italian tomatoes, chopped

2 tablespoons finely chopped flat-leaf parsley

4 cups water

2 cups chopped Savoy cabbage

2 celery ribs, chopped

1 medium carrot, sliced

Salt and freshly ground black pepper or hot pepper flakes

½ pound Italian sweet sausages

½ cup rice

Grated Parmesan cheese or extra virgin olive oil, for garnish

Heat 2 tablespoons of the olive oil in a large soup pot over medium heat. Add the onion and garlic and cook until the onion becomes translucent, about 5 minutes. Add the tomatoes and parsley. Cover and simmer for about 10 minutes, until the tomatoes break up. Add the water, cabbage, celery, carrot, and salt and pepper to taste. Cover and boil gently for 15 minutes.

Heat the remaining 1 tablespoon of olive oil in a medium skillet over medium heat. Prick the sausages and cook them in the skillet for about 10 minutes, until they are brown all over. Remove the sausages and slice.

Add the rice and sausages to the soup and continue cooking until the rice is tender, about 10 to 15 minutes.

Serve each portion with grated cheese or a drizzle of extra virgin olive oil.

Serves 4

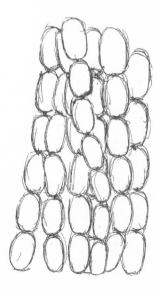

Linguine with Blue Crab Sauce

We serve this pasta every Christmas Eve, as part of the Cena della Vigilia feast. The recipe comes from Edward's godfather, Tomasso, an Italian fellow who worked in the Pennsylvania coal mines. He never spoke English, and sent his money home to Abruzzo. An elegant man, he wore a derby hat and smoked his cigars in a holder he made from a rabbit bone. Tomasso was famous in the neighborhood for this pasta sauce, which the local ladies could never reproduce, although Edward's mother said the secret was he never washed his pots well. It is very light and powerfully tasty. A version of this recipe was first published in Italian Family Cooking *in 1971.*

6 live blue crabs

4 tablespoons olive oil

1 large red or green bell pepper, seeded and finely chopped

3 garlic cloves, minced

Salt and hot pepper flakes

3 cups whole canned Italian tomatoes, chopped

4 tablespoons finely chopped flat-leaf parsley

1 teaspoon dried basil

3/4 pound linguine

Clean the crabs: Remove the top shell by forcing a heavy knife blade under the flap on the underside of the crab. Push the knife in and wedge off the shell. Discard the shell. Remove the gills and discard. Wash the crabs. You can also ask your fishmonger to clean the crabs.

Heat the oil in a large skillet over medium heat. Add the bell pepper, garlic, and salt and hot pepper flakes to taste. Cook until the garlic begins to take on color, about 3 minutes. Add the tomatoes, 2 tablespoons of the parsley, the basil, and the crabs. Cover and boil gently for 1 hour, until the vegetables in the sauce have completely broken down. Remove the crabs. Save them to serve as a second course, or to make crab stock (see page 260).

Bring a large pot of salted water to a boil over high heat. Add the pasta and cook until it is almost al dente. Drain and add the pasta to the sauce. Finish cooking the pasta in the sauce over moderate heat, mixing constantly, for about 4 minutes, until the pasta is al dente.

Serve each portion with a sprinkling of the remaining 2 tablespoons of parsley.

Note: You can substitute 2 lobsters for the crabs in this dish. Kill the lobsters first by plunging a sharp knife between the head and body, severing the spinal cord. Cook the lobsters as you do the crabs, and substitute fresh chopped mint for the basil.

Serves 4

Spaghettini with Maine Shrimp

Because it is so light, this is an excellent first-course pasta.

Maine shrimp, or sweet shrimp, have never been frozen, and their season is short, January through March, if you're lucky. They are small, sometimes minuscule, but usually about 2 to 3 inches long with the heads on, and run about 40 to the pound. We buy them from our local fishmonger, but you can also find them at Farm 2 Market (www.farm-2-market.com).

2 pounds Maine shrimp, washed, heads and shells removed and reserved

1½ cups dry white wine

6 tablespoons olive oil

6 garlic cloves, minced

Salt

¾ pound spaghettini

Hot pepper flakes

1 cup grated Parmesan cheese

4 tablespoons finely chopped flat-leaf parsley

In a skillet, combine the shrimp heads and shells, the wine, 3 tablespoons of the oil, and 1 tablespoon of the garlic over medium-high heat. Add salt to taste. Cook the shells until they are pink, crushing them down into the wine with a wooden spoon as they cook. Cover and cook for about 20 minutes. Strain the shells and save the liquid. Discard the shells.

Bring a large pot of salted water to a boil over high heat. Add the pasta and cook until it is al dente. Drain.

In the meantime, heat the remaining 3 tablespoons of oil over medium heat in a skillet large enough to hold the pasta. Add the remaining garlic and cook for about 3 minutes, until the garlic begins to take on color. Add the shrimp and cook about 3 minutes, until the shrimp begin to turn pink and curl up. Add salt and hot pepper flakes to taste. Add the drained pasta and the shrimp broth. Stir, mixing well. Add ¾ cup of the cheese and the parsley, mixing gently. Adjust the seasoning.

Remove the pasta from the heat, and garnish with the remaining ¼ cup of cheese.

Serves 4

Spaghettini alla Foriana

This recipe has been in the family of our friend Salvatore Del Deo for generations. It was the required pasta for the Cena della Vigilia supper in Salvatore's ancestral home of Forio, on the island of Ischia, in the Bay of Naples.

12 to 14 anchovies, preferably cured in salt, or 24 anchovy fillets packed in oil

²/₃ cup olive oil

4 garlic cloves, minced

¾ pound spaghetti or spaghettini

½ cup walnut meats, broken

½ cup golden raisins

½ cup pignoli nuts

1 tablespoon dried oregano

Salt and freshly ground black pepper

4 tablespoons finely chopped flat-leaf parsley, for garnish

If you use anchovies packed in salt, remove the fillets from the bone, then allow the fish to soak in warm water for about 10 minutes, then take the fillets off the bone. If you use anchovy fillets packed in oil, drain the anchovies.

Heat the oil in a large skillet over medium heat. Add the garlic and all but 4 of the anchovy fillets. Cook until the garlic takes on color, about 3 minutes, and the anchovies have broken up.

Bring a large pot of salted water to a boil over high heat. Add the pasta and cook until it is al dente. Scoop out about 1 cup of cooking water and drain the pasta. Add the pasta to the skillet with the walnuts, raisins, pignoli nuts, oregano, and salt and pepper to taste. Toss over low heat, until the ingredients are heated through. Add cooking water as needed if the pasta seems dry.

Garnish each serving with parsley and a reserved anchovy fillet. Serve immediately.

Serves 4

Trenette with Baccala and Walnuts

This is a Christmas Eve specialty from Liguria. Baccala, which is dried salt cod, must be soaked before cooking, so plan ahead.

1 pound baccala, soaked in cold water for 3 days, with water changed twice daily, drained

4 tablespoons olive oil

1 small onion, finely chopped

2 garlic cloves, finely chopped

1 tablespoon finely chopped flat-leaf parsley

Hot pepper flakes (optional)

2 cups whole canned Italian tomatoes, chopped

1 heaping tablespoon golden raisins

1 teaspoon dried basil

Salt

4 tablespoons dry white wine

1½ cups fresh breadcrumbs

¾ pound trenette, spaghettini, linguine, or spaghetti

½ cup chopped walnuts, toasted in a small dry skillet for about 4 minutes

Place the baccala in a soup pot and cover it with water. Boil the baccala gently over medium heat for 10 minutes. Remove the baccala and let it cool. Remove the skin and bones from the baccala and break up the fish into small pieces.

Heat 3 tablespoons of the oil in a large skillet over medium heat. Add the onion, garlic, parsley, and hot pepper flakes (if using) to taste. When the onion becomes translucent, about 5 minutes, add the tomatoes, raisins, basil, and salt to taste. Cover and simmer for 10 minutes, until the tomatoes break up.

Add the fish and the wine to the tomato sauce, cover, and simmer for about 15 minutes.

Heat the remaining 1 tablespoon of oil in a skillet over medium heat. Add the breadcrumbs and toast them, stirring often, until they are lightly browned, about 3 minutes.

Bring a large pot of salted water to a boil over high heat. Add the pasta and cook until it is al dente. Scoop out about 1 cup of the cooking water and drain the pasta. Combine the pasta and sauce in a serving bowl, adding pasta water to keep the sauce very loose.

Garnish each serving with the walnuts and breadcrumbs.

Serves 4

Penne with Ham and Potatoes

This is a great pasta to make for large groups as the recipe easily doubles and triples. Have the ham cut in a ½-inch thick slice.

8 tablespoons extra virgin olive oil

1 large onion, chopped

½ pound sliced boiled ham, cut into ½-inch cubes

Salt and freshly ground black pepper

¾ cup dry white wine

1 tablespoon finely chopped flat-leaf parsley

1 teaspoon dried marjoram

¾ pound cut pasta, such as penne or ziti

2 large potatoes, peeled and diced (we prefer Yukon Gold)

Half a head Savoy cabbage, cored and shredded

1 cup grated Pecorino or Parmesan cheese, for garnish

Heat 5 tablespoons of the oil in a large skillet over medium heat. Add the onion and cook until it becomes translucent, about 5 minutes. Add the ham and season with salt and pepper to taste. Add the wine, parsley, and marjoram and simmer, covered, over low heat until the wine is absorbed and no longer smells winey, about 5 to 10 minutes.

In the meantime, bring a large pot of salted water to a boil over high heat. Add the pasta, potatoes, and cabbage. Boil the pasta and vegetables until the pasta is al dente. Drain the pasta and vegetables and put them in a serving bowl. Add the remaining 3 tablespoons of oil and the sauce. Toss well and garnish with grated cheese.

Note: Broccoli florets may be added as well. Add the broccoli to the boiling water a couple of minutes after you add the pasta and other vegetables.

Serves 4

Penne with Cauliflower and Ground Pork

We've eaten this simple, addictive pasta as both a first course and as a second course followed by a green salad. It is very hearty but not rich.

4 tablespoons olive oil

3 medium onions, chopped

4 garlic cloves, chopped

1 pound lean ground pork

¾ cup dry white wine

4 cups beef or chicken stock

4 ounces dried porcini mushrooms, soaked in 1 cup of warm water for about 15 minutes, then chopped (optional)

2 tablespoons chopped flat-leaf parsley

2 tablespoons chopped basil

Salt and freshly ground black pepper

¾ pound cut pasta such as penne

2 pounds cauliflower, cut into florets

Freshly grated Parmesan cheese, for garnish

Heat the oil in a large skillet over medium heat. Add the onions and garlic and cook until the onions become translucent, about 5 minutes. Add the pork and cook, stirring frequently, until it browns, about 10 minutes. Add the wine and continue cooking until the wine is absorbed and no longer smells winey, about 5 minutes. Add the stock, mushrooms (if using), parsley, and basil. Cover and cook over medium-low heat for 1 hour, until the sauce takes on the consistency of a thick ragu. Add salt and pepper to taste.

Bring a large pot of salted water to a boil over high heat and add the pasta. After 5 or 6 minutes, add the cauliflower. Continue boiling another 5 to 6 minutes, until the pasta is al dente and the cauliflower is tender. Drain the pasta and cauliflower.

Toss the sauce, pasta, and cauliflower together in a large serving bowl and garnish with grated cheese.

Serves 4

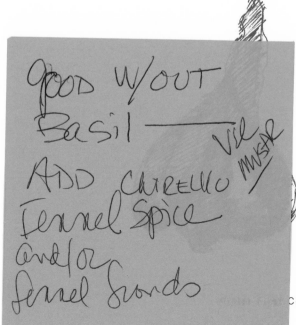

good w/out
Basil —
ADD Chirello
Fennel spice
and/or
fennel fronds

Chicken Gnocchetti with Sauce

This is a perfect dish to make after you have prepared a big pot of chicken stock. The recipe for stock (below) can be doubled. The leftover boiled chicken is used in the gnocchetti (so called because they are smaller than regular gnocchi), and the stock is used for boiling them. Use the marinara sauce, or simply dress the gnocchi with butter and chopped sage.

For the chicken stock

1 chicken (3 pounds)

1 large beef bone

4 quarts water

3 large carrots

3 celery ribs

2 large onions, each stuck with 2 whole cloves

5 sprigs flat-leaf parsley

2 bay leaves

1 teaspoon dried basil

Salt and freshly ground black pepper

For the gnocchetti

2 cups boiled chicken, finely chopped

2 cups plain mashed potatoes, cooled

2 eggs plus 1 egg yolk

1 scant tablespoon grated lemon zest

$\frac{1}{2}$ teaspoon grated nutmeg

Salt and freshly ground black pepper

All-purpose flour for dredging

For the chicken stock: In a large pot, place the chicken, beef bone, water, carrots, celery, onions, parsley, bay leaves, basil, and salt and pepper to taste. Simmer gently for 2½ hours. Remove the chicken and set aside. When it is cool, skin and bone the chicken, and chop 2 cups finely for the gnocchetti. Discard the beef bone, vegetables, and bay leaves. Defat the chicken stock.

For the gnocchetti: In a large bowl, mix together the chicken, mashed potatoes, eggs and egg yolk, lemon zest, nutmeg, and salt and pepper to taste. Shape the chicken mixture into 24 dumplings and roll them in the flour. Be careful, they are very soft.

To assemble

2 cups marinara sauce
(see page 258, optional)

2 quarts chicken stock

2 tablespoons unsalted butter

Salt and freshly ground black
pepper

Grated Parmesan cheese, for garnish

To assemble: Heat the marinara, if you're using it.

Bring the stock to a simmer over medium-low heat. Carefully drop in the gnocchetti and simmer them for 10 minutes. Remove with a slotted spoon and save the stock for another use.

Toss the gnocchetti in the butter and salt and pepper to taste on a serving platter and pour the marinara sauce over them. Garnish with grated cheese.

Note: You can also serve these gnocchetti in chicken broth. Bring the broth to a simmer, then add the dumplings a few at a time. Cover and cook gently. After 5 minutes, add the juice of half a lemon and cook another 5 minutes. Serve the soup with grated cheese.

Serves 4

Spaghettini with Broccoli and Egg Whites

We like to serve this recipe followed by a hearty dish such as Ground Pork with Brussels Sprouts (see page 277) or Parchment-Wrapped Sausage with Fennel and Onions (see page 279).

2 pounds broccoli florets, stems
peeled and cut into 2-inch pieces

3 tablespoons olive oil

1 medium onion, finely chopped

2 garlic cloves, minced

Salt and freshly ground
black pepper

2 egg whites

6 cups chicken stock

3/4 pound spaghettini

1 tablespoon finely chopped
flat-leaf parsley

Grated Parmesan or Pecorino
cheese, for garnish

Bring a large pot of salted water to a boil over high heat. Blanch the broccoli, uncovered, for 1 minute. Drain the broccoli, rinse in cold water, and set aside.

Heat the oil in a medium skillet over medium heat. Add the onion and garlic and cook until the onion becomes translucent, about 5 minutes. Add the broccoli and salt and pepper to taste, and cook, uncovered, until the broccoli is tender, about 10 minutes.

Beat the egg whites in a large bowl until foamy.

Heat the stock in a large soup pot over medium heat and add the spaghettini. Cook until the spaghettini is al dente. The pasta will absorb most of the stock. Drain the pasta (save the reserved stock for another use), and immediately toss it in the egg whites. (The heat from the pasta will cook the egg whites.) Add the broccoli mixture and toss gently. Toss in the parsley and garnish with grated cheese.

Serves 4

Mashed Potato Ravioli

It is not unusual for Italians to serve two kinds of pasta as a first course. This dish calls for ravioli prepared two ways: ravioli with mashed potatoes and ricotta, and ravioli with mashed potatoes (and truffles, should you want to add them). Serve the raviolis garnished with butter and sage, marinara, or meat sauce. We like to serve butter and sage sauce with the mashed potato ravioli, and marinara sauce with the mashed potato and ricotta ravioli. If making the ravioli with truffles, serve only with butter.

This comforting recipe is an adaptation of a dish Edward ate at Il Drappo, a wonderful Sardinian restaurant in Rome. Be sure to mash potatoes by pushing them through a ricer.

For the pasta dough

3 cups unbleached all-purpose flour

Salt

4 eggs, at room temperature

2 to 4 tablespoons warm water

For the plain mashed potato stuffing

3 cups mashed potatoes (about 3 to 4 Yukon Gold potatoes, peeled, boiled, and pushed through a ricer)

1 egg, beaten

3 tablespoons truffle paste, or 1 tablespoon for every cup of mashed potato stuffing (optional)

3 tablespoons grated Parmesan or Pecorino cheese

2 teaspoons dried mint

Dash of grated nutmeg

Salt and freshly ground black pepper

For the pasta dough: Place the flour and salt to taste together on a breadboard or countertop and make a well in the center. Break the eggs into the well. Beat the eggs with a fork, gradually working in part of the flour. When half of the flour is in, start working in the remaining flour with your hands. Continue to blend the eggs and flour, working slowly in a circular motion. Scrape the board occasionally with a pastry scraper or knife so that all the ingredients are thoroughly mixed.

Gradually add approximately 2 tablespoons of warm water, kneading constantly. Then add more as necessary. The dough should be dry and not sticky, so add the water gradually, in tiny amounts. If too sticky, add a little flour.

Sprinkle the surface lightly with flour so that the dough does not stick to the surface, taking care not to add too much. The dough must remain soft and pliable. Knead the dough in a rolling motion, pushing it away from you with the heels of your hands. Knead for 15 to 20 minutes, or until the dough is velvety and smooth. Cut the pasta in half and roll each half into a ball. Flatten the balls into disks. Rub each disk lightly with oil to prevent drying. Put the disks in separate plastic bags and let the dough rest at room temperature for at least 1 hour.

For the plain mashed potato stuffing: In a large bowl, combine the mashed potatoes, egg, truffle paste (if using), cheese, mint, nutmeg, and salt and pepper to taste. Mix well.

For the mashed potato/ricotta stuffing

1 cup mashed potatoes (about 1 to 2 Yukon Gold potatoes, peeled, boiled, and pushed through a ricer)

1 cup ricotta

3 tablespoons grated Parmesan or Pecorino cheese

1 egg, beaten

1 teaspoon dried mint

Dash of grated nutmeg

Salt and freshly ground black pepper

For the garnish

½ cup (1 stick) unsalted butter

4 tablespoons minced sage or 2 tablespoons crushed dried

2 cups marinara or meat sauce (see page 258), heated (optional)

Grated Parmesan or Pecorino cheese, for garnish

For the ricotta/mashed potato stuffing: In a large bowl, combine the mashed potatoes, ricotta, Parmesan, egg, mint, nutmeg, and salt and pepper to taste. Mix well.

Make the ravioli: Either roll out the ravioli by hand on a large floured surface, or crank it through a pasta machine. When rolling out by hand, roll out one disk of dough at a time, to a circle about 20 inches in diameter. Place about 20 separate tablespoons of either filling on one half of the dough, and then fold over the remaining half of the dough. Cut around the individual raviolis and seal the edge with a damp fork. If you use a ravioli mold, place a cut sheet of the pasta into the bottom of the mold, add the filling, and place another cut sheet on top. Seal the edges by pressing down on the ravioli with the top portion of the mold.

For the garnish: In a small saucepan or skillet, melt the butter with the sage.

To assemble: Bring a large pot of salted water to a boil over high heat. Carefully add the mashed potato ravioli. Do not crowd the ravioli; you will have to boil them in batches. Cook the ravioli for 2 to 3 minutes, until they float to the surface of the water. Lift the ravioli out of the water with a small strainer or slotted spoon. Place the cooked ravioli on a serving dish. Repeat with the mashed potato/ricotta ravioli. Be sure to put the different ravioli in separate platters, as they take different sauces. Add a couple of tablespoons of the appropriate sauce to each platter, to keep the ravioli moist as you finish cooking them.

When the ravioli is cooked, add the butter and sage sauce to the mashed potato ravioli and the marinara sauce to the mashed potato and ricotta ravioli and sprinkle Parmesan on top.

Serves 8 (about 40 ravioli)

Meat Lasagne

This dish is often served as a first course before our Christmas Day meal. This lasagne has three sauces, all of which are extremely easy to make. The marinara sauce, which is very sweet and versatile, can be made ahead of time, and used for other purposes as well. Indeed, since this marinara sauce appeared in an article by Craig Claiborne back in the 1960s, every time Eugenia publishes an article someone writes her a letter asking for the recipe, saying they had lost it or given it away decades before, and have been looking for it ever since. This can be assembled and frozen for up to 3 months. We use either homemade or Delverde no-boil lasagna, which we think is very good. It is not made with eggs, and is corrugated to give it strength because it is so thin.

For the marinara sauce

½ cup olive oil

3 medium onions, chopped

2 medium carrots, peeled and sliced

3 garlic cloves, minced

6 cups whole canned Italian tomatoes, with their juice

Salt and freshly ground black pepper

½ cup (1 stick) unsalted butter

1 tablespoon finely chopped flat-leaf parsley

2 tablespoons chopped basil or 2 teaspoons dried

1½ teaspoons dried oregano

For the meat sauce

2 pounds ground lean pork

Salt and freshly ground black pepper

½ pound wild mushrooms, sliced (or 1 ounce dried porcini mushrooms, soaked in warm water for 15 minutes, plus ½ pound sliced white mushrooms)

2 teaspoons minced garlic

For the marinara sauce: Heat the oil in a large saucepan over medium-low heat. Add the onions, carrots, and garlic. Cook until the vegetables are golden and the carrots are tender, about 15 minutes.

Meanwhile, work the tomatoes through a food mill or sieve into a bowl. Discard the skins and seeds.

Add the pureed tomatoes to the vegetables. Add salt and pepper to taste. Partially cover the pan and simmer for 15 minutes.

Press the sauce through the food mill or sieve again (using a foodmill or sieve will reduce the volume but create a smoother sauce; pureeing in a food processor will retain the volume but make a less refined sauce). Pour the sauce back into the pan, and add the butter, parsley, basil, and oregano. Partly cover the pan and simmer 30 minutes more, stirring occasionally. This makes about 6 cups of sauce.

For the meat sauce: Place the pork in a nonstick skillet over medium-high heat, and season it with salt and pepper to taste. Sauté the pork about 10 minutes, stirring often to break it up, until it loses its raw look and begins to brown. Pour off excess fat. Add the mushrooms (if you are using dried porcini, add the water too) and garlic. Cook until the mushrooms give up their liquid, about 5 minutes.

In the meantime, heat the marinara sauce in a large saucepan over medium-low heat. Add the ground pork and mushrooms to the sauce and continue to cook over medium-low heat for 45 minutes, stirring occasionally.

For the besciamella

2 tablespoons unsalted butter

2 tablespoons all-purpose flour

1 cup milk

¼ teaspoon grated nutmeg

Salt and freshly ground
black pepper

To assemble:

4 sheets no-boil lasagna,
preferably Delverde, or 12 strips
imported Italian lasagna (see Note,
page 37)

½ cup grated Parmesan cheese

For the besciamella: Melt the butter in a saucepan over low heat. Using a wire whisk, stir in the flour until it is blended. Gradually add the milk, whisking constantly until the sauce is thickened, about 3 to 5 minutes. Add the nutmeg and salt and pepper to taste. Use the sauce immediately.

To assemble: Heat the oven to 375°F. If you are using a lasagna noodle variety other than Delverde, bring a large pot of salted water to a boil and cook the lasagna until it is al dente. Drain off half the water and set the pot under cold running water to cool the lasagna. Lay the lasagna on paper towels. Do not overlap, as they will stick together.

Spoon a layer of meat sauce into the bottom of the Delverde tray or a 9-inch square baking dish. Lay down a layer of lasagna and spoon over another layer of meat sauce. Spoon about 4 tablespoons of besciamella over the meat sauce. Arrange another layer of lasagna, and so on, until all of the lasagna is used, ending with a layer of meat sauce and the grated cheese.

Cover the lasagne with aluminum foil and bake for about 45 minutes, until it is piping hot and bubbling throughout.

Serves 8

Risotto with Crabmeat

This very elegant dish is worth the effort. The stock may be cooked ahead of time, but the rest of the recipe should be prepared right before serving. You can substitute fish stock (see page 25) for the crab stock.

For the crab stock

1 dozen blue crabs, shells and gills removed (see Note)

6 cups water

2 carrots, peeled

1 fennel bulb, coarsely chopped

1 large onion, peeled, or 1 leek, rinsed

3 tablespoons finely chopped flat-leaf parsley

4 bay leaves

Salt and freshly ground black pepper

For the risotto

3 tablespoons extra virgin olive oil

Half a medium onion, finely chopped

4 garlic cloves, finely chopped

1 cup Arborio rice

½ cup dry white wine

2 tablespoons finely chopped flat-leaf parsley

4 cups warm crab stock (or fish stock), or more if needed

Salt and freshly ground black pepper

4 tablespoons grated Parmesan cheese

For the crab stock: In a large soup pot, place the crabs, water, carrots, fennel, onion, parsley, bay leaves, and salt and pepper to taste. Bring to a boil over high heat. Reduce the heat to medium and cook for 2 hours at a low boil.

Strain the stock. Discard the solids.

For the risotto: Heat the oil in a deep saucepan over medium heat. Add the onion and garlic and cook until the onion becomes translucent, about 5 minutes. Add the rice and stir to coat with oil. Cook for a few minutes, until the rice begins to take on a little color. Add the wine and parsley. Bring the wine to a boil, and cook, covered, until the wine is absorbed, about 5 minutes. Then add enough stock to cover the rice (about 1 cup). Stir periodically until the rice absorbs the stock. Add more stock and continue stirring, adding stock as the rice absorbs it. When the rice is tender, about 15 minutes, add salt and pepper to taste, and the cheese.

For the crab garnish

2 tablespoons olive oil

2 garlic cloves, finely chopped

8 ounces lump crabmeat

2 tablespoons finely chopped
flat-leaf parsley

¼ cup dry white wine

Salt and freshly ground
black pepper

3 tablespoons finely chopped dill

For the crab garnish: Heat the oil in a small skillet over medium heat. Add the garlic. When the garlic begins to take on color, about 3 minutes, add the crabmeat, parsley, wine, and salt and pepper to taste. Cover and simmer for about 5 minutes, until the wine is absorbed.

Serve each portion of risotto with a helping of crabmeat on top and garnish with the dill.

Note: To clean the crab, remove the top shell by forcing a heavy knife blade under the flap on the underside of the crab. Push the knife in and wedge off the shell. Discard the shell. Remove the gills and discard. Wash the crabs. You can also ask your fishmonger to clean the crabs.

Serves 4

Rice with Fennel and Ricotta

This is a delicate and aromatic dish. Because it bridges two seasons (the fennel is a winter vegetable and ricotta is, traditionally, a spring product), it will work as a first course with second courses from either season.

2 cups water

1 fennel bulb, cut in half, cored, and thinly sliced (including greens, which should be kept whole)

Salt

1 cup rice (we prefer Uncle Ben's or basmati)

1 pound ricotta

1 tablespoon finely chopped flat-leaf parsley

¼ teaspoon grated nutmeg

Freshly ground black pepper

⅓ cup grated Parmesan cheese

Bring the water to a boil in a medium pot over high heat.

Add the fennel slices and stems to the water, with salt to taste. Boil the fennel for about 15 minutes, until it is tender. Remove the fennel from the water with a slotted spoon or small strainer. Discard the stems. Reserve the water.

Heat the broiler.

Add the rice to the fennel water. Bring to a boil over medium-high heat, then cover, reduce the heat to medium-low, and simmer the rice until it has absorbed all of the liquid, about 10 to 15 minutes.

In a bowl, combine the fennel, rice, ricotta, parsley, nutmeg, and salt and pepper to taste. Pour the rice mixture into a 9-inch ovenproof dish. Add the grated cheese and place the rice under the broiler for about 5 minutes, until the cheese melts and browns.

Serves 4

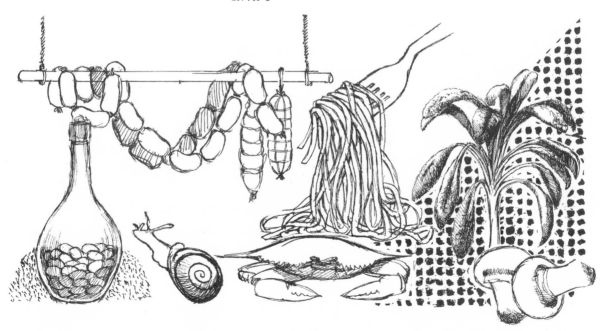

NEW YEAR'S EVE

When I was young, my brother and sister and I were shipped off to my mother's parents' house in West Palm Beach for ten glorious days of swimming and sunning and dressing up for Lost Tree Club's "boo-fay" dinner. During those years, my parents headed for Craig Claiborne's house in East Hampton, where Dad and Pierre Franey and Roger Vergnes and other chefs upended the house cooking a New Year's Eve dinner, and the wives hung out together and drank whiskey and grumped about how they'd be just as happy with a sandwich. As children, we attended a few times, but the only person who ever paid attention to us was Henry, a longtime boyfriend of Craig's. Henry was not much of a cook, or at least, not compared to Craig's set, and so he would visit with us kids, and annoy the chefs as he fussily crowded the kitchen to make us fudge—the one dish he had perfected.

Craig's first New Year's Eve party was in the early 1960s, held at his New York City apartment in the Osborne, a fine old building on West 57th Street. Though his means were modest, Craig definitely had style. For that party, he removed every bit of furniture out of his one-bedroom apartment and put it in the hallway. He rented tables and chairs and had a caterer roast a pig for twenty. After a couple of years, Craig moved the party to East Hampton. At first they were small affairs, no more than twenty-five interesting, hard-partying people, and a buffet consisting of oysters, brandade de morue, and pâtés; then roast goose, coulibiac, and sometimes a whole baby pig. But eventually the party expanded to one hundred people, and my parents didn't have as much fun anymore. There were strangers showing up, and the chefs didn't like the feeding frenzy at the buffet. I guess it hit rock bottom the year Craig decided he was going to have a potluck. There were thirty platters of veal stew that New Year's Eve, and they all looked to be made from the same recipe. To this day my father abhors potlucks, because of what he believes will be the inevitable onslaught of veal stews.

My parents now spend New Year's Eve at home, with dinner for no more than six people. They prepare cranberry beans with caviar, a tiny beef tenderloin with black pepper, a green salad, and one of my mother's delicate flans, with champagne. If they stay up until midnight, great. And if they don't, well, they get a good night's sleep.

By the time I was in my twenties, I was living in New York City. Sometime in the early 1980s, the food writer Jay Jacobs began inviting me to his New Year's Eve parties. Jay, a petite, wrinkled cynic with a hilarious deadpan delivery, had been a friend of my parents for decades, and I suppose we were like family; but I was, nonetheless, hugely flattered to be included. Jay's parties were far swankier than those I usually attended in dark grimy loft spaces, sporting a table laden with half-drunk bring-your-own bottles, and where attempts at decoration usually ended in small fires. Jay's parties were grown-up. Usually too smashed to mingle, Jay stood at the end of a glorious buffet, comprised of a huge baked ham, with mustard and bread, seared steak and potato salad, and home-cured gravlax, blinking blearily and periodically cracking an urbane witticism. After greeting me with a kiss, he would say, "Find yourself a drink and some grub, if you can stand it."

After I was married, New Year's Eve parties changed again. For years we went to a party at Carson's godfathers' apartment, a wild dressy affair where our hosts would serve trays and trays of Chinese dumplings stuffed with pork, crab, and scallops. Then Lisa and I hosted formal sit-down dinners. Our first—seared foie gras with apples, Spaghettini alla Foriana, a veal tenderloin with wild mushrooms, and pumpkin soufflé—was a success, except for the small fire lit by the grease from the foie gras pan, the too-cool veal, and the burn-your-mouth-hot soufflé. The wines, however, were wonderful, and made up for a multitude of sins. We learned an important lesson about parties that night: Serve the good stuff, and no one will notice that the clams are chewy.

Currently, we take it easy. We open a bottle of Amarone and make cotechino with lentils, traditional Italian fare for New Year's Eve. If we stay up until midnight, great. And if we don't, well, we get a good night's sleep.

WINTER
SECOND COURSES

Scrambled Eggs with Oysters

An easy, elegant dish, this is very good for a light dinner with a salad afterward, and a glass of white wine or champagne, followed by a couple of homemade chocolates. You can substitute about 30 small, peeled, deveined shrimp or bay scallops for the oysters. We have also made this dish with smoked scallops and tarragon.

8 eggs

Salt and hot pepper flakes

2 tablespoons unsalted butter

2 garlic cloves, finely chopped

24 oysters, shucked

2 tablespoons finely chopped
flat-leaf parsley, for garnish

Break the eggs into a small bowl and whisk them together. Add salt and hot pepper flakes to taste.

Melt the butter in a large nonstick skillet over medium heat. Add the garlic and cook for 1 minute, just to soften a bit. Add the oysters and cook them until they just begin to whiten, about 2 minutes, and then add the eggs. Reduce the heat to medium-low. Allow the eggs to set for 2 minutes or so before you start to scramble them. Scramble the eggs to your taste, but we like them soft, about 5 minutes.

Garnish with parsley.

Serves 4

Baccala alla Marchigiana

Edward's mother used to make this recipe for baccala (salt cod). Be sure to soak the fish for 3 days, changing the water once or twice a day.

1½ pounds baccala, soaked

2 cups whole canned Italian
tomatoes, chopped

4 medium potatoes, peeled and
cut in half (we prefer Yukon Gold)

1 fennel bulb, cut into quarters and
cored

1 large onion, sliced

6 tablespoons extra virgin olive oil

2 tablespoons chopped flat-leaf
parsley

1 teaspoon dried marjoram

Salt and hot pepper flakes to taste
(optional)

Heat the oven to 450°F.

Place the baccala in a baking dish. Put the tomatoes, potatoes, fennel, onion, oil, parsley, and marjoram around and on top of the fish and add salt to taste and some hot pepper flakes, if you like. Cover with aluminum foil and bake for about 45 minutes, until the fennel and potatoes are fork-tender.

Note: You can also add cardoons to this dish. You will need 2 cups cardoons, cut into strips 2 inches long and ½ inch wide, the juice of half a lemon, and 1 tablespoon flour. Soak the cardoons in cold water with the lemon juice for 30 to 45 minutes. Drain the cardoons and place in a small pot with 2 cups water and the flour. Gently boil the cardoons for about 30 minutes over medium-low heat. Drain, and add to the dish with the fennel and potatoes.

Serves 4

Striped Bass with Sweet Potatoes

You can also make this sweet, cozy dish with scrod or halibut fillets. Avoid really delicate fillets, though, like sole, as they tend to fall apart in the sauce. This is a perfect second course following risotto or pasta with a fish or vegetable sauce.

4 small sweet potatoes (about 1 pound)

2 tablespoons olive oil

2 medium onions, finely chopped

4 garlic cloves, finely chopped

1 cup whole canned Italian tomatoes, chopped

Salt and freshly ground black pepper

1½ pounds fresh striped bass fillet, cut into 2-inch pieces

4 tablespoons extra virgin olive oil, for garnish

Heat the oven to 450°F.

Place the sweet potatoes in the oven and bake them until they are tender, about 45 minutes. (Poke them with a fork to see if they are cooked all the way through.) Remove the sweet potatoes and when they are cool, peel them and cut them into thick slices. Leave the oven on at 450°F.

Heat the olive oil in a medium, ovenproof skillet over medium heat. Add the onions and garlic and cook until the onions become translucent, about 5 minutes. Add the tomatoes. Cover the skillet and simmer the vegetables over medium-low heat for 10 minutes, until the tomatoes break up. Add the sweet potato slices and salt and pepper to taste.

Place the fish pieces in the sauce so that the pieces do not overlap. Add salt to taste and cover the skillet. Place the skillet in the oven and bake for about 10 minutes, until the fish is white and flaky. Adjust the seasoning.

Sprinkle the fish and sweet potatoes with the extra virgin olive oil and serve immediately.

Serves 4

Codfish with Brocoletti di Rape

This is one of our favorite dishes, and we eat it frequently during the winter. You can substitute any large, white fish, like striped bass, for the cod. You can also substitute chunks of fish, like monkfish.

2 bunches brocoletti di rape, washed, with tough stems removed

5 tablespoons olive oil

6 garlic cloves, minced

1 dried hot pepper or hot pepper flakes

1 cup black olives cured in oil

4 codfish steaks, about 2 inches thick (about 1½ pounds)

Salt to taste

Extra virgin olive oil, for garnish

Heat the oven to 450°F.

Bring a large pot of salted water to a boil. Dunk in the rape. When the water comes back to a boil, drain the rape and set aside.

In a small skillet, heat 3 tablespoons of the olive oil over medium heat. Add the garlic and hot pepper and cook until the garlic takes on color, about 3 minutes.

In a large baking pan, dribble the remaining 2 tablespoons of olive oil. Add the drained rape, the olives, and the cooked garlic and oil. Place the rape in the oven and bake it for 10 minutes, until the rape is tender when pierced with a fork. (If the rape overcooks, it's okay. The leaves will get a little crispy, but the taste will just get sweeter.)

Remove the rape from the oven and push aside the vegetable to make room for the codfish steaks. Nestle them into the pan, season to taste with the salt, and return the pan to the oven for another 10 to 15 minutes, until the fish is cooked.

Garnish the fish with extra virgin olive oil and serve.

Serves 4

Monkfish with Leeks

This dish is very delicate and light—perfect as a second course after a pasta like Trenette with Baccala and Walnuts (see page 251).

Monkfish is a great bargain: It has something of the taste of lobster, but the tenderness of a fin fish. The monkfish in this recipe can be replaced by other firm-fleshed, non-oily white fish, like black bass or cod.

1½ pounds monkfish fillet, skinned, cut into 4-inch pieces

⅓ cup dry white wine

2 tablespoons olive oil

2 tablespoons finely chopped flat-leaf parsley

1 tablespoon chopped rosemary or 1 teaspoon crushed dried

1 large garlic clove, finely chopped

Salt and freshly ground black pepper

2 leeks, whites only

Heat the oven to 350°F.

Put the fish in a mixing bowl and add the wine, oil, parsley, rosemary, garlic, and salt and pepper to taste. Mix well.

Wash the leeks. (To wash, trim off the root end of each leek and split the leeks partly in half lengthwise. Rinse between each layer to wash away sand.) Cut the leeks crosswise into 2-inch lengths. Cut these pieces into thin julienne strips, like matchsticks.

Lay a piece of parchment paper, about 30 × 15 inches, on a baking tray. Place the fish pieces and the oil and herb mixture in the center of the paper. Top the fish with the leeks. Fold over the paper and crimp the edges to seal. Place the baking tray in the oven and cook for about 15 minutes, until the parchment package is browned and puffy.

Remove the tray and carefully open the bag—the steam is hot. Serve the fish in its juices.

Serves 4

Broiled Sardines with Breadcrumbs

We like to serve these sardines with Tomaso's Baked Brocoletti di Rape, following a light fish pasta like Spaghettini with Maine Shrimp. On special occasions we will serve a slice of Meyer Lemon Tart afterward (see pages 292, 249, and 302).

6 tablespoons extra virgin olive oil

16 fresh sardines (each 7 inches long), with heads on (about ¾ pound), butterflied (see Note)

Salt

2 cups fresh breadcrumbs

6 garlic cloves, minced

2 tablespoons finely chopped flat-leaf parsley

Hot pepper flakes (optional)

Heat the broiler.

Lightly oil a baking tray with 2 tablespoons of the oil and place the butterflied sardines side by side, skin down. Sprinkle them with salt.

In a small bowl, combine the remaining 4 tablespoons of oil, the breadcrumbs, garlic, parsley, and hot pepper flakes (if using) to taste. Sprinkle this mixture over the sardines.

Place the sardines under the broiler and broil them for about 4 minutes, until the breadcrumbs are browned.

Serve immediately.

Note: To butterfly the sardines, slit the sardines along the belly and remove the innards and the gills but leave the heads on. Open the fish as you would a book and press the sides of the fish back until the spine is bulging forward. Pull the spine up and out of the fish and discard. Or ask your fishmonger to butterfly the sardines.

Serves 4

Fresh Maine Shrimp in Wine

The shells of the Maine shrimp are extremely tender once cooked. Remove the head and suck out the juices, then eat the shrimp whole, discarding the tail fin.

Sweet Maine shrimp are never frozen. They are often available, during their short season, from Farm 2 Market (see Sources on page 305).

½ cup extra virgin olive oil

6 tablespoons finely chopped flat-leaf parsley

6 to 8 garlic cloves, minced

Hot pepper flakes

2 pounds Maine shrimp
(with heads and shells on)

1 cup dry white wine

Salt

4 slices bruschetta, for serving
(see page 17)

Heat the oil in a medium skillet over medium heat. Add the parsley, garlic, and hot pepper flakes to taste. Cook until the garlic takes on color, about 3 minutes. Add the shrimp and turn the heat up to high. Cook, stirring often, for about 60 seconds. Add the wine, reduce the heat to medium-high, and cover. Simmer the shrimp until the shells turn pink and the shrimp curl, about 2 minutes. Add salt to taste and serve immediately with bruschetta.

Serves 4

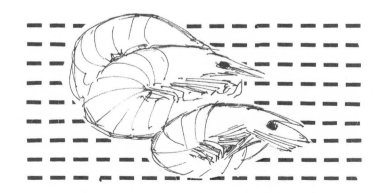

Smelts in Garlic and White Wine

Smelts are a seasonal freshwater fish harvested during winter and spring (the best are caught by ice fishing with a hand line). If they are very fresh, smelt will smell like cucumbers. In our family, we prepare smelts two ways: fried and steamed in wine. In both cases, we leave the heads on after cleaning and leave the roe in the fish. We do not recommend frozen smelts that are cleaned and headless. Be sure you use smelts that are at least 8 inches long, as smaller smelts are just not meaty enough.

½ cup extra virgin olive oil, plus additional for garnish

½ cup finely chopped flat-leaf parsley

8 garlic cloves, finely chopped

Hot pepper flakes

1 cup dry white wine

12 large smelts (each about 8 inches long), cleaned, with heads on

Salt

4 slices bruschetta (see page 17)

Juice of 1 lemon

Heat the oil in a medium saucepan over medium heat. Add the parsley, garlic, and hot pepper flakes to taste. When the garlic begins to color, about 3 minutes, add the wine. Cover and simmer for about 3 minutes, until the wine is boiling rapidly.

Place the fish in a skillet. Do not overlap. Pour the wine and garlic mixture over the fish, add salt and hot pepper flakes to taste, and cover tightly. Simmer over medium heat until the smelts are cooked: The eyes will turn white, about 5 minutes.

Place the bruschetta on a warm plate and place 3 fish on top of each slice. Pour the pan juices over the fish. Add one quarter of the lemon juice to each serving and drizzle with extra virgin olive oil.

Serves 4

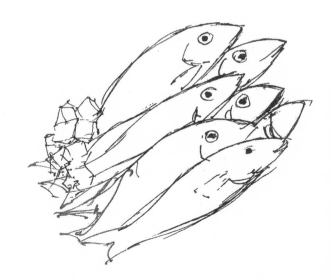

Fillet of Sole Stuffed with Crabmeat

We often serve this light and fancy dish as the final course at the Cena della Vigilia. The shrimp sauce is also excellent on top of risotto cooked in fish broth.

For the shrimp sauce

3 tablespoons olive oil

Half a medium onion, chopped

4 garlic cloves, minced

Shells from 24 medium shrimp

½ cup dry white wine

2 tablespoons finely chopped flat-leaf parsley

4 cups whole canned Italian tomatoes, chopped

Salt and freshly ground black pepper

For the stuffing

4 ounces lump crabmeat

1 cup ricotta

3 tablespoons grated Parmesan cheese

3 tablespoons finely chopped flat-leaf parsley

Pinch of grated nutmeg

Salt and freshly ground black pepper

To assemble

8 fillets of sole (about 4 ounces each)

⅓ cup dry white wine

24 medium shrimp, shelled and deveined

Finely chopped flat-leaf parsley, for garnish

For the shrimp sauce: Heat the oil in a saucepan over medium heat. Add the onion and garlic and cook until the onion becomes translucent, about 5 minutes. Add the shrimp shells, wine, and parsley and cook until the wine no longer smells winey, about 5 minutes. Add the tomatoes and salt and pepper to taste; cover, and cook over medium-low heat for 45 minutes.

Puree the shells and sauce in a food processor. Press the puree through a sieve. What solids you can't press through, wrap in a cheesecloth and squeeze the juice into the sauce. This makes about 4 cups of sauce. Keep 2 cups of the sauce warm, for assembly, and refrigerate the rest for another use.

Heat the oven to 450°F.

For the stuffing: In a large mixing bowl, combine the crabmeat, ricotta, Parmesan cheese, parsley, nutmeg, and salt and pepper to taste.

To assemble: Lay the fillets out on a work surface and season with salt and pepper. Place about 2 tablespoons of the stuffing in the center of each fillet. Roll up the fillets and place seam side down in a 13 × 9-inch baking dish. Add the wine to the dish. Bake for 20 minutes, until the fish is white and cooked through. Add the shrimp and the reserved shrimp sauce and bake for about 5 minutes, until the shrimp turn pink.

Serve the fish garnished with parsley.

Serves 8

Capon Stuffed with Clementines

We vastly prefer capon—a moist, tender bird—to the dry, bland meat of the grotesque commercial turkey. However, organic turkeys are becoming increasingly available, and they are delicious. You can substitute an organic turkey of the same weight for the capon in this recipe.

We prepare this dish on Christmas Day.

1 capon (10 pounds) or
organic turkey

8 garlic cloves, sliced

4 tablespoons crushed dried
rosemary

Salt and freshly ground
black pepper

1 tablespoon crushed fennel seeds

2 clementines or small tangerines

3 cups white wine (red wine is
okay), plus another cup on hand

10 dried figs

Heat the oven to 450°F.

With your fingers, loosen the skin from the breast and slip the garlic and half the rosemary under the skin. Rub the bird with salt, pepper, crushed fennel seeds, and the remaining 2 tablespoons of rosemary. Salt and pepper the cavity. Stuff the bird with the clementines.

Place the capon breast-up in a large roasting pan and pour about 2 cups of wine into the pan. Roast the capon for about 45 minutes, until it begins to brown. Add the figs to the pan and turn the capon over. Continue roasting until the back of the bird turns brown, about 30 minutes. Turn the capon back over, so it is breast-up again, and add the remaining 1 cup of wine. Continue to cook, basting often, for another 30 minutes or so, for a total cooking time of about 1 hour and 45 minutes, until the leg separates easily from the torso and the juices from the bird run clear. If the pan juices dry out, add some more wine.

Remove the bird from the oven and let it rest for 30 minutes. In the meantime, strain and defat the pan juices. Carve the bird and dribble the pan juices over the meat.

Note: Reserve the carcass and the clementines for Capon Broth with Angel Hair Pasta (see page 246), and make a salad with any leftover meat.

Serves 10

Osso Buco with Tripe

While there are many kinds of tripe available in Italian markets, we primarily find white beef or veal honeycomb tripe. Boiling it first removes all traces of the cleansing agents used in preparing tripe for sale. Tripe is rich in gelatin, which is very good for bone and tendon health, and it is quite sweet.

1½ pounds tripe

4 veal shanks (osso buco) about 2 inches thick, tied with culinary string

Salt and freshly ground black pepper

All-purpose flour for dredging

4 tablespoons olive oil

2 cups leeks, whites only, rinsed and finely chopped

6 garlic cloves, finely chopped

1 cup dry white wine

3 tablespoons dried basil

3 bay leaves

4 cups whole canned Italian tomatoes, chopped

4 carrots, coarsely chopped

2 cups fresh cranberry beans (about 2 pounds in the shell) or 1 can (15 ounces) cannellini beans

For the gremolata

2 tablespoons finely chopped flat-leaf parsley

Grated zest of 1 lemon

1 garlic clove, finely chopped

1 teaspoon chopped sage or ½ teaspoon dried sage

Bring a large pot of salted water to a boil over high heat and add the tripe. Boil the tripe for 10 minutes. Drain, then rinse in cold water. Flip over the tripe so that the comb side is facedown. Remove the fat from the skin with a sharp knife. Discard the fat. Cut the tripe into pieces about ¼ inch wide by 2 inches long.

Season the veal shanks with salt and pepper and dredge in flour.

Heat the oil in a deep skillet with a fitted cover over high heat. Add the veal shanks and brown them on both sides, about 5 minutes on each side. Brown the edges, too, another 10 minutes. Add the leeks and garlic. Cook over medium heat, until the garlic begins to take on color, about 3 minutes. Add the wine, basil, and bay leaves. Cover and simmer until the wine no longer smells winey, about 10 minutes. Add the tomatoes, carrots, and tripe. Cover the skillet and boil gently for about 1 hour. Add the cranberry beans and cook for an additional 45 minutes to 1 hour, until the beans are tender. (If you use canned beans, let the veal and tripe cook for 1½ hours before adding them; the canned beans will cook in about 15 minutes in the sauce.) Remove the bay leaves.

For the gremolata: In a small bowl, combine the parsley, lemon zest, garlic, and sage.

Garnish the osso buco with the gremolata and serve immediately.

Serves 4

Pork Shoulder with Fennel

Pork shoulder seems to be one of the few cuts of pork that haven't had all the fat bred out of it. We don't even eat tenderloin that much anymore, because the meat is so dry and tasteless. Shoulder, however, has lots of fat, and as a result, the meat is rich and sweet.

1 pork shoulder (5½ pounds), tied

4 to 5 garlic cloves, slivered

8 to 10 1-inch pieces fresh rosemary or 2 tablespoons crushed dried

Salt and freshly ground black pepper

3 tablespoons olive oil

3 cups red wine

2 cups beef or chicken stock

1 fennel bulb, cored and coarsely chopped, or 2 tablespoons fennel seeds

2 large carrots, cut into 2-inch lengths

1 medium onion, peeled and cut into quarters

4 tablespoons chopped flat-leaf parsley

5 bay leaves

3 tablespoons golden raisins

Heat the oven to 350°F.

Make 8 to 10 slits in the pork meat with a sharp knife. Shove a sliver of garlic and a piece of rosemary into each slit. Rub salt and pepper all over the meat.

Heat the oil in a large Dutch oven over medium-high heat. Add the pork and sear the meat on all sides, about 15 minutes. Add 1 cup of the wine and cook until the wine no longer smells winey, about 5 minutes. Add the stock, the remaining 2 cups of wine, the fennel, carrots, onion, parsley, and bay leaves. Cover and place in the oven. Bake for 1 hour. Turn the roast over. Bake for another hour, and add the raisins. Bake for an additional hour, for a total of 3 hours baking time.

Remove the roast from the pot. Set aside and keep warm. Strain and defat the pan juices and return them to the pot. Cook over medium-high heat for about 15 minutes, until the sauce is reduced by half.

Garnish each serving with a tablespoon of sauce.

Serves 8

Ground Pork with Brussels Sprouts

The fennel and raisins make this a deliciously sweet winter dish. It is great served on its own, followed by a green salad. If you serve a pasta course first, omit the potatoes from this dish.

4 small potatoes (we prefer Yukon Gold)

1 pound Brussels sprouts, stem ends trimmed and light, outer leaves removed

2 tablespoons olive oil

1 fennel bulb, cored and thinly sliced

1 medium onion, thinly sliced

4 garlic cloves, finely chopped

1 pound lean ground pork

4 tablespoons golden raisins

3 tablespoons finely chopped flat-leaf parsley

Salt and hot pepper flakes

Extra virgin olive oil, for garnish

Bring a medium pot of salted water to a boil over high heat. Add the potatoes and boil them, uncovered, for about 10 minutes. Add the Brussels sprouts and continue boiling for about 5 to 10 minutes, until the potatoes are tender. Drain and run cold water over the vegetables to stop the cooking process. Cut the Brussels sprouts in half, lengthwise.

In a nonstick skillet, heat the olive oil over medium heat. Add the fennel, onion, and garlic. Cover and cook until the onion becomes translucent, about 5 minutes. Add the pork, raisins, and parsley, and cook, uncovered, over medium-low heat for about 10 minutes, until the pork begins to brown. Add the drained Brussels sprouts, cover, and simmer for another 10 to 15 minutes, until the Brussels sprouts are tender. Add salt and hot pepper flakes to taste.

Peel and slice the boiled potatoes. Add salt and pepper to taste.

Serve the pork and vegetables with the boiled sliced potatoes. Garnish with a drizzle of extra virgin olive oil.

Serves 4

Stuffed Cabbage

This version of stuffed cabbage is lighter than you'd expect (note there is very little pork), but because there is rice in the dish, we recommend you serve a soup as a first course, or no first course, and a salad following.

For the stuffing

2 tablespoons olive oil

1 medium onion, finely chopped

3 tablespoons finely chopped
flat-leaf parsley

½ pound lean ground pork

½ cup golden raisins

½ cup cooked rice

Salt and freshly ground
black pepper

For the sauce

2 tablespoons olive oil

Half a medium onion, finely
chopped

3 garlic cloves, finely chopped

2 cups whole canned Italian
tomatoes, chopped

1 tablespoon dried basil

Salt and freshly ground
black pepper

To assemble

8 large Savoy cabbage leaves,
blanched and drained

Heat the oven to 375°F.

For the stuffing: Heat the oil in a medium skillet over medium heat. Add the onion and parsley and cook until the onion becomes translucent, about 5 minutes.

In a large mixing bowl, combine the pork, cooked onion, raisins, cooked rice, and salt and pepper to taste. Mix well.

For the sauce: Heat the oil in a medium skillet over medium heat. Add the onion and garlic and cook until the onion becomes translucent, about 5 minutes. Add the tomatoes, basil, and salt and pepper to taste. Cover and simmer for 10 minutes, until the tomatoes break up.

To assemble: Place a cabbage leaf on a flat surface and place 2 tablespoons of stuffing on the lower third of the leaf. Roll the leaf up and just before reaching the end, fold the edges of the leaf in and tuck under the final roll. Place, seam side down, in a 9-inch square baking dish. Continue with the remaining 7 leaves.

Pour the sauce over the stuffed cabbage, cover, and bake for 1 hour.

Serves 4

Sausage with Cabbage

This is a very quick second course that we prepare often. You can substitute or add 12 Brussels sprouts. Treat them the same way as the cabbage, except blanch them for an additional 5 minutes.

4 tablespoons olive oil

2 pounds sweet pork sausages

1 pound Savoy cabbage, outer leaves discarded, cut into 1-inch thick slabs

4 garlic cloves, minced

1 tablespoon crushed fennel seeds

Salt and hot pepper flakes

Heat the oven to 375°F.

Heat the oil in a large skillet over medium heat and add the sausages. Prick them and cook them until they are brown all over, about 10 minutes. Remove the sausages and cut them into bite-size slices.

Bring a large pot of salted water to a boil over high heat and add the cabbage. When the water starts to boil rapidly again, remove the cabbage and drain.

Add the sausage and cabbage to an ovenproof casserole with a fitted top. Add the garlic, fennel seeds, and salt and hot pepper flakes to taste. Cover and bake for 25 to 30 minutes, until the cabbage is tender.

Serves 4

Parchment-Wrapped Sausage with Fennel and Onions

Sausages cook nicely in parchment. If you plan to serve a pasta course before this dish, omit the potatoes.

4 tablespoons olive oil

1 medium onion, thinly sliced

2 cups whole canned Italian tomatoes, chopped

1 large fennel bulb, cored and thinly sliced

2 medium potatoes, boiled, peeled, and sliced (we prefer Yukon Gold)

2 tablespoons chopped flat-leaf parsley

1 teaspoon dried tarragon

Salt and freshly ground black pepper

1 pound sweet pork sausages

Heat the oven to 400°F.

Heat the oil in a Dutch oven or heavy-bottomed ovenproof pot with a fitted lid over medium heat. Add the onion and cook until the onion becomes translucent, about 5 minutes. Add the tomatoes and simmer for about 5 minutes, then add the fennel, potatoes, parsley, tarragon, and salt and pepper to taste. Cover and place in the oven. Bake for about 45 minutes.

In the meantime, place a sheet of parchment paper on a baking dish. Prick the sausages with the tines of a fork and place in the center of the sheet. Fold over the sheet and crimp the edges. Place the sausages in the oven next to the vegetables and cook them for about 30 minutes. Remove the sausages and discard the fat and liquids. Separate the sausage links and add them to the fennel mixture. Cook an additional 5 minutes.

Serves 4

Cotechino in Galera (Cotechino in Prison)

Italians eat cotechino with lentils on New Year's Eve. It is a lovely, soft sausage, very flavorful and easy to make.

You can find cotechino in most Italian delis and butcher shops around the holidays, or you can use the recipe below to make your own.

1 homemade cotechino (about 1½ pounds) or 1 store-bought cotechino (about 1 pound)

1 thin slice beef shoulder, pounded large enough to wrap around the cotechino (about 1 pound)

Salt and freshly ground black pepper

9 thin slices pancetta

2 tablespoons olive oil

1 medium onion, finely chopped

3 garlic cloves, finely chopped

1½ cups beef or chicken stock

1½ cups red wine

1 celery rib, finely chopped

3 bay leaves

Heat the oven to 400°F.

Bring a large pot of water to a boil over medium heat. Add the cotechino and cook for about 15 minutes. Drain and remove the casing.

Place the slice of beef on a work surface. Season the beef with salt and pepper, then place the sausage on the beef and roll the cotechino in the beef. Then wrap the pancetta around the cotechino and beef. Tie up the package, using butcher's twine. We make a slip knot every 1½ inches.

Heat the oil in a large Dutch oven or heavy-bottomed ovenproof pan. Add the cotechino and brown it all over, about 10 minutes. Add the onion and garlic. Cook until the onion becomes translucent, about 5 minutes. Add the stock, wine, celery, and bay leaves. Cover the pot and place it in the oven. Cook the cotechino for about 1 hour. Remove the meat from the pan, set aside, and keep it warm.

Move the pan to the stovetop and cook the liquid over medium-high heat until it has reduced to about 1½ cups, about 15 minutes. Remove the bay leaves.

Serve the cotechino sliced, with the sauce dribbled over it.

Serves 4

Cotechino Sausage

Saltpeter is used to preserve the color of the sausage, but we prefer not to use nitrates. You can individualize this dish by adding a couple of tablespoons of fresh, minced herbs, or a jigger of grappa or other brandy.

Ask your butcher to get you the pork casing.

1 pork casing, about 2 inches in diameter and 2 feet long

3 pounds lean coarsely ground pork butt

2 garlic cloves, finely chopped

¾ tablespoon freshly ground black pepper

1½ teaspoons salt

½ teaspoon grated nutmeg

½ teaspoon saltpeter (optional)

Wash the pork casing well and let it soak in cold water for at least 1 hour.

In a large bowl, combine the ground pork, garlic, pepper, salt, nutmeg, and saltpeter (if using).

Rinse and drain the casing thoroughly. Tie one end of the casing with a knot. Spoon the pork mixture into the casing, squeezing it as you fill. Gradually release space in the casing as it fills. If the casing breaks, tie off both ends and continue anew. Continue until the casing is filled. Squeeze down the pork so that there are no air pockets, tie off the second end, and then tie off two sausages.

Sausages keep in the refrigerator for about 1 week. They freeze for 3 months.

Makes 2 sausages (each about 1½ pounds)

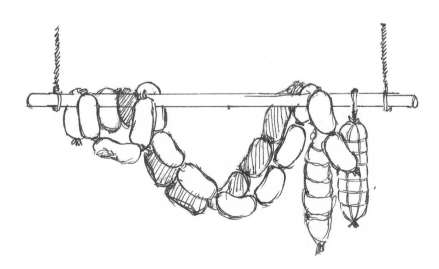

WINTER GREENS

Winter does not have to be a vegetable wasteland. Nor do you have to depend on imported vegetables that were grown in South America, picked under-ripe, shipped for thousands of miles in vehicles spewing fossil fuels, and, when cooked, taste like sawdust. There are many wonderful fresh winter vegetables: Brussels sprouts, cardoons, speckled cranberry beans, crinkly Savoy cabbage, kale, leeks, sweet mustard greens, cauliflower, and frilly puntarelle, to name a few. But I think our favorite is brocoletti di rape.

Brocoletti di rape, also known as broccoli rabe (actually dialect) and rapini (the second growth on the plant), is an Italian winter staple. My parents keep it in a box on the porch— as long as it doesn't freeze, the vegetable is happiest in the cold weather. Rape is a member of the cabbage family. It is similar to broccoli, only leafier, with longer stems, and a slightly bitter taste. The inflorescences are the sweeter aspect of the plant, so when shopping for rape, be sure to look for bunches with lots of flowers—the more the better.

To prepare rape, we cut off the stems. You can peel rape stems as you would broccoli, but they are quite narrow and probably not worth the effort. We often blanch rape in boiling salted water first. This softens the vegetable up and ensures a bright green color. Seal the color by plunging the blanched rape in cold water. There are many ways to cook rape, despite what some folks say. Most often, we simply sauté chopped, blanched rape in a skillet with olive oil, garlic, hot pepper flakes, and some of the blanching water. To turn it into a first course, we add orecchiette boiled until al dente, or spaghettini broken into pieces and added to the rape with a cup of the blanching water—the spaghettini will cook in the vegetables and the scant broth. Sometimes we add scallops or shrimp to garnish.

Other times we will make polenta, combine it with cooked brocoletti di rape that has been finely chopped, and pour the mixture in a pie plate to set, and then sprinkle Parmesan cheese on top and run it under the broiler to make a delicious side dish.

We also bake brocoletti di rape. Again, the vegetable is blanched, and then placed in a baking pan with olive oil, black olives cured in oil, raw garlic, and hot pepper flakes and baked in a hot oven until it is soft, even crispy. This really brings out a sweet taste to this otherwise bitter vegetable. The other way we bake rape is by placing it raw into the hot oven. While we lose more volume with this method, the results are equally sweet and delicious. To turn this dish into a second course, we often set a few fillets of some white fish, like cod or striped bass, into the rape, sprinkle with olive oil, and continue cooking until the fish is done. To prepare baked brocoletti di rape with sausages, we add cooked fresh cranberry beans and sliced, browned sweet sausages to the baking pan with the blanched rape and cook in a hot oven for about twenty minutes. For us, there is nothing more seasonal than the smell of rape in the oven.

Puntarelle is a seasonal salad green that is not to be missed. Also called Roman wild chicory or Catalan chicory, it is less leafy than its cousins in the botanical family, *Cichorium*. Indeed, a literal translation of the name is "little points." That there's more stalk than leaf is good news: Only the crisp white stalks are eaten, as the deep green leafy tips are very bitter. And even the stalks can be too bitter to eat if they are chopped across the plant. But sliced lengthwise, their bitterness is transformed into a taste delicately sharp and peppery. Italians believe puntarelle, like chicory and chard, cleans the stomach, and is good for the blood. It is high in iron and vitamins A and C.

While this herb (it's not a vegetable) is flavorful when sautéed quickly with garlic, olive oil, and a splash of water, or served Pugliese-style — braised with fava beans — or wilted into delicate, clear soups, it is as a salad that puntarelle truly excels. Preparation of this Roman specialty is simple: Puntarelle must be washed and the green leaves discarded. The white-greenish tips are split with a knife lengthwise and dipped in cold water. This allows the leaves to curl and lose some of their bitter taste. The puntarelle is served with a dressing made of garlic and anchovy fillets crushed in a mortar, and combined with olive oil, lemon juice, salt, and pepper. Puntarelle may be exotic, but it's not weak or precious — like most winter vegetables, this is a green that can hold its own.

WINTER VEGETABLES
AND SALADS

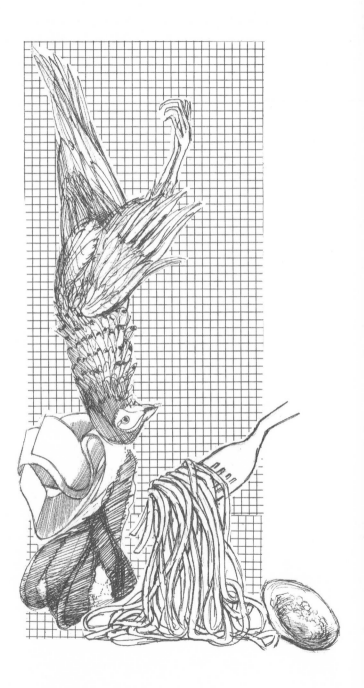

Cranberry Beans with Fennel

This is a perfect side dish to grilled and stewed meats. We ate it one Sunday lunch with Pork Shoulder with Fennel, Brussels Sprouts with Mint, and Tomaso's Baked Brocoletti di Rape (see pages 276, 286 and 292). Our first course was Mashed Potato Ravioli (see page 256), with a nice bottle of Dad's homemade wine, a petite syrah and zinfandel combination. It was a wonderful meal, celebrating Cham's 41st birthday, with lots of kids on board.

2 tablespoons olive oil

1 small onion, finely chopped

2 garlic cloves, finely chopped

2 cups fresh cranberry beans (about 2 pounds in the shell)

1½ cups chicken stock

1 tablespoon finely chopped flat-leaf parsley

Salt and freshly ground black pepper

1 fennel bulb, cored and thinly sliced

Extra virgin olive oil, for garnish

Heat the olive oil in a medium soup pot over medium heat. Add the onion and garlic and cook until the onion becomes translucent, about 5 minutes. Add the cranberry beans, stock, parsley, and salt and pepper to taste. Cover, reduce the heat to low, and simmer for 45 minutes. Add the fennel and cook for an additional 45 minutes.

Adjust seasoning and serve garnished with extra virgin olive oil.

Serves 4 to 6

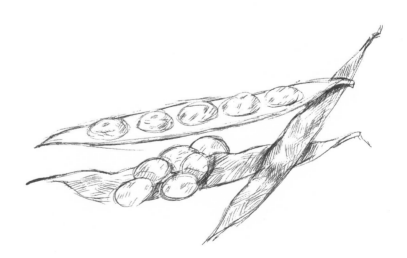

Brocoletti di Rape, Broccoli, and Potatoes

The addition of broccoli sweetens this dish.

2 medium potatoes (we prefer Yukon Gold)

1 bunch brocoletti di rape, washed, with stems removed

1 bunch broccoli, washed, with stems cut and peeled, and florets separated

3 tablespoons olive oil

6 garlic cloves, sliced

Salt and hot pepper flakes

Extra virgin olive oil, for garnish

Place the potatoes in a large pot and cover with salted water. Bring to a boil over high heat. Cook for 5 minutes, and then add the rape and broccoli. Boil the vegetables, uncovered, for 2 minutes. Reserve 1 cup of the cooking water, then drain and rinse the vegetables in cold water to retain the color. As soon as you can handle them, peel and slice the potatoes. Set aside.

Heat the olive oil in a large skillet over medium heat. Add the garlic and cook until the garlic begins to take on color, about 3 minutes. Do not brown. Add the vegetables to the skillet, season with salt and hot pepper flakes to taste, and add ½ cup of the reserved cooking water. Cover, reduce the heat to medium-low, and simmer the vegetables until the potatoes begin to dissolve, about 15 minutes. Add a bit more cooking water if the vegetables start to dry out.

Garnish with a dribble of extra virgin olive oil.

Serves 6

Brussels Sprouts with Mint

If you can find fresh mint this time of year, that would be best. Just double the quantity you would use for dried.

4 cups fresh Brussels sprouts, stem ends trimmed and light, outer leaves removed, cut in half

3 tablespoons olive oil

3 garlic cloves, finely chopped

2 cups chicken stock

2 teaspoons dried mint

Salt

Hot pepper flakes (optional)

Bring a large pot of salted water to a boil over high heat and add the Brussels sprouts. Cook, uncovered, for about 4 minutes. Drain.

Heat the oil in a large skillet over medium heat. Add the garlic and cook until the garlic takes on color, about 3 minutes. Add the Brussels sprouts and the stock and mint. Season with salt and hot pepper flakes (if using) to taste. Simmer, uncovered, for about 10 minutes, until the sprouts are very tender.

Serves 4

Cabbage with Beans

We harvest leeks and Savoy cabbage from our garden after the first frost in the late fall. Because these vegetables come in season at the same time, they are very compatible. This recipe has a lovely, sweet taste.

2 tablespoons olive oil

¼ pound pancetta cut into ½-inch cubes, or Canadian bacon

1 medium onion, chopped

1 leek, white only, rinsed and chopped

2 garlic cloves, finely chopped

½ cup whole canned Italian tomatoes, chopped

1 tablespoon finely chopped flat-leaf parsley

Salt and hot pepper flakes

Half a head Savoy cabbage, cored and chopped

1 cup fresh cranberry beans (about 1 pound in the shell)

1 cup chicken stock

1 bay leaf

Heat the oil in a soup pot over medium heat. Add the pancetta and cook until the fat is rendered, about 5 minutes. Add the onion, leek, and garlic. Cook until the onion is translucent, about 5 minutes. Add the tomatoes, parsley, and salt and hot pepper flakes to taste. Cover and simmer for 10 minutes, until the tomatoes break up. Add the cabbage, beans, stock, and bay leaf. Cover and simmer over medium-low heat, until the beans are tender but firm, about 1 hour, or more if necessary. Check frequently to be sure the cooking liquid doesn't evaporate. If it looks like it is getting low, add more stock. The vegetables need to stay moist while cooking, but not soupy. Remove the bay leaf before serving.

Serves 4

Savoy Cabbage with Fennel

This is a recipe from southern Italy that Edward first ate in a little trattoria in Florence. This is a sophisticated yet simple dish, perfect served with any meats or fish.

Half a head Savoy or green cabbage, cored and chopped

1 fennel bulb, cored and sliced

1 medium potato, cut into eighths (we prefer Yukon Gold)

2 tablespoons olive oil

2 tablespoons chopped pancetta or Canadian bacon

1 medium onion, finely chopped

3 garlic cloves, finely chopped

1 tablespoon finely chopped flat-leaf parsley

Salt

Hot pepper flakes (optional)

Bring a large pot of salted water to a boil over high heat. Add the cabbage, fennel, and potato and boil for about 8 minutes, until the vegetables are tender. Reserve 2 cups of the cooking water, then drain.

Heat the oil in a large skillet over medium heat. Add the pancetta and cook until it renders its fat, about 5 minutes. Add the onion and garlic and cook until the onion becomes translucent, about 5 minutes. Add the cooked vegetables, the parsley, 1 cup of the reserved water, and salt and hot pepper flakes to taste. Boil gently for about 15 minutes, until the vegetables are tender and the flavors melded. If the vegetables seem dry, add a little more of the reserved water.

Serves 4

Fried Cardoons

Cardoons are harvested in northeast Italy during the winter. We like to eat fried cardoons with fish dishes.

3 cardoon ribs, strings removed, cut into lengths about 3 inches long and ½ inch wide

Juice of 2 lemons

4 cups water

8 tablespoons all-purpose flour, plus additional for dredging

½ cup light beer or white wine

1 egg white, beaten

½ teaspoon baking powder

Salt

Vegetable oil for frying

1 teaspoon fresh or dried rosemary

In a medium bowl, cover the cardoons in cold water. Add the lemon juice and soak for 30 to 45 minutes. Drain the cardoons and place in a small pot with 4 cups water and 2 tablespoons of the flour. Gently boil the cardoons over medium-low heat for about 30 minutes. Drain.

In the meantime, combine the beer, the remaining 6 tablespoons of flour, the egg white, baking powder, and salt to taste. Refrigerate the batter for about 1 hour.

Fill a large nonstick skillet with about 1 inch of oil. Add the rosemary. Heat the oil over medium-high heat until it is very hot. You can test the hotness by throwing a pinch of flour into the oil. If the flour pops, the oil is ready.

Dry the cardoons. Dredge them in flour, and then dunk them in the batter. Place the cardoons—a few at a time—in the hot oil and fry them until golden brown, about 2 minutes on each side. Drain on paper towels. Allow the oil to come back to heat before you add more cardoons.

Add salt to taste and serve immediately.

Serves 4

Fennel with Potatoes

We eat this dish with roasted capon on Christmas Day.

1 large fennel bulb, cut into large pieces about 3 inches long

2 medium potatoes, peeled and cut into quarters (we prefer Yukon Gold)

2 tablespoons olive oil

Salt

4 tablespoons grated Parmesan cheese

Heat the oven to 450°F.

Place the fennel and potatoes in a baking dish. Sprinkle with the oil and salt to taste and place in the oven. Bake for 45 minutes, until the potatoes are tender and the fennel looks translucent. Remove the fennel and potatoes from the oven.

Heat the broiler. Sprinkle the cheese over the vegetables, and place under the broiler. Broil until the cheese browns slightly, about 3 minutes.

Serves 4

Baked Fennel with Tomatoes

This is a wonderful side dish to serve with fish.

2 fennel bulbs, cored and cut into ¼-inch slices

1 medium onion, thinly sliced

1 cup whole canned Italian tomatoes, chopped

3 tablespoons extra virgin olive oil

2 garlic cloves, minced

Salt and freshly ground black pepper

½ cup grated Parmesan cheese, or fresh breadcrumbs

Heat the oven to 425°F.

In a medium bowl, mix the fennel, onion, tomatoes, oil, garlic, and salt and pepper to taste. Pour the ingredients into a baking dish about 2 inches deep. Cover the dish with aluminum foil and bake for 45 minutes, until the fennel is soft.

Heat the broiler. Remove the foil from the dish and sprinkle the grated cheese (or breadcrumbs) over the fennel. Broil for about 3 minutes, until the cheese begins to brown.

Serves 4

Kale with Turnips

This is a delicious vegetable to serve with meats and poultry.

1 pound kale, tough stems removed, chopped

2 medium white turnips, cut into quarters and sliced

4 tablespoons olive oil

4 garlic cloves, coarsely chopped

Hot pepper flakes

Salt

Bring a large pot of salted water to a boil over high heat and add the kale and turnips. Boil the vegetables, uncovered, for about 3 minutes. Scoop out 2 cups of the cooking water, then drain.

Heat the oil over medium heat in a skillet large enough to hold the vegetables. Add the garlic and hot pepper flakes to taste and cook until the garlic begins to take on color, about 3 minutes. Add the drained vegetables and 1 cup of reserved water to the garlic. Add salt to taste. Cook the vegetables, partially covered, over medium heat for about 1 hour, until the turnips are very tender. If the vegetables get dry, add a little of the remaining reserved water.

Serves 4

Puntarelle with Brocoletti di Rape

We often serve this vegetable dish as a second course, after a pasta or bowl of soup.

8 cups puntarelle, green leaves discarded, sliced lengthwise, soaked in cold water for about 15 minutes

4 tablespoons extra virgin olive oil

8 garlic cloves, sliced

Hot pepper flakes

1 bunch brocoletti di rape, stems removed

Salt and freshly ground black pepper

Bring a large pot of salted water to a boil and add the puntarelle. Boil for 5 minutes, and then remove the puntarelle with a slotted spoon. Do not discard the water. Keep it boiling.

In the meantime, heat the oil in a large skillet over medium heat. Add the garlic and hot pepper flakes to taste and cook until the garlic is slightly brown, about 4 minutes. Add the puntarelle to the skillet and continue cooking.

Dump the rape into the boiling water. Blanche, scoop out about 1 cup of the cooking water, then drain and add the rape to the puntarelle. Add salt and pepper to taste, and cook, uncovered, for about 10 minutes, until the vegetables are soft. If the vegetables look dry, add a little of the reserved water.

Serves 4

Tomaso's Baked Brocoletti di Rape

This is Edward's godfather Tomaso's recipe. It calls for cooking the rape until the leaves dry out and become crispy: What might be perceived as overcooking actually sweetens the vegetable. Normally one bunch of rape will serve four. This style of cookery produces only two servings per bunch.

2 bunches brocoletti di rape

6 tablespoons olive oil

6 garlic cloves, sliced

12 black olives cured in olive oil, pitted

Salt and hot pepper flakes

Heat the oven to 450°F.

Discard the discolored and large leaves from the rape. Cut off the tough stem ends.

Pour the oil into a baking dish and add the garlic and olives. Place the dish in the oven, and when the garlic begins to take on color, about 3 minutes, add the rape and salt and hot pepper flakes to taste. Spread the rape on the bottom of the dish and bake, uncovered, for about 25 minutes, until the edges of the leaves become crispy, flipping the rape over in the oil with tongs a couple of times.

Serves 4

Butternut Squash with Potatoes

This is a very luxurious dish that tastes creamy, but doesn't call for any cream.

1½ pounds butternut squash

Extra virgin olive oil

Salt and freshly ground
black pepper

3 medium potatoes (we prefer
Yukon Gold)

1 medium onion, coarsely chopped

3 tablespoons olive oil

2 tablespoons chopped flat-leaf
parsley

4 tablespoons grated Parmesan
cheese

Heat the oven to 400°F.

Cut the squash in half lengthwise and scoop out the seeds. Rub the squash with extra virgin olive oil and season with salt and pepper. Place the squash in a baking pan and bake for about 30 minutes, until fork-tender. Scoop out the flesh from the skin and place in a bowl. Discard the skin.

Fill a medium saucepan with water, add the potatoes, and bring to a boil over high heat. Cook for about 20 minutes, until the potatoes are tender. Drain and set aside.

Heat the broiler to hot.

When the potatoes are cool enough to handle, peel them. Push the potatoes through a potato ricer, or mash by hand in a large bowl. Add the squash, onion, 2 tablespoons of the olive oil, the parsley, and cheese. Combine well. Spoon the potato and squash mixture into a 13 × 9-inch baking dish. Sprinkle with the remaining 1 tablespoon of olive oil.

Place the pan under the broiler and brown the vegetables until a crust forms, about 5 to 6 minutes.

Serves 6

293

Fennel Salad

Fennel makes a delightful winter salad on its own. It is also a wonderful, crunchy addition to green salads.

1 large fennel bulb, cored and thinly sliced

Half a medium red onion, thinly sliced

3 tablespoons extra virgin olive oil

Juice of half a lemon

Salt and freshly ground black pepper

In a large bowl, mix together the fennel, onion, oil, and lemon juice. Season with salt and pepper to taste, and toss.

Note: You can dress this salad 30 minutes ahead of time as the fennel will stay crisp.

Serves 4

Orange Salad with Olives

Edward first tasted this dish in his Uncle Quintillio's home in Italy in 1951 and first published the recipe in Italian Family Cooking *in 1971. Quintillio was a dapper man, well educated and quite discerning about food. He served the oranges sliced thinly, with the rinds still on. Some people might find the rinds objectionable, so they can be removed. Orange salad is perfect after broiled or baked fish. Try to buy blood oranges, which are in season in the winter. You can substitute 2 heads of endive, thinly sliced, for the fennel.*

2 medium oranges (preferably blood orange)

1 fennel bulb, thinly sliced

2 tablespoons extra virgin olive oil

Salt and freshly ground black pepper

12 dried black olives cured in oil, pitted and sliced

4 tablespoons shaved Parmesan cheese, for garnish (optional)

Slice the oranges—with the rind on—into ¼-inch thick slices.

In a small bowl, combine the fennel, oil, and salt and pepper to taste.

Arrange the oranges on a platter—do not overlap—and spread the fennel mixture on top. Surround the oranges with the olives. (The olives will stain the oranges black, so add the olives just before serving.)

Garnish with the shaved cheese, if using.

Serves 4

ECONOMY CANDY

There's a swanky new hotel going up near the corner of Rivington and Essex Streets in Manhattan's Lower East Side. The nasty garbage-strewn vacant lots are being filled in by tidy new apartment buildings. The shuttered, graffiti-covered businesses are reopening as trendy frock shops and quirky mid-century modern furniture stores. The neighborhood is definitely changing.

Except for Economy Candy, praise God. Since 1937, the Cohen family has been operating one of the great candy/cookie/dried fruit and nut establishments in the city. The Lower East Side used to have many such places that catered to the local Jewish population. These days, high rents and changing demographics have led to the disappearance of all but a few outposts. People from all over the city flock to this Mecca of sweets, particularly around specific holidays—like Christmas, Passover, Easter, Purim, and Halloween—when the Cohens stock their shelves with holiday-specific items. We shop there for our chocolate-making essentials: Mercken's chocolate break up—milk, bittersweet, dark, and white—sold in planks big enough to renovate a kitchen; walnuts, pistachios, hazelnuts, and pecans; dried sour cherries, cranberries, and apricots. But there is so much more.

The store is long and narrow, with wobbly metal shelving that almost touches the fluorescent lights overhead. In the front are bins of wrapped and boxed candies, like Sweet Tarts, Tootsie Rolls, Runts, Zours, Jujubes, and Sno-Caps. There are thousands of varieties, from Hot Tamales to Goobers, chocolate cigarettes to gummy fangs. There are thirty-six flavors of jelly beans, nine colors of Jordan almonds (the gold and silver ones are stashed elsewhere), and twenty-two colors of large M&Ms. Incongruously, heavy metal music plays on the sound system. It is a penny candy paradise, lorded over by the current, third-generation owner, Jerry Cohen. Indeed, there's no tasting allowed, unless Jerry says it's okay.

Center aisles sport candies and cookies from all over the world: hamentashen from Brooklyn ("the best in the world," according to one mink-coated grandma); licorice from Finland; Turkish Delight from Turkey; shortbread from Scotland; Swiss, Belgian, Italian, and French chocolates packaged in fancy boxes. Jerry says folks often come in with a wrapper of a chocolate brought home from abroad and ask him to find it. "And 90 percent of the time it's worth stocking," he says, weighing up a bulging bag of Mary Janes. "But it always comes down to this," he says, handing over the bag to a customer. "Mary Janes and Bit-O-Honeys. That's our bread and butter."

Walk deeper into the store, and you are greeted with the smell of sesame seeds and honey. Huge blocks of halvah, plain and marbled, rest on a table, the big cutting knife nearby; cardboard boxes filled with dried prunes and figs from California and Turkey; dried blueberries, peaches, nectarines, and strawberries so deliciously sweet and gummy they are in themselves a candy; deep barrels of nuts, roasted, salted, raw; seeds of all sorts; and plastic containers of sugared sliced orange, spearmint, cherry, and ginger.

We shop at Economy Candy and buy the ingredients to make orange-flavored Chunkies (remember those chunks of chocolate studded with nuts and dried fruits?), which we wrap in white paper and pink ribbon to give as gifts on Christmas and Valentine's Day. We exit under floating piñatas—at $4.99 each, a bargain—laden with bags . . . and some lingering regrets. It's not that we worry about having purchased so many sweets. Just the opposite: We can't help but wonder how that German chocolate bar "mit cornflakes" would have tasted.

WINTER DESSERTS

Orange-Clove Soufflé

In general, sweet soufflés are based on pastry cream, and savory soufflés are based on besciamella. We, however, like to base our sweet soufflés on a besciamella sauce. We find it a little simpler and quicker. We make this dish when the Honeybell tangelos come in (see Sources on page 305).

4 tablespoons unsalted butter

2 tablespoons plus ¼ cup sugar

2 tablespoons all-purpose flour

½ cup milk

2 egg yolks

¼ cup fresh orange juice (preferably from a Honeybell)

1 tablespoon orange extract

2 tablespoons Cointreau, or other orange liqueur

1 tablespoon grated orange zest

Pinch of ground cloves

4 egg whites

Confectioners' sugar, for garnish

Heat the oven to 400°F.

Use 2 tablespoons of the butter to butter 4 individual 3-inch ramekins. Use 2 tablespoons of the sugar to sugar the ramekins, swishing it around to coat the bottom and edges.

Melt the remaining 2 tablespoons of butter in a medium heavy-bottomed pan, preferably one with rounded sides, over medium heat. Add the flour and cook, whisking, for about 3 minutes, until the butter mixture is pale and bubbling.

In the meantime, bring the milk to a boil in a small pot. Pour the milk slowly into the butter mixture, whisking all the while, until all of the milk is incorporated. The mixture will bubble vigorously and become quite pasty. It's okay. Take the sauce off the heat and add the egg yolks, one at a time, whisking all the while. Add the orange juice, orange extract, Cointreau, orange zest, and cloves and whisk well. The mixture should be thick, like a cake batter. Transfer to a large bowl.

In a separate bowl, beat the egg whites until they are almost stiff. Add the remaining ¼ cup sugar in a slow dribble, beating all the while until stiff and glossy.

Add about one-third of the egg whites to the orange and egg batter, and mix well. This should lighten the batter. Add the remaining egg whites carefully, folding in with a spatula. Do not mix too much, just enough to incorporate the egg whites.

Turn the oven down to 375°F.

Pour the batter into the buttered ramekins and place them in the center of the oven. Bake for about 20 minutes, until the soufflés have risen a few inches above the rim of the ramekins and are light brown on top.

Dust with confectioners' sugar and serve immediately.

Serves 4

Panettone Bread Pudding

We make this bread pudding during the Christmas season, when panettone are in abundance.

6 slices panettone, about 2 inches thick, lightly toasted

4 tablespoons unsalted butter, softened

2 eggs

2 egg yolks

²/₃ cup sugar

2 cups milk

3 tablespoons Amaretto

1 teaspoon grated orange zest

Confectioners' sugar, for garnish

Heat the oven to 350°F, with a rack set in the center of the oven.

Smear one side of the panettone slices with the butter. Lay them in a 9 × 5 × 3-inch loaf pan, butter side up. Try to fit the slices in the pan so that there are no empty spaces. Or tear the slices up and add the butter in dabs to the pan.

In a small bowl, beat the eggs, egg yolks, and sugar until light. Add the milk, Amaretto, and orange zest. Pour the custard over the panettone slices and let it sit for a few minutes while you heat the water.

Bring a kettle of water to a boil. Place the loaf pan into a larger pan. Pour the hot water into the larger pan, to come about halfway up the sides of the loaf pan. Place on the center rack in the oven. Bake for about 50 minutes, until a knife slipped into the center of the pudding comes out clean.

Remove the bread pudding from the oven and allow to cool slightly. You can flip the bread pudding over onto a serving platter, but it isn't the most beautiful dessert. It's better to bring out individual servings, garnished with confectioners' sugar.

Serves 8

Homemade Chunkies

We make these candies for Valentine's Day. You can use any combination of fruit and nuts. Sometimes we even add Red Hots cinnamon candies.

1 pound bittersweet chocolate, chopped

¾ teaspoon orange extract

3 tablespoons dried cranberries

3 tablespoons dried sour cherries

3 tablespoons broken walnut meats

3 tablespoons pistachios

3 tablespoons finely chopped dried apricots

Lightly oil a 9 × 5 × 3-inch loaf pan.

Fill a medium pot ¾ full of water and bring to a simmer over medium heat. Place a metal bowl over the hot water and add the chocolate. The chocolate will melt in about 5 minutes. Stir to smooth. Take the bowl off the hot water, add the orange extract, cranberries, cherries, walnuts, pistachios, and apricots to the chocolate, and mix well.

Pour the chocolate mixture in the loaf pan. Refrigerate the chocolate for about 6 hours. Remove the chocolate and turn it over onto a large piece of wax paper, so the rough side is up for cutting.

Heat a large knife by pouring boiling water over it and drying it off. Gently cut the chocolate into 2-inch squares. Wrap in wax paper and store in the refrigerator.

The chocolate will be fine for up to a month. If the chocolate is exposed to varying temperatures, a bloom will appear. It does not affect the taste of the chocolate.

Makes about 12 chocolates

Variation:

Line a baking tray with wax paper and drop on about 1 teaspoon melted chocolate. Drop a combination of nuts and dried fruits onto the chocolate. Chill.

Walnut Orange Cake

The tastes of walnut and orange are very distinctive in this delightful cake, which is an adaptation of a traditional walnut cake from southwestern France. It is best served with whipped cream or vanilla ice cream. Walnut oil can be found in most gourmet shops.

3 large eggs

1⅓ cups sugar

½ cup walnut oil

⅓ cup fresh orange juice

1½ cups all-purpose flour

2 teaspoons baking powder

Salt

½ cup chopped walnuts

2 teaspoons orange extract

Confectioners' sugar or vanilla ice cream, for serving (optional)

Heat the oven to 350°F. Butter a 9-inch round cake pan.

In a large bowl, beat the eggs and gradually add the sugar, beating all the while. Continue beating until the mixture is light and fluffy. Add the oil and orange juice and mix well.

Sift together the flour, baking powder, and a pinch of salt. Add the flour mixture to the egg mixture and stir until combined. Add the walnuts and orange extract and stir until combined.

Pour the batter into the cake pan and bake for 40 minutes. Do not open the oven and jiggle around the cake to see if it is done earlier. You will smell it when it is done. Remove the cake from the oven and let it cool on a rack for about 10 minutes. Then turn the cake out onto the rack and cool completely. Serve with a dusting of confectioners' sugar or a scoop of vanilla ice cream, if you like.

Serves 8

Meyer Lemon Tart

Meyer lemons are available during January and February. They are thought to be a cross between a lemon and an orange, with less acidity than regular lemons. We make Meyer lemon marmalade from a wonderful recipe by Edon Waycott in Preserving the Taste *(Hearst Books, 1993). This tart is a baked adaptation of that marmalade. Vanilla ice cream is a nice accompaniment, if you like.*

For the filling

2 pounds Meyer lemons (about 6 ripe lemons)

2 cups sugar

2 large eggs, slightly beaten

2 tablespoons unsalted butter, melted

1 tablespoon all-purpose flour

For the pastry

1 cup all-purpose flour

¼ teaspoon salt

8 tablespoons (1 stick) unsalted butter, very cold

1 tablespoon cold water

Vanilla ice cream, for serving

For the filling: Remove the lemon skins and, with a sharp knife, cut most of the white pith off the skins. Julienne the skins. Cut away any white pith remaining on the fruit. Cut the fruit in quarters and remove as many seeds as you can. Place the fruit (not the julienned skins) in a food processor and pulse to coarsely chop. The yield should be about 2 cups. Place the fruit and julienned skins in a nonreactive bowl. Add the sugar, cover, and allow to rest for 4 hours at room temperature, or overnight in the refrigerator.

For the pastry: In a large bowl, combine the flour and salt. Cut in the butter until the mixture has a sandy texture. Work quickly so the butter doesn't get soft. Add the cold water and combine, handling the dough as little as possible. You may need more water to make the dough come together—add it in very small amounts. Do not form into a ball.

You will need to work on a marble countertop or other very smooth surface. Grab a walnut-size piece of the dough (it will be loose and crumbly—it's okay) and smear it with the heel of your hand against the work surface. The process causes the butter to integrate with the flour in long streaks. Gather the smear and set aside. Repeat with the remaining dough.

Form the dough into two disks, one large and one small, wrap in plastic, and refrigerate for at least 30 minutes.

In the meantime, pour the sugared lemons into a medium heavy-bottomed saucepan and bring to a boil, uncovered, over medium-high heat. Lower the heat to medium and cook at a low boil for 15 to 20 minutes, until the color becomes a deeper orange and the fruit looks glossy. The remaining seeds will float to the top. Remove them. Take the marmalade off the heat and allow the marmalade to come down to room temperature. It will become quite thick.

Heat the oven to 400°F. Butter a 10-inch tart pan.

Roll the large disk of pastry out on a floured surface. Place the pastry into the tart pan.

In a bowl, combine the lemon with the eggs, butter, and flour. Pour the lemon filling into the pastry.

Roll out the remaining disk and cut into 1-inch strips. Use the strips to create a crosshatch pattern over the top of the tart.

Bake the tart for about 30 minutes, until the edges begin to brown, then reduce the heat to 350°F and bake for an additional 15 minutes, until the crust is golden brown and the filling has set. Allow the tart to come to room temperature before serving.

Serve with a scoop of vanilla ice cream.

Serves 10

Lemon Sorbet with Spumante

This ambrosial dessert can be served any time of year. We just tend to serve it during the winter, especially during the holiday season, when we drink more sparkling wines in general. It's fantastic after fish meals.

1 bottle (750 ml) imported sweet Italian spumante

2 pints good-quality lemon sorbet

Strips of lemon zest, for garnish

Open the spumante and let it sit for a few minutes so the bubbles can settle.

Working in batches, place the lemon sorbet into the bowl of a blender. Pour in the spumante and blend. Pour into champagne glasses and garnish with the lemon zest. Serve immediately with a long spoon.

Serves 8

Chocolate Meringue Pie

This pie is adapted from a lemon meringue pie recipe from the 26th edition of The Memphis Cookbook, *published by the Junior League of Memphis. Elinor and all her female relatives were members at one time or another, going back generations.*

For the pastry

1 cup all-purpose flour

¼ cup superfine sugar

1 egg yolk

5 tablespoons unsalted butter

For the filling

5 ounces semisweet chocolate

3 eggs

3 egg yolks

1 cup superfine sugar

5 tablespoons warm water

4 tablespoons unsalted butter

For the meringue

3 egg whites

Cream of tartar

6 tablespoons superfine sugar

Heat the oven to 350°F, with a rack set in the center of the oven.

For the pastry: In the bowl of a food processor, combine the flour, sugar, egg yolk, and butter and pulse for about 1 minute, until the dough comes together into many little balls. Remove and press the dough together. Wrap in wax paper and refrigerate for about 30 minutes.

Roll out the dough on a well-floured surface. Press down on the dough with the rolling pin in all directions, and gradually roll out, starting from the center of the ball. Roll the dough up on the rolling pin, or fold into thirds, and place in a 9-inch pie plate. If the dough is too tender and falls apart when you try to put it in the pie plate, just press the pieces into place. Line the pastry with parchment paper and fill the crust with beans or a pie chain.

Place the crust on the center rack of the oven and bake for about 20 minutes, until lightly brown. Remove but leave the oven on.

For the filling: Melt the chocolate in a double boiler over medium heat. In a large bowl, beat the eggs, egg yolks, and sugar until light. Add the egg and sugar mixture to the melted chocolate, still over simmering water in the double boiler. Add the water and mix well. Add the butter and continue mixing. Stir the filling as it cooks in the double boiler over medium heat until the filling is thick enough to fall in ribbons from the spoon, about 15 minutes. Do not overcook. Pour the filling into the crust.

For the meringue: Beat the egg whites and a pinch of cream of tartar until soft peaks form. Add the sugar gradually, beating until stiff and glossy. Pour the meringue over the chocolate filling.

Bake the pie for about 5 minutes, until the meringue turns golden brown. Allow the pie to cool thoroughly before cutting, to allow the filling to set.

Note: You can substitute ½ cup fresh lemon juice plus the grated zest of 1 lemon for the chocolate to make lemon meringue pie.

Serves 6

SOURCES

Biancardi's
2350 Arthur Avenue
Bronx, NY 10458
718-733-4058
Game, meat, and poultry

Calandra's Cheese
2314 Arthur Avenue
Bronx, NY 10458
718-365-7572
Ricotta

D'Artagnan
280 Wilson Avenue
Newark, NJ 07105
800-327-8246
Game, poultry

DiPalo's Fine Foods
200 Grand Street
New York, NY 10002
212-226-1033
Ricotta

Economy Candy Corporation
108 Rivington Street
New York, NY 10002
212-254-1531
Supplies for Chunkies (page 300)

Farm 2 Market
www.farm-2-market.com
Maine shrimp

N.Y. Cake & Baking Distributors
56 West 22 Street
New York, NY 10010
212-675-CAKE
Candy- and cake-making supplies

Randazzo's Fish Market
2327 Arthur Avenue
Bronx, NY 10458
718-367-4139
Seafood, including Maine shrimp

Teitel Brothers Wholesale and Retail Grocery
2372 Arthur Avenue
Bronx, NY 10458
800-850-7055
Delverde no-boil lasagna,
Parmesan cheese, olives, capers

Ter Marsch Groves
13900 U.S. Highway #1
Juno Beach, FL 33408
561-626-1177
Honeybell tangelos

Tino's Delicatessen
609 East 187 Street
Bronx, NY 10458
718-733-9879
Pasta, black rice, faro, oils, vinegars,
tuna fish

INDEX